Village Life in Bengal
Hindu Customs in Bengal

VILLAGE LIFE IN BENGAL

by

Tara Krishna Basu

and

HINDU CUSTOMS IN BENGAL

by

Basanta Coomar Bose

Edited by

Richard Stevenson

iUniverse, Inc.

New York Lincoln Shanghai

Village Life in Bengal
Hindu Customs in Bengal

Copyright © 2005 by Lionheart LLC

iUniverse books may be ordered through booksellers or by contacting:

iUniverse
2021 Pine Lake Road, Suite 100
Lincoln, NE 68512
www.iuniverse.com
1-800-Authors (1-800-288-4677)

ISBN-13: 978-0-595-36233-2 (pbk)
ISBN-13: 978-0-595-80678-2 (ebk)
ISBN-10: 0-595-36233-8 (pbk)
ISBN-10: 0-595-80678-3 (ebk)

Printed in the United States of America

CONTENTS

▼

VILLAGE LIFE IN BENGAL

HINDU CUSTOMS IN BENGAL

VILLAGE LIFE IN BENGAL

Tara Krishna Basu

assisted by
Hasim Amir Ali
and
Jiten Talukdar

Edited by Richard Stevenson

Editor's Foreword

India is best understood, perhaps, as being two countries, one a modern, wealthy country of two to three-hundred million persons, and the other a timeless ancient country of seven to eight-hundred million persons. Of course, modern techniques and ideas are entering the periphery of timeless India, just as modern India retains its reliance on astrology and caste and on ancient social customs. The cement which binds these two countries is religion, both Hindu and Muslim, and nothing can really be understood about both countries without some understanding of the religions which permeate everything. Modern India can be seen by going to Bombay or Calcutta or Bangalore. But such observation completely passes over timeless India which can only be understood, partially, by living in a village and also by study of the complex society. It is in this spirit that this book is presented to the public.

This book is a re-publication of a treatise originally published in 1962 by the Indian Statistical Institute of Calcutta under the title *The Bengal Peasant from Time to Time*. The new title, *Village Life in Bengal*, is much more descriptive for an edition directed at the general reader.

The Indian Statistical Institute is a very distinguished learned society usually devoted to mathematical statistics. One might wonder how it generated a book on sociology and population statistics. The original intent of the book (the third in a series) was to provide survey information about a rural village in West Bengal. There are tens of thousands of such villages and the particular village was chosen because its life had been the subject of a realistic novel written about a century ago, followed by sociological studies of the village described in the novel. The present book found its way into the huge Calcutta book market, but has been largely unknown, perhaps, in the West.

The statistical information given in the original edition of *The Bengal Peasant from Time to Time* is outdated by now and much has been omitted in the present edition for the sake of easy readability. Only very minor changes have been made in the text, mainly to smooth out references to omitted tabular data. Undoubtedly there has been a great improvement in physical conditions over the last forty years. The book itself is a great classic in the description of human life and deserves the attention of a wider audience. Life in Bengal changes slowly and the customs described a generation ago will still be found largely as they were described by Tara Krishna Basu. It is both informative and entertaining, and it is written in a beautiful style of the Bengali version of English—a language of great expressiveness and imagery. Also, apart from its inherent interest, it is an excellent starting point to attempt some understanding of Bengal and of India itself.

Richard Stevenson

Author's Introduction

In the year 1887 the Reverend Lal Day wrote a novel in English under the caption *Govinda Samanta* to illustrate the social and domestic life of the rural population and working classes of Bengal. The story attempted only to delineate the everyday life of an actual raiyat of Bengal in the middle decades of the nineteenth century. It is proper to state also that this book of the Rev. Day was written in response to an offer of a prize of £50 made by the late Sri Joy Kissen Mookerjea of Uttarpara, a benevolent and illustrious zamindar of Bengal. The book of the Rev. Day was adjudicated as the best among the essays submitted, and its worthy author obtained the aforesaid prize. In the opening chapter of his book the Rev. Day, remembering that brevity is the soul of wit, pithily explained that the reader was to expect there only a plain and unvarnished tale of a plain peasant living in the plain country of Bengal, told in a very plain manner.

Now the days of the Rev. Day were not the days of social surveys or studies of the pattern with which we are at present familiar. He had little problem in selecting his village or in collecting or analyzing the primary data, or expressing his findings in terms of statistical constants and formulae. Moreover, he was neither a statistician nor an economist nor a sociologist presenting his report according to an accepted scientific pattern. He described the social life of the rural Bengal of his times, and in so doing provided also a work of some literary merit. The author simply took his readers to his native village Shona Palashi to which he gave the pseudonym of Kanchanpur, and with this village as a setting he wrote out the biography of a real raiyat, a Bengal peasant of the Ugra-Kshatriya caste. But, chapter-by-chapter, as the author was unfolding the career of his hero, he was also engaged in giving a detailed interwoven picture of the culture and problems of the rural Bengal of his days. It was not a quantitative study at all, but there is much to commend in the method of describing social and domestic life of a people in this way. The business of life with its network of relationships of a complex social structure is perhaps more intelligibly understood through such biographical studies. They perhaps give us more insight in the understanding of the intimate human attitudes, values and problems that arise in a complex living situation, than collecting and heaping up of data on the basis of questionnaires and schedules.

The Bengal Peasant Life, for that was the title of the Rev. Day's book in subsequent editions, was prescribed for general reading in the schools for many years. The last of its many editions was published in 1926. Being still available in the second-hand book market it stands as a classic in the village life studies of Bengal.

In the years 1931 to 1934 the present writer was assisting Dr. Hashim Amir Ali in his research into the socioeconomic conditions of the villages around Tagore's Sriniketan. There one day in 1933, as he was discussing the place of *Bengal Peasant Life* in rural literature with Dr. Ali, the latter suggested that it might be worthwhile to locate and make a re-study of Kanchanpur that might throw a great deal of light on our present rural problems. Accordingly, the village was traced out with considerable difficulty and was actually visited in August 1933. Thereafter, the present writer again spent some three weeks there from the end of December 1933 to the middle of January 1934. To get glimpses of life of the village of the Rev. Day, as it was sixty years later, was indeed a pleasant adventure.

During these two visits this writer did not make any routine survey, but simply entered some notes in his diary, which were later typed out and handed over to his teacher and chief. That was twenty-five years ago; both the teacher and the student left Sriniketan—one for Hyderabad and the other for Bihar and proceeded in different walks of life.

Years passed by and Kanchanpur became a forgotten village, so far as that old student was concerned.

After a full cycle of twenty-five years the teacher and the student met again. The latter old pupil was invited by the old teacher to make a restudy of Kanchanpur on a one-year project to be sponsored by the Indian Statistical Institute, and much to his surprise he also learnt that his old notes on Kanchanpur had been sent to the world of publication—under the title *Kanchanpur Revisited*. The teacher's forecast of twenty-five years was fulfilled overnight: the pupil found himself an author.

Kanchanpur Revisited presented a picture of that village as it was in 1933 and this present investigation deals with it in 1958. That had been a year of the "Great Depression", and this was a year of rising prices. That had been a year of bondage and fear, and this was a year of freedom and hope. There was a psychology of courage and progress in the atmosphere of 1958. Then the people had been deep in gloom and chaos and now they were planning their future with confidence and strength. What then have been the specific changes effected in the pattern of rural life as represented by Kanchanpur?

In other words, the question arises as to how much the village has actually altered under the impact of these changing years? The mid-nineteenth century pattern of a culture gradually declining in prosperity was nicely outlined in the Rev. Day's book, *Bengal Peasant Life*. The notes presented in *Kanchanpur Revisited* gave a somewhat different picture of the village in the early thirties of this century. There the first few lines under the caption, "Distant Footsteps", read as follows:

> Kanchanpur sleeps on. But when some government representative or exciting piece of news comes to disturb it, it gets up and attempts to get a view of what is happening inside its own arena as well as outside in the world beyond. Its torpor is broken but only for a while.

Evidently the footfalls approached nearer and nearer and in the India of 1958 the village is now involved in and dependent on relations of the wider social environment. Has the basic texture of Kanchanpur's cultural individuality proved to be sufficiently tough to resist the changes and to remain undisturbed? What are the noticeable changes in different sectors of living? Are the old values and faiths still clinging to men, or is the village moving out to embrace new ways of thoughts and forms? If some light is thrown on the present situation and on the above questions, this survey, I hope, will justify itself.

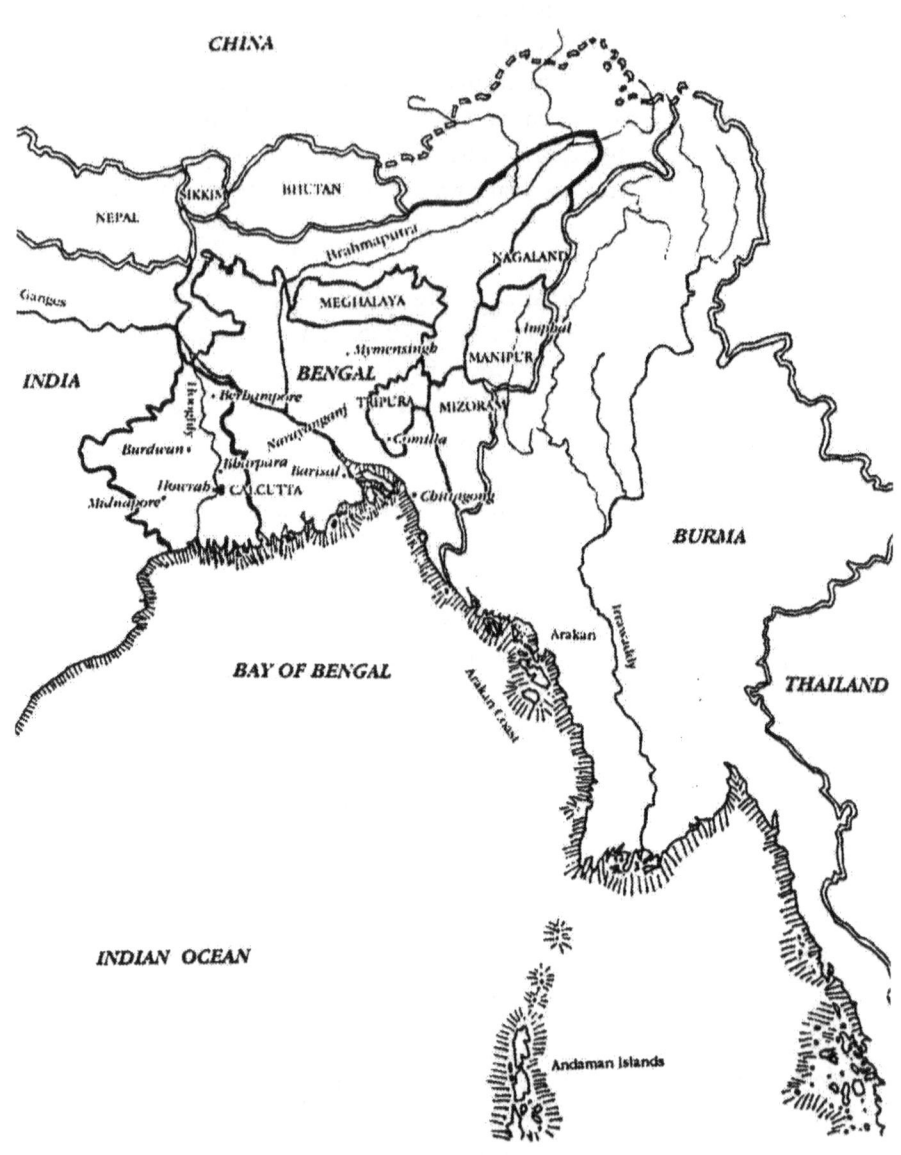

CHAPTER 1

▼

THE ENVIRONMENT

1.1—LOCATION

As already mentioned, Kanchanpur, meaning Golden Habitation, was the pseudonym which the Reverend Lal Behari Day had given to the village of his birth when writing *Bengal Peasant Life* in 1872. The official name of the village is Palashi.

Partly to distinguish it from another village of the same name, located some twenty miles northeast, partly because of its erstwhile wealth and prosperity and perhaps also because it was for long the abode of many families of the gold-merchant (Subarna Banik) caste, this village has come to have Shona, meaning "golden", affixed to its name; even officially it is generally referred to even now as Shona Palashi, Golden Palashi. So Lal Behari Day's name for the village was both a veil and an indication.

In 1933 the village had actually to be traced out through pointers given in *Bengal Peasant Life*. *Kanchanpur Revisited* mentions how even people who had searched for Kanchanpur had failed to locate its identity. But that brief inquiry about Govinda Samanta's (hero of *Bengal Peasant Life*) surviving descendants had sown the seed of curiosity in the mind of the village people and had enhanced the pride and self esteem of the family that still claims to be at least a branch of the Day family. Anyway, the pseudonym no longer serves as a veil of anonymity for the village and, thanks to the fame which has begun to be attached to Reverend

Day and his book, *Bengal Peasant Life*, the present inhabitants would accept the name Kanchanpur as readily as Shona Palashi; that is why we have used two names indiscriminately for the same village throughout the present study.

This Kanchanpur or Shona Palashi then is a middle-sized village of the Gangetic delta area in that part of Eastern India which is now known as West Bengal with Calcutta as its metropolitan city. From Calcutta if one wants to pay a visit to Kanchanpur, the first step is to reach Vardhamana which, in its Anglicized form is known as Burdwan. The railway station adjoining the town of Burdwan lies on the Eastern Railway and is sixty-six miles northwest of Calcutta. An express or mail train takes about one hour and a half for the journey, and nowadays even the slower local electric trains take the traveler from Calcutta to Burdwan in about two and half hours. The village lies to the northeast of Burdwan, and in dry seasons there runs a bus on the Burdwan-Kusumgram road which passes by Kanchanpur on the north at a distance of less than a mile from the village proper. If there is a heavy shower the road becomes muddy even in other than rainy seasons, and the bus service is temporarily discontinued. In the rainy season and early autumn, the road is in such a condition that even ox cart treks become hazardous. The distance from Burdwan to Kanchanpur via this road is about nine miles and presents the most formidable part of the journey when the rains have set in.

1.2—THE ROAD TO KANCHANPUR

When it was decided that a restudy of Kanchanpur was to be made, the present writer made several attempts to pay a visit to Kanchanpur during the rainy season in 1958. But the roads were bad and he was discouraged at the Burdwan station from proceeding towards the village. To get across these nine miles he had to wait for three months: the rains kept Kanchanpur inaccessible till the end of September. The problem which he had faced twenty-five years ago confronted him again. A trek on foot was the only solution as it had been in 1933.

Below are extracted the lines from *Kanchanpur Revisited*, which described the situation at the time of this author's first visit in August 1933. This might well have been written in September 1958:

There then on the map was Kanchanpur, six miles from Burdwan in a straight line, but almost double the distance by road. Up to Kolgaon (Kaligram) village, eight miles from Burdwan, I learnt there was a metaled road and that then it became Kachha. During other seasons horse carriages and motorcars can go as far as Palashi; but now, in the rainy season, they cannot go because the road is too muddy even for bullock carts. I tried to engage a cart and found that even so far as Kolgaon the minimum fare asked was three rupees. The rest of the way, l would have to walk, because there, as one carter said, "we won't go on the cart; the cart will ride on our shoulders".

The counsel of perfection was not to go to Palashi during this season at all. But I did not heed their advice, and started on foot next morning for the village, which I had had so much difficulty in locating.

It was raining hard when I left Burdwan. Up to Kolgaon, which lies on the metaled road, it was not very difficult. But from there the Kachha road was but a stretch of quagmire where one sank in up to the knees. It was hard exercise to walk even for a hundred yards. l overtook a villager who was carrying a seven-year-old boy on his shoulders. It was impossible for the child to walk, and the father almost wept for the road. l could not but pity his position; but, realizing that mine would be no better if I were to walk upon the remainder of this unmetaled road, I hit upon another plan. There was Palashi hidden in a thicket. Between me and the village stretched a vast expanse of watery paddy fields barely separated from each other by the raised embankments. l abandoned the road—if it could be so called—and walked zigzag along the narrow bunds between the rice fields.

But this time, having grown twenty-five years older, I had not the youthful zest to face the task on foot and there was also a miscellany of equipment to be carried to the village where I would have to stay for several months.

"Go there even on a duli (litter) if you can get one"—such were the instructions of Alida when we parted at Santiniketan this time. But the days of duli are gone in the villages. Decades ago it was in vogue, a kind of indigenous litter for carrying women of the less wealthy classes, while palli (palanquin) was the only vehicle available to the well-to-do when the roads were in such a state that not even two-wheeled carts could pass on them. Journeys by palanquin have also fallen into disuse, and at Kanchanpur, I found out later, its existence is noted only on nuptial occasions or when a man in a sick bed has to be sent to the town for medical treatment.

At the end of September the visit could be delayed no longer. By then things were only slightly better, but no bus had begun to ply. The only recourse for me in such circumstances was to chance the bullock cart, and I set out to hire one for getting across those nine miles. The condition of the road even now demanded certain precautions. There must be strong and fresh bullocks with no heavy load to carry. The carter should be an expert in his job, and he should also take one or two assistants with him to help him in case of difficulties, as it would be often necessary to lead the bullocks by hand through stretches of sticky mud and also put human muscles to the wheels simultaneously.

I agreed to pay Rs.12/as cart fare and settled the matter with a carter. Next morning we were to start. But the road was in a horrible mess. I came to understand that the road was to be macadamized under the Second Five Year Plan and as a prelude to construction a good quantity of earth had been thrown and spread over it. Then the rains set in and made the road a stretch of quagmire. In some spots within the villages through which we had to pass portions of the road were submerged in water, and they served as so many merry pools for the village ducks to swim and dive. There was also an endless number of undulations in the road that not only caused painful jerks but also threatened to make the cart turn turtle in some cases.

The bullocks apparently did not like the idea of moving through such a road, and the carter was doing his best to make a headway towards the goal. The poor creatures were alternately scolded or coaxed, beaten or caressed. From inside the chhai (mat roof) of the cart, I could hear the goading address of the carter to his animals.

> You, sala (wife's brother), are you so fond of your feet that you can not step in the mud?

> You, brother-in-law of a brute, why don't you like to move or get down in the mud?

> These salas are only making intermittent efforts…

Off and on the voice of the carter turned soft and persuasive. I heard him shower flatteries on his animals, and such appealing words also came to my ears:

> Babas, you know that we have to go on, then why are you refusing, my children?

or

My jewels, this is but an empty cart, then why are you finding it difficult to go? Proceed, my treasures: proceed without any stop anywhere.

Occasionally it appeared that the cart would remain stuck in the mud; often the carter submitted that he did not know what was in God's mind and whether he would be allowed to carry his Babu safe to Palashi. But his prayers were answered, and having left Burdwan at seven in the morning I eventually found myself safe in Kanchanpur at two in the afternoon; my friends were anxiously awaiting my arrival.

Here I should thankfully refer to the kindness shown to me by Dr. Khan, a medical practitioner, and Sri P. R. Paul, a rice mill owner, both carrying on their respective business in the northern suburbs of Burdwan. This time, along with the problem of access to the village, I had the question of securing friendly introductions as well. A relative of mine, my nephew's cousin and a resident of Burdwan, took me to his friend, the said Dr. Khan, as he used to get occasional calls from many villages of this area. He, in his turn, took us to Sri Paul, a native of Kurman, a sister village of Palashi. If Sri Paul was rich and influential, he was no less kind. He helped me to arrange the cart, and got a chance of speaking of me to the president of Sakti-Sangha (a young men's association) of Kanchanpur. On his way back from Burdwan where he had come on some business, Sri P. M., the president of Kanchanpur's Sakti-Sangha met Sri Paul just after our visit to him in the day. While getting up on the cart next morning, for the memorable trek described above, it was a pleasant surprise to me to learn from Sri Paul that he had already arranged for my stay at Palashi, and a hearty reception would cheer me as soon as the difficulties of the journey were over.

The first impression that I had on entering the village was to feel that I was in a besieged town. It was difficult either to come in or go out until the roads had dried up. The people here make requisite arrangements in advance for this period of isolation so that they can tide over minor difficulties. But cases of emergency arise, such as the need of bringing a doctor from the town or taking of paddy stocks for sale at the rice-mills of Burdwan; it is then that the magnitude of the problem is brought home. Easy communication with the town is the most keenly felt need here; and the people are looking hopefully for the days when macadamization of the main road will be completed at least up to the spot where their village cart-track branches off.

In this connection it may be noted that growing in comparative isolation, Kanchanpur seems to have retained a high degree of hospitality. I was forced to notice this trait twenty-five years ago, and have to do so here again. When greetings were over, my new friends at once declared that I should be treated as a guest of the village at least for the first few days. Visitors from outside are welcome as food does not require cash and is plentiful in the village household. The villagers, living in areas where communications from town are poor, love to hear news of the outside world. Religion also lays down an injunction that one should treat his guests as gods. Our rural culture continues, therefore, to reserve an amount of hospitality declining in city conditions.

1.3—LAYOUT OF THE VILLAGE

Now that Kanchanpur has been reached, I intend to take my readers through the village and present a sketch of it in the lines given below:

The Rev. Day in his book spoke of two distinct parts of Kanchanpur—first the village itself or the cluster of homesteads inhabited by the members of the community, and second, the "arable mark", consisting of some thousands of bighas of land and forming a circle of cultivation of a radius of about half a mile.

Human habitation indeed forms the nucleus of the village, but the surrounding area is oval two miles north to south and one mile east to west, and covers approximately two square miles. To be more exact, the moiuza consists of 1461 acres. Roughly speaking only one fourth of this area forms the human habitation.

On the south through the fields of the village, runs the main canal from the Damodar River. There was no canal in the days of the Rev. Day. In *Kanchanpur Revisited* (1933), it was noted:

> A projected distribution of the Damodar Canal would run through the fields of Kanchanpur. The peasants see nothing but the disadvantages of the new scheme of things. The free passage of their carts from one village to another would be obstructed. The water-tax, amounting to as much as Rs.3/-per acre, would be an additional item on their already overburdened shoulders. True, they would get a supply of water, but they doubt whether they would get it when the demand of the crops is most urgent, and they definitely know that

famine is not unknown even where canals have been constructed. Malaria will be less—this they doubt.

The stagnant water of the canal—stagnant because the sluice gates will not allow a free flow from the river—and the jungles that will flourish profusely on both sides of the canal will become additional breeding places for mosquitoes...

The canal did come, but the jungles, as apprehended, did not flourish. Paths on the embankments of the canal make a trek on foot easier, and the distance from Burdwan to Kanchanpur is less when the village is approached direct from the southwestern side instead of the roundabout way via Dewan Dighi, that is, the main road to Kusumgram running north of the village. Even in the rains, if the weather is dry for a couple of days, one can ride on a bicycle on these embankments and there are at present no less than fifty cycles in the village of Kanchanpur: This has brought the village in closer contact with Vardhamana.

Branching out from the main canal two distributary channels run northwards. One of these flows through the eastern fields of Kanchanpur, while the other passes through Kaligram just west of the village. The main canal has separated the southernmost fields of Kanchanpur and there is no bridge over the canal at this place. As a result a Kanchanpur raiyat who has any land on the southern side of the canal has to make a circuitous round in order to attend to the agricultural operations on those lands. The inconvenience is caused to a good many cultivators, and the inhabitants are making repeated applications to the authorities for construction of a bridge over the canal at this point. But hitherto no action has been taken.

The village has a natural decline from the south to the north. On the north side again, the east-west run of the land shows an undulating picture, and the waters of the fields flow down in ditches that run northwards and take the surplus water to the river Khori (or as it is sometimes called, Khargeswari). This river flows in a northeastern direction and passing by the neighbouring villages of Parui and Kurman carries the waters of the valley down to the Ganges.

The village is situated between fifty to one hundred feet above sea level and has a fertile soil. Like other villages of Bengal, Kanchanpur also is a stage for the six seasons that come and play their respective roles year after year. The callously rude and indifferent summer, the drunk and hilarious rains, the serene fore-autumn with its clear blue sky, the golden after-autumn with its basket of corn and ripe fruits, the dry bitter winter with cold north winds, and the season of transition, the ever-fickle queen of the seasons, the prodigal spring, all pass by casting sunshine and shadow on the round of human life that flows on at Kanchanpur.

A few common specimens of the flora and fauna of Kanchanpur may be named here, before we come to the geography of the village proper. When approached from the road on the north, Kanchanpur stands completely camouflaged by the green foliage of its stately trees. Its houses and temples are screened from the eyes of the approaching visitor until he has actually entered their precincts. Numerous kingly trees give shade and beauty to the village—the big batas (*Ficus indica*) with scores of downward branches, the heavy trunked asvathvas (*Ficus religiosa*), the mango (*Mangifera indica*), topes and bamboo (*Bambos*) clusters, the bael (*Aegle marmelos*), the kathbael (*Feronia elephantam*), the tamarind (*Tanmarindus indica*), the neem (*Melia azadrachta*), the palm (*Borassus flabetuniformis*), the bakul (*Mimusops elangi*), the palash (Butea frondosa) and various other glories of vegetable creation. The smaller fruit trees like the plum (*Prunum*), guava (*Psidium guayaba*), lime (*Citrus medica acida*), papya (*Carica papaya*), plantain (*Plantoginem*) and various shrubs are scattered throughout the village. The villagers take pride that such richness of vegetable creation is not to be found in all the neighbouring villages of Kanchanpur.

Of the domestic animals, buffaloes, bullocks and cows, goats and sheep, ducks and hens, and pigs belonging to the extraneous castes are quite common. Peacocks, pigeons, hares, kittens, pups and various singing birds are also kept as pets in several households. The kittens and pups are not, however, cared for when they grow into cats and dogs; they have then to make their living by their own efforts. Of the non-domestic animals, there may be seen in the village a good number of jackals and wild cats after evening. The monkeys that had been so troublesome in 1933 have been scared away by repeated massacres organized by the villagers with the help of the monkey-killers. Many birds, rats, mice, snakes, flies, mosquitoes and various insects refuse to abandon human company.

Besides the glories of vegetation and the ruins of old buildings, the things that strike a visitor when strolling in the village are its temples. Some of the temples, like that of Dayanath of the Pauls, are completely dilapidated, but several are still standing. Some of them appear to have been made nearly 200 years ago and in one the date of establishment is given as 1189 B.S. or 1783 A.D. In some, the outer walls have pictures in relief on the bricks depicting religious stories of the epics. These are mainly Siva temples and number about twenty-five in all.

There are no less than forty tanks (ponds), some of which are amongst the finest and most picturesque ones in the district. The roads of the village are also very well-laid and compare favorably with any other village in this respect although the straight road running through the center of the village which Rev. Day had so proudly mentioned has become somewhat undulating as will be seen in the maps shown below.

As the various Figures below indicate, the village is divided into two main wards the Uttapara (Northside) and the Dakshinpara (Southside). The Southside again has three parts known as Purabpara (east end), Dakshinpara (south end) and Paschimpara (west end). Apart from these regional divisions, there are several caste-wise paras such as the Banerjeepara, Mashaipara, Kotalpaia, Goalapara and so on, but the subject of dispersion of the castes may be reserved for a later discussion.

The central road of the village runs from north to south and small streets from the eastern and western divisions come and merge in it The central road which goes to meet the Burdwan-Kusumgram main road about three quarters of a mile north of the village is called the feeder road in village terminology. Lately, at the request of the villagers, the improvement of this feeder road has been taken up by the District Board. The condition of this road in the winter is good, but it needs some dressing if cars are to be driven up to the heart of the village even then. In the dry season, jeeps bring visitors and goods are brought in trucks. After harvest is over, bags of paddy and stacks of straw are also sometimes carried away in lorries. The days when such vehicles enter the village offer great jubilation for the village children. Excited and hilarious, they run with the moving vehicles, through dust and noise while the driver and the august passengers shout their utmost to caution the village urchins.

1.4—Neighbourhood of Kanchanpur

A village community is bound to be affected by its neighbourhood. Mention has already been made in the beginning of the chapter of the Burdwan-Kusumgram road which links the village with the nearest city which is Burdwan. The geographical position of the village in relation to Burdwan and the surrounding area is illustrated in Figure 2.

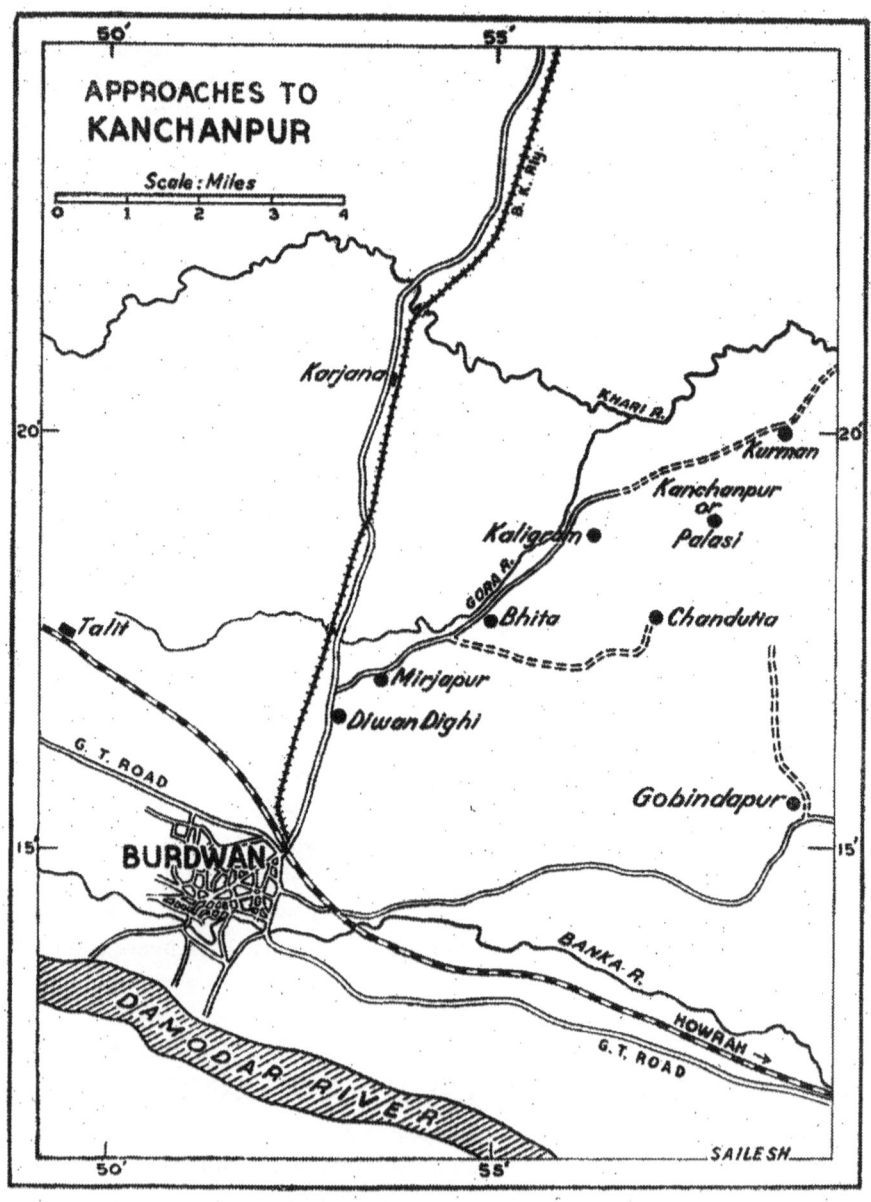

There is another bus route—the Burdwan-Kahlna road which runs a few miles south of Kanchanpur and passes through Gobindapur, an important village in the locality. It is convenient for travelers coming from the southern or the southeastern sides to approach Kanchanpur through Gobindapur. It is interesting to note that this Gobindapur has acquired an adjective, namely, Hat (market) and is generally referred to as Hat Gobindapur, possibly because of the market relations that it has developed with the surrounding villages. On Mondays and Thursdays vegetable hats are held at Gobindapur, and on all days there are some aratdars (commission agents) ready to buy, store or sell paddy; Gobindapur has also a cinema house, the only one in the neighbouring area. On Asharnabami, during the puja of the god Panchanan, a fair is held at Gobindapur which is fairly attended by the villages of the neighbourhood.

Though connected with ties of economics and rituals, Hat Gobindapur is five miles away to the south and on the west-east pucca road from Burdwan to Kalna. The surrounding villages whose fields meet those of Kanchanpur are Kaligram in the west, Parui in the north, Kurman in the northwest, Debagram in the east, and Belgona, Malkita and Chandrahati in the south. Of these surrounding villages Kanchanpur (Palashi) has special relations with Debagram, as these two villages taken together constitute one gram sabha, and therefore have one and the same gram panchayat. Besides this Shona Palashi gram sabha, there are five other constituent gram sabha that go to form the anchal of the region in which Kanchanpur is situated. It is to be noted that the adjoining villages of Parui, Kaligram and Chandrahati do not fall in this particular anchal. Kaligram, however, especially its hattala (market place) as a center of different services to the local people, affects the life of Palashi in several ways. After passing from the F. P. School of the village, many students of Palashi go to read in the classes of the Junior High School at Kaligram hattala. There is also an arat there for buying, storing and selling of paddy. There is a dehusking machine where many householders, including those of Palashi, send their boiled paddy for hulling. The buses plying on the Burdwan-Kusumgram road stop for a few minutes at this hattala where there are a few sweetmeat and tea shops. Formerly the place was the terminus of the bus traffic, but in recent years the service has been extended to Bhanderdih. The passengers love to get down here a few minutes for some conversation and refreshment. Many passengers of Kanchanpur get in or out of the bus stop of Kaligram and make their way through the fields instead of going more than two miles further towards the northeast where the feeder road from the village joins the main road.

Beyond the main road to the north lies Parui, the nearest riverbank village in the area. The Khori River, rising somewhere from the high lands of Chotonagpur flows down to the Ganges. A few decades ago, I am told by some elders of the village, people used to bring their goods down from Calcutta on this river, and natives of Kanchanpur used to get their merchandise transported from the banks of the Khori at Parui to their own respective places.

On the first of Magh of the Bengali year when according to the Hindu almanac the sun just begins to take its path towards the north, the villagers of Kanchanpur and the neighbouring area observe a river bathing ceremony. Men, women and children of Kanchanpur go to Parui that day for their baths and there they also participate in a fair that gathers on the occasion. The Vaishinabs of the village also hold a mahotsab (great festival) at this time, on the banks of the river at the fair where kirtans (mass prayers) are sung for hours and people are fed with khitchuri (hotchpotch of rice and dal) and tarkari (hotchpotch of various vegetables).

Parui, Kurman and Palashi are three villages that have close ties in the rituals that are practiced at the great festival of Siva's gajan celebrated at the end of Chaitra each year. The sannyasis from Parui as well as from Kurman have to visit Palashi with their god of *gajan*. They march in a dancing procession through the village and are warmly received in embrace by the Kanchanpur sannyasis. They make due obeisance to the old Siva, and thereafter return to their own villages. Next day the sannyasis of Kanchanpur make their return visits both to Kurman and Parui.

Kurman, to the northeast, has various other ties with Palashi. It is the seat of the anchal panchayat, in which Kanchanpur is represented by four of its members. On Wednesdays and Sundays, it holds vegetable hats which are attended by a considerable number of men from Kanchanpur as the latter has no longer any such hat. The hats on Tuesdays and Saturdays that used to be held at Kanchanpur were shifted to Belgona, another neighbouring village, long before 1933, and Kanchanpur had lost its position in this respect.

At Kurman there is a High School which prepares students for the School Final. No less than thirteen students from Palashi daily attend the classes at Kurman. There are also a rice-hulling machine and a paddy arat, which have developed the economic relations already existing between the villages.

The anchal of the locality consists of the following nine villages (see the map below)

1. Kurman
2. Chhota Belun
2. Burar (Ramchandrapur)
4. Palashi
5. Debagram
6. Sadya
7. Singhapara (part of Karori mouza)
8. Belgona
9. Mallcita

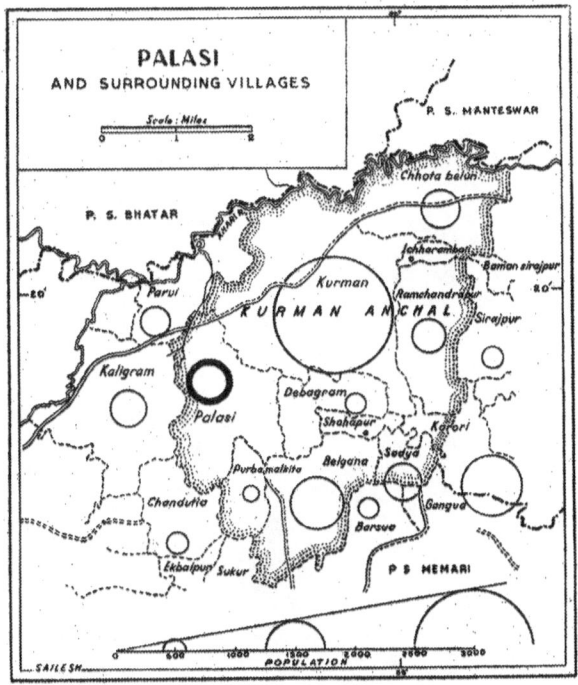

Of these, Kurman, Chhota Belun and Burar (Ramchandrapur) each consti-
tutes a gram sabha (village assembly) and consequently has a gram panchayat as
well. Devagram, Singhapara and Malkita are not viable units to compose a gram
sabha independently and have therefore been merged respectively with the
adjoining bigger villages of Palashi, Sadya and Belgona for formation of the gram

sabhas. Thus there are six gram sabhas each represented by a gram panchayat in the anchal, and over the entire area functions the anchal panchayat.

As regards numbers of households and population, Kurman is the biggest amongst the anchal villages. Belgona stands second while Kanchanpur occupies the third position. The Ugra-kshatriyas are the predominating caste in the area. Both in wealth and number they are in majority in six villages out of nine. Of the other three Chhota Belun and Burar are Sadgop villages while the Brahmins predominate at Kanchanpur. There is however a considerable number of influential Sunbarnabaniks both at Kanchanpur and its sister village Belgona.

CHAPTER 2

▼

THE HERITAGE OF CASTE: A SOCIOLOGICAL ANALYSIS

Caste plays such an important place in Kanchanpur and permeates so effectively the everyday life of its people that we shall first try to obtain a bird's eye view of this social phenomenon before going on to a demographic or economic analysis of the village population.

2.1—CONCENTRIC GRADATION AND GROUPINGS OF CASTE

Many attempts have been made to delineate the patterns of caste on the bias of status. The concepts emerging from such efforts have always assumed a vertical structure with the Brahmin at the "top" and the untouchables at the "lowest" rung of the ladder.

But a close examination of the relations between different castes as they live in Kanchanpur has suggested that a more realistic way of presenting the pattern of caste, and one that would make the inherent significance of caste more comprehensible, would be to represent the different caste groups in concentric circles with the Brahmins occupying a place not at the top but in the very center of the village society. (Please see Figure 6)

Similarly attempts have been made by sociologists to devise a scale for measuring the social distance between the different caste groups, and these attempts have succeeded in giving names to existing sociological phenomena such as "consanguinity, "commensality", etc. etc. But each of these phenomena is found to be interwoven with another presenting in each region a different pattern too intricate to be seen or understood dearly.

Long conversations with peoples of different castes, however, have suggested that to the village people themselves this problem of defining social distance between caste groups presents no complexity. They simply place each caste in one or another of four concentric circles. The Brahmins, as explained above, occupy the center; those from whom Brahmins can accept water to drink, or the "Jal-chal" ("jal" means water), fall in the immediately outer ring, the "Jal-achal", or those from whom Brahmins do not take water, are placed in the next outer ring but they are still within the fort walls of caste, the so called Sudras. Then come the segregated and the servile castes—those outside the pale of decent society, the "mlechhas" among the Hindus. It is a paradox of Hindu social development that these groups have been absorbed and exteriorized at the same time. The epithet "low" has been attributed to them, but here they have been classed as "exterior castes", though the concept of the latter term has been questioned by many sociologists. Muslims, Christians and in fact all those who resist the tendency to become absorbed in the Hindu fold are not regarded as "low" castes—they are the non-Hindu "mlechhas" and the distance at which they are kept from the central circle is no less.

The hierarchical importance of different social groups may be noted as early as the institution of the Varnashram Dharma of the ancient Hindus, which lies at the background of the present complex caste-system. In fact it is mentioned even in the "srutis" that from the body of Manu were born all human beings: the Brahmins from the face, the Kshatriyas from the breast, the Vaishyas from the thighs and the Sudras from the feet.

> sruti—The literature regarded as revelation of deity, as the Vedas and parts of Upanishads.

> Manu—The mythological ancestor of mankind according to the Hindus.

The text ascribed to the Rig Veda is famous: *brahmano'sya mukhamasid vahu rajanyah krtah uru tadasya yadvaisyah padbhynm sudra ajayata.* There is a text in the Ramayana: *mukhatah brahmana jatah urasah ksatriyastatha urubhyam jajnire vaisyah padbhyam sudra iti srutih, (aranyakanda, canto 14 sl. 30).)*

Each of these four rings or circles is allotted to the four groups of castes; each individual caste and religion occupies a different segment in one or another of these four rings.

Let us examine each of these four circles in turn.

2.1.1—The High Castes

Among the high castes, the Brahmins as a rule stand at the very center. They are the men of "great birth" (mahajanam). They are the gurus, the teachers of all the varnas.

The majority of the Brahmins at Kanchanpur, as was observed by the Rev. Day in the last century, are of the Srotiya order, better known in this area as the Radhi Brahmins. There is only one Brahmin householder of the Vedic order. Strictly speaking he belongs to another village, but is a resident of Kanchanpur for many years and is settled here as the headmaster of the local Primary School. There are families of the Goswami Brahmins. They are followers of Sri Chaitanya, and are therefore Vaishnabs. The Srotriya and the Vedic Brahmins claim to be followers of Sakti and are therefore Saktas. They consider themselves nearer to the center of the circle than the Goswamis because they offer ministrations only to clean castes, while the Goswamis have many disciples even amongst the jal-achal castes. A Radhi Brahmin will not give his girl-child in marriage to a Goswami boy, though Goswami girls may be accepted in a Brahmin household. However, nowadays, this rule is often violated, and Radhi brides are often married to Goswami young men but chiefly because in such cases suitable bridegrooms may be found at a lower price. As a result the Goswamis are coming to be considered almost equal to the Radhi Brahmins, and there is seen to be no strict restriction as to commensality and marriage between the two groups at Kanchanpur.

The Vaidyas and the Kayasthas also occupy the inner circle but come next to the Brahmins, but the Subarnabanik Brahmins are not accorded the high respect due to the true Brahmins. Even the Vaidyas and the Kayasthas consider themselves superior to the Subarnabanik Brahmins who are derogatorily termed in the village parlance as the Bene-Bamun (that is, Brahmins of the Banias). They are considered to be degraded because they officiate at the ceremonial functions of the Subarnabaniks, who fall amongst the jal-achal castes of the Hindu society. Thus the Goalas have their Goala Brahmins, and the Kotals their Kotal Brahmins, the Bagdis their Bagdi Brahmins, and so on. Even the exterior caste sannyasis of the Old Siva, have their Gajan Brahmin, and the unclean dead at the crematory have their Mafia-Brahman to minister in the prescribed rituals. Except the Subarnabanik Brahmins, the degraded Brahmins catering to other low castes do not live in Kanchanpur but come from other villages to help their clients in the performance of their ritual ceremonies.

2.1.2—Jal-chal Castes:

Now let us look at the castes of the jal-chal group, i.e., the castes from whose hands the Brahmins occupying the *sanctum sanctorum* may accept water to drink. They occupy a circle outside that of the high castes, but as they form a group of non-polluting status, they occupy distinct segments in this next-to-the-inner circle and are traditionally known as the "Nabasakhs" (that is, the nine branches). Amongst them fall the Sadgop, the Gandhabanik, the Napit, the Modak, the Karmakar, the Tanti and the Tili. The last mentioned caste, that is, the Tili as merchants in oil seeds, are accepted within the respectable class of the Nabasakhs, but the Teti (the extractors of oil) are looked down upon as following a degrading occupation of destroying life by crushing the seed. The Teli is therefore considered inferior in status and from his hands no water can be taken by a Brahmin. There are only three Ugra-Kshatriya families at Kanchanpur at present. But the Ugra-Kshatriyas were an influential class in the village and, as we have seen earlier, they are at present a predominating caste in the neighbourhood of Kanchanpur. Though not in the traditional group of the Nabasakhs, their status was considered equivalent to the Jal-chal group in 1931 and much earlier. This caste chiefly abounds in this part of Bengal, and forms a strong, courageous community. The men of this class are now trying to improve their social position further. Claiming their origin from a Kshatriya father, they are now claiming themselves to be Kshatriyas and are trying to acquire the status of the twice born themselves. In fact they already perform rites and ceremonies reserved for those of the innermost citadel only.

In Bengal, the Pallav Gops are not amongst the traditional Nabasakhs and in 1931 they were classed in the third group of castes having doubtful status. Since then the Gops have improved their positions in this area, and in common behavior they are more or less accepted as a jal-chal caste. Manu gave them a degraded status, as they used to geld their male calves but as a class of milkmen, they are in a position of vantage and who is there so bold as to say that not a drop of water has been accepted by him from the milkman? According to tradition the "Sadgops" and the ordinary "Gops" originally belonged to the same stock. Among them those who took to cultivation were ranked as "Sadgop", that is, the clean Gops; and those who took to cattle-breeding here given a lower status because of the reasons stated above. The latter are colloquially known as the "Goalas", but they love to call themselves "Pallava Gops" in our Kanchanpur. The result, however, is that people seldom refuse to take water from the Gops, and many even class them amongst the Nabasakhs. But the conservatives among the Brahmins still reject the Gops as polluting and they specially behave in that manner in all ceremonial and ritual situations.

2.1.3—Jal-achal Castes

Neither treated as outside the pale of caste nor accepted within the respectable circle of the jal-chals, there is a group of castes termed in the village parlance as jal-achal, i.e., from whose hand water is not acceptable.

The Subarnabaniks, the Sunnis, the Chunaris, the Kaibartas and the adhars are amongst them. At present there is one Vaishnab household in the village. He is a refugee settler and before joining the Vaishnab sect, was a Namasudra by caste. A great majority of the present Vaishnabs of the mendicant order come from low and lost castes.

They simply take the bhek, that is, put on the garb of a mendicant and become Vairagis. The Vairagi order is more or less becoming a caste but from them water is not usually acceptable to a high caste villager. As one of these remarked: "I am not prepared to accept water from a Vaishnab who has turned so on losing his caste". "*Jat hariye Bostom*"—as they say in village parlance.)

The Subarnabaniks claim to be descendants of traders from Rajputana, who belonged to the Vaishya caste, i.e., the third estate of the Vedic Aryan society. It is said that at one time these Baniks were held in high esteem in our society, but owing to their refusal to finance King Vallal Sen of Bengal (1158-1179 A.D.), they were degraded in status by a royal fiat. They were supposed to pursue an occupation of greed, and hence came to be looked down upon. Indeed even in these days their social position is considered to be so inferior that in the marriage of a Vaidya boy of our village in recent years, the vessels and plates used by his Subarnabanik friends in the dinner became of no further use to the owner, and they were, thereafter, given away to some low caste neighbours. During my stay in the village I personally saw an elderly Brahmin widow refuse treatment from our Subarnabanik Doctor on the ground that she could not accept water from a Banik—as medicine is usually mixed in water for service. In serious crises, however, I found on enquiry, such scruples do not come in the way.

The Subarnabaniks of this village are noted for their wealth, and with education and culture they are trying to raise their caste position in the society. But this seems not very easy to achieve against the thwarting attitude of superiority of the higher castes in the village. But, as individuals, many Subarnabaniks are held in consideration and esteem in the village and their contributions to the community festivals and rituals are accepted with grace.

The Sunris, the caste of liquor sellers, have also got an inferior social status as a caste community. None of them has at present any liquor shop, and they have turned into an agricultural caste in the village. The Kaibartas are a class of fishermen. Their occupation of fishing bore a stigma and consequently water would not be accepted from them. At Kanchanpur they have acquired, like the Sunris, land for cultivation which is their main occupation at present. Fishing is still the subsidiary occupation for all the Kaibarta households at Kanchanpur.

The Kaibartas are of two broad classes: (i) the "Hele", the plowing "Kaibartas" and (ii) the "Jele", that is, the fishermen "Kaibartas". As cultivators the former have a socially favorable position, and are otherwise known as "Mahishyas" in Bengal. They are not however ever represented in Kanchanpur where the "Kaibartas" are of the "Jele" group.

The Chunaris are a class of lime makers. The name of the caste has been derived from the Bengali word chun which means lime and Chunari therefore means "a manufacturer of lime". Most of them have taken to share-cropping at present though some of them still make lime from shells by an indigenous process which they practice as a subsidiary occupation. The Chunaris of the village consider their place in the social hierarchy at least as high as the Subarnabaniks, Sunris and Kaibartas, but their complaint is that they are not given the esteem due to them because of their comparative poverty. They also state that they are the Varnakar (color maker) Tamulis, and perhaps by this claim they expect their status to be raised to that of the clean castes to which the Tamulis undoubtedly belong. It is a familiar method of raising the status of a caste—that of adopting the name of a much higher caste and qualifying it by a suitable adjective. It is hoped that in the course of time, the adjective will have less significance than the caste name chosen and thus the status of the group will be raised in the estimation of others.

There is now only one Sutradhar household in the village, and the man there is living in single blessedness. He is the village carpenter, as well as an idol maker, as he has acquired some skill in the making of the earthen images of the Hindu deities. The villagers do not like to lose the services of this Sutradhar, so much so that they are quite lenient with him even when he does not follow the correct behavior pattern approved by the society.

2.1.4—The Exterior Castes

The fourth group in Kanchanpur is what might be called the Exterior Group which consists of the Outcastes, the Santhals and the Muslims. Theoretically the Santhals and the Muslims belong to other groups than the Hindu castes. The former are a tribe, but apparently on their way to becoming a caste; the latter as represented in Kanchanpur profess to practice a different faith, but apparently consist of converts from the low castes and have much in common with them. Paradoxically enough, the Outcastes, too, are a part of the caste system and yet excluded from the inner circle of Hinduism. Many have called them the Exterior Castes as opposed to what may be called the Interior Castes. Some have labeled them as Depressed Classes; the British Government has listed them as Scheduled Castes. Gandhiji classed them as Harijans, that is, "the beloved of God", but none of these euphemisms helped to raise their position materially, each becoming only another synonym for the others.

Examining this fourth group in our village community more closely, we find that they are "below the sort", they are the chhota-loks (i.e., the debased or small men) of the village society. There is a traditional social barrier which prevents them from moving upwards. They hang around and move on the periphery, neither allowed to come within nor allowed to detach themselves from Hindu village society.

It has already been noted that while jal-chal and jal-achal classification is a useful line of describing the caste society, it is not of much use as a test for exterior castes. Thus the Subarnabaniks and some others, as discussed earlier, are amongst the jal-achal group but they are not considered "exterior" in our village.

The psychology of social gradation imposed upon the exterior castes has introduced caste distinctions within the exterior castes also. In Kanchanpur, the Bagdis occupy the highest place among the exterior castes. They love to call themselves Bagdi-Kshatriyas, thereby persuading themselves and trying to persuade others to regard them of a Kshatriya origin. But among themselves there are four sub-castes, three of which are represented in Kanchanpur—the Tentule, the Kush-Mete and the Dule. Of these the Tentule Bagdis consider themselves of superior status and do not intermarry with their own sub-castes.

The distinctive status of the Bagdis amongst the exterior castes is borne out by the fact that they are privileged to have the services of the village barbers and the dais (midwives), while other exterior castes do not receive such services. The Dhawa Muslims of the village, however, are entitled to these privileges, though they are outside Hindu society. It is surmised by the villagers that the Muslim families got these privileges at the time when the Nawabs ruled, and the tradition is still continuing.

Among the exterior castes, the Kotals of the village are an influential class and have taken to agriculture as their occupation. The term Kotal, it is understood, is an adopted name in the place of the word Chandal to which tradition has attached a terrible stigma. The first Chandala, it is said, was the offspring of a pratiloma (hypogamous) marriage between a Brahmin woman and a Sudra man. Such marriages were highly disfavored by the Aryan invaders, and tradition gave its offsprings the lowest place in the Hindu society. In some places these people go by the name of Namasudra, and possibly they originally belonged to an aboriginal tribe. In fact it seems that all the exterior castes at one time were such tribes, and were in course of time transformed into castes and admitted in the Hindu society but not allowed within the respectable social pale.

At Kanchanpur, the Kotals are more advanced in wealth and education in comparison with the other exterior castes and are consequently trying to raise their social status.

The three Kora families have been settled here only for the last two generations but are claiming to be Hindus. Originally a Kolarian tribe, they have grown into a caste here, but they have not yet been able to appoint a Brahmin priest to minister at their rituals. The village barbers do not render them service, and the dais do not visit their houses overtly. But they have accepted the gods of the village and cast derogatory looks on the new Kora immigrants who come from their native districts to seek work in Kanchanpur.

2.1.5—Ulterior Groups

Eight Santhal families are now settled in the village. They claim that they are kin to the Hindus and have begun to adopt the Hindu customs and practices like the Koras. It was noted in *Kanchanpur Revisited* that there was only periodical immigration of the Santhals and there was not a single Santhal settler in the village at that time. Besides these eight settled families there is of course a regular ebb and tide in the flow of Santhal labour in the village, and, especially in the harvest season, a large number of temporary settlements of the Santhals still spring up at Kanchanpur.

In 1874 there were no Muslim families in Kanchanpur, in 1931 there were no less than eleven, their number has dwindled again into only two in 1958. The increase in the number of Hindu field labourers put them into difficulty, and many of them also liked to migrate to neighbouring Muslim villages to live there with their coreligionists. The remaining two householders prefer to stay on in the village where, in the ties of master and servant, they are almost members of Hindu households and, living in an Hinduized atmosphere, they appear more like Hindus than Muslims. It is true that they worship Allah, and follow the ritual of the Muslim life cycle. But the great gods of the Hindus—the old Siva, the Great Kali, Mother Manasa and so on, all command respect from them and they promise sacrifices to them in times of difficulties. They observe and participate in the village parvans and festivals such as the Navanna and the Pitha-sankranti. They share in the joys and the merriments during the pujas and though they are not supposed to worship the earthen gods, they have no objection to help shouldering the earthen images in the processions round the village.

2.2—PATTERN OF PARTICIPATION

All that has been said above regarding the inter-caste and intra-caste relations will be borne out by the following description of a festival meal in which all the people of the village participate annually.

Sri N. Chakravarti, a rich, childless householder celebrates the Basanti Puja honoring the Goddess Annapurna each year and gives a banquet to the villagers on the occasion coinciding with March-April. The host is a Brahmin and all food is also prepared by authentic Brahmins. Moreover, it is Devi Annapurna's prasad (leavings of food partaken of by a deity). There are therefore, no inhibitions to participating and all are glad to come. Formerly a 100% of the villagers were invited, but in recent years the proportion of the villagers participating in it has been reduced. Still, all relatives and intimate friends and representatives from all Hindu households of the village are invited to the feast

In the morning of the day of the feast, a Brahmin was deputed by the householder to invite the high castes; a Napit was similarly asked to go round the village for inviting the jal-chal, the jal-achal and the exterior castes. According to custom, the invitees were to be again called to the feast at the proper time, by a Brahmin and a Napit respectively; a person who is not thus reminded again would not come to the feast

The villagers attach great significance to the caste status of the person who is deputed for conveying the invitations. The deputy, I understand, may be a person of higher caste status than the person invited; he must be at least of equal status. His position cannot be lower, and if it be so it is an affront. The system of delegating a Brahmin for the high castes and a Napit for the rest has taken almost the force of a custom.

What happened once in the times of an influential zamindar of the village has left behind an imprint in the form of a jocular phrase—"the barber as the mean"—still current in the village. On the occasion of a feast in his house, the said zamindar sent his Nagdi (peon) for conveying the invitations to the middle and the lower castes. As it happened the Nagdi was a Hari, and the middle castes, and especially the Sadgops, felt insulted and there was great dissatisfaction and agitation. The zamindar was made aware of the situation and he understood that his procedure for the invitations had not been proper. But it was then time for the dinner, and what could be done? A shrewd Brahmin, a friend to the zamindar, suggested that the situation might be remedied if a Brahmin instead of a Napit could be deputed to make the second call for dinner. The zamindar requested the adviser himself to do that "honorable" task and a zamindar's request could not be refused in those days. The Hari and the Brahmin deputies, taken together, must have produced the "barber as the mean", and the zamindar came out of the situation with good grace.

Let us now attend the feast at the house of the Chakravartis. The dinner starts after one o'clock in the day and ends at sunset. In the first batch, the high castes are seated—the Brahmins, the Subarnabanik Brahmins, the Goswamis, the Vaidyas and the Kayasthas. They are, no doubt, grouped in different rows according to their caste, but all the dishes are served to them at the same time.

In the other villages of the region the Kayasthas, I understand, have a little lower social position, and in such feasts they have to wait till the Brahmins have practically finished their eating. In other words it is not the custom to distribute rice (the first item) to Kayasthas until tak (sour relish served at the end of dinner) is served to the Brahmins. The Kayasthas of this village, therefore, avoid all outside intervillage social dinners. Their social position in this village was raised possibly in the regime of the Kayastha zamindars, and their influence is still continuing in the traditions of this village.

When the first batch has finished, the upper caste women, and the middle caste men come for their seats. The women of the high castes take their seats in the rooms as well as the raised verandahs of the houses. The men of the middle castes, including the jal-chal and the jai-achal groups, usually sit on the lower verandahs or the uthan (courtyard) below. Needless to say all the castes sit in different groups in different rows.

An adjoining house was also requisitioned for the arrangement of the seats. Service started and all these groups began to eat at the same time. When this batch also finished their meals, the third group sat for theirs. This consisted of the women of the middle castes and the men of the exterior castes. These women did not go inside the rooms, but took their seats in the verandahs, while the low-caste men all sat on the uthan, i.e., the earth yard of the two houses. In the fourth batch the women of the exterior castes came to eat when their men-folk had finished, and took their seats on the same uthans.

Lastly, when evening was drawing near the Santhals came and took their seats and when their eating was over the feast had come to an end.

2.3—THE RESIDENTIAL DISPERSION OF THE CASTES

Figures 4 and 5 illustrate the residential dispersion of the castes in the village of Kanchanpur.

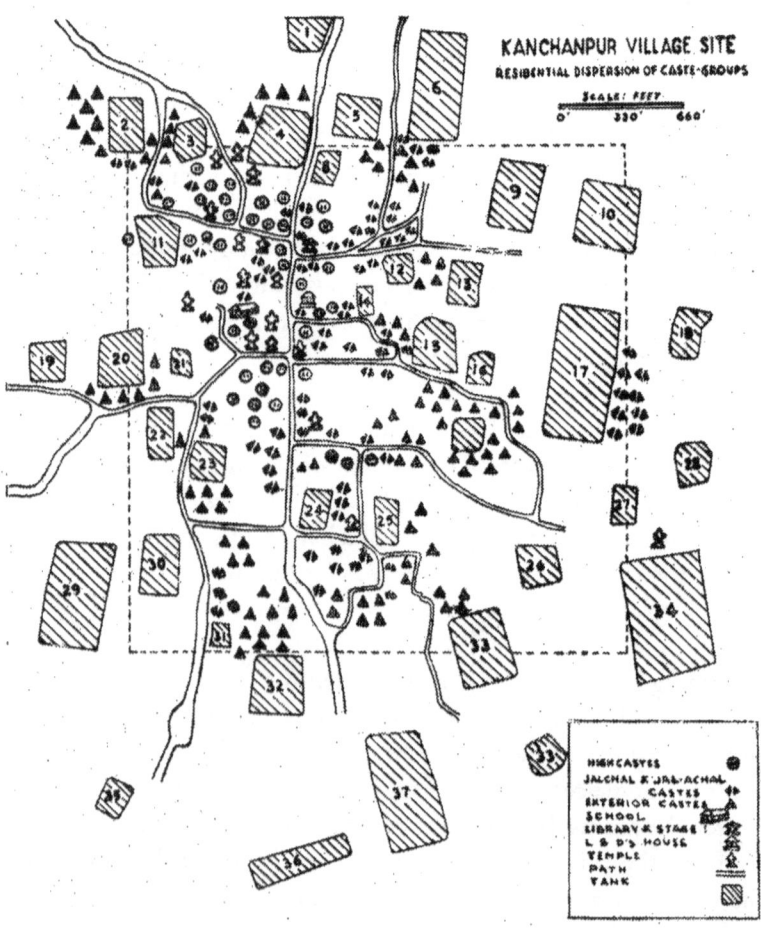

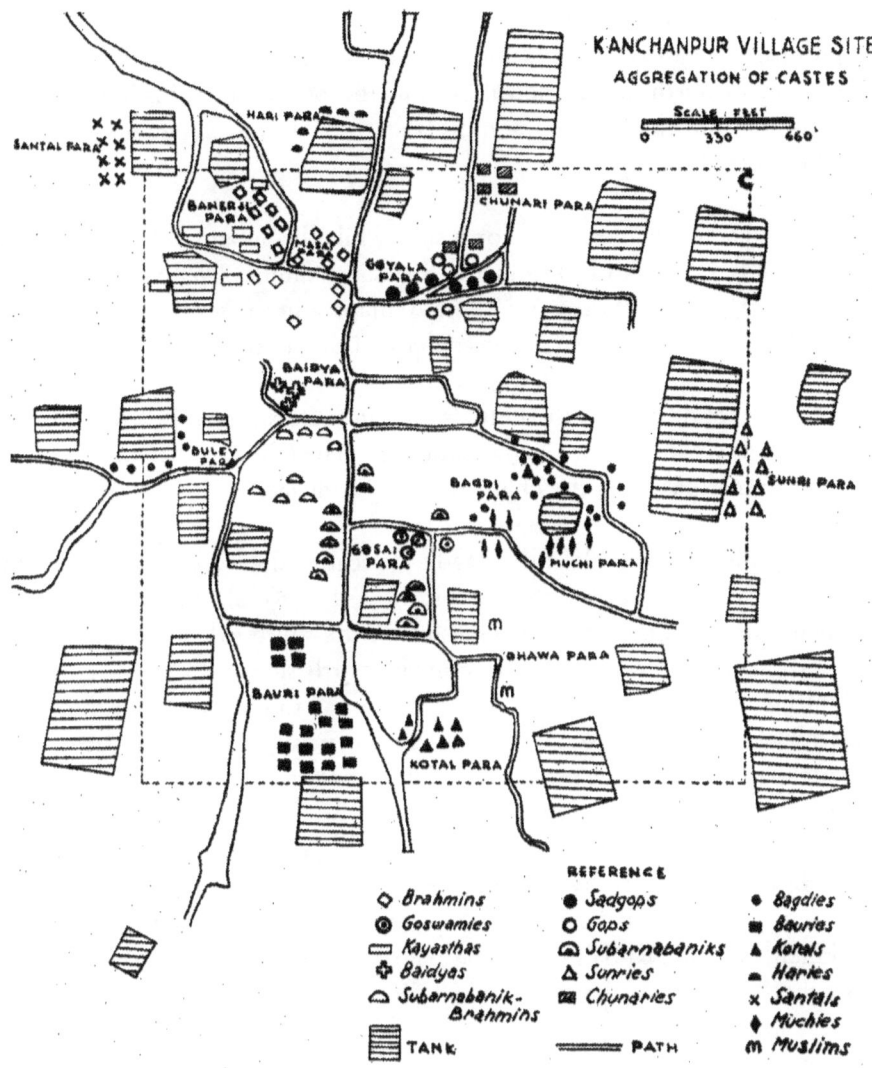

KANCHANPUR VILLAGE SITE
AGGREGATION OF CASTES

SCALE: FEET
0'   330'   660'

REFERENCE

◇ *Brahmins*	● *Sadgops*	• *Bagdies*
◉ *Goswamies*	○ *Gops*	▦ *Bauries*
▭ *Kayasthas*	◠ *Subarnabaniks*	▲ *Konals*
✚ *Baidyas*	△ *Sunries*	▬ *Haries*
◠ *Subarnabanik-Brahmins*	▦ *Chunaries*	✕ *Santals*
		♦ *Muchies*
▦ TANK	═══ PATH	⋒ *Muslims*

Generally speaking, the interior of the village is inhabited by the upper castes, while the exterior castes are scattered on the outskirts, as shown in Figure 4. The local saying is: "The Haris must be kept in segregation, and the Donis on the fringe". That is to say there must be respectable distance between the dwelling places of the "clean castes" and the polluting ones.

Figure 5 further clarifies the aggregation of castes within each of the three main groups. A majority of the Brahmins and all the Kayastha households are in the Uttarpara or north side of the village. The rest of the Brahmins including the Goswamis, the Subarnabanik Brahmins and the Vaidyas are in the Dakshinpara—the south side.

The Sadgops mainly live in the north side, while the Subarnabaniks, excepting two households, belong to Dakshinpara. Five Gop families live in the Goylapara (the northeast), and six of them are in the Aymapara in the southwest. The other four Gop families are sprinkled in the center and the south.

The Sunnis reside beyond the Dutta's tank in the east, in an isolated compact group and their ward is known as the Sunripara. The Chunaris live in one block, known as Chunaripara near the Dighi tank of the village.

The forty-nine households of the Bagdis are scattered in four clusters in all the four directions—north and south, east and west. The Kotals, excepting the family of their Sardars in the north side, all live in the south side in two clusters of homesteads. One of these just borders on the north side and the other is to be found in the extreme south. At a little distance away to the west from the village there is a settlement of the Kotals in the area known as Barabagan, but as it is not an integral part of the village proper, and falls in Kaligram mouza, it has not been taken into account in this survey.

The Haris are found to live in three groups—beyond the Patkel tank on the north, near Poddar tank in the southeast and also in the southwest on the embankments of the Nanda's tank. The Bauris however are concentrated in one group—the Bauripara of the village which lies at the southern end of Kanchanpur.

The Muchis live to the east of the village near the Bagdipara of that area. The Koras are in the southeast, and further to the end of that side are the two families of the Dhawa Muslims—living in the area known as the "Dhawapara" in the village. The settlement of the Santhals is to the northwest of the embankments of the Bene-tank, and has come to be known as the Santhalpara. The rest of the smaller castes are sprinkled here and there.

2.4—TRADITIONAL CASTE CHARACTERS

Living together generation after generation and continuing to play the roles assigned to them by society, most castes have come to possess some peculiar qualities of their own. This has resulted in the fixation of a traditional character type for many of the castes. There have also come into currency many sayings and proverbs in our rural society to illustrate such popular "caste" characters. For example, of the men of great birth, the Brahmins, it is said:

Bamun, Badal, Baan
Dakhina pelei jan.

That is, the Brahmins, the rains and the flood all three go away as soon as they get the dakhina. Here is a pun on the word dakhina in the couplet; it means the "southern wind" in case of the rains and the flood, but "fees" in the case of the Brahmins. The Brahmins render important services to the community by offering ministrations in all ritual situations. But they think more of the fees that are given to them at the end of the functions and lose interest in the occasion after being duly paid. According to another saying, "a Brahmin is a beggar even when he owns a lac of rupees". Apart from greed the Brahmins are also said to be very fond of feasts and are proverbially great smokers. A kalki (a small earthen pot containing, tobacco for puffing through a hookah) which has been puffed away by a Brahmin is said to leave no tobacco in that pot, and the next smoker who takes the kalki gets nothing, and this has given rise to the phrase "like a kalki puffed away by a Brahmin!".

The Goswami Brahmins, known in the village parlance as the Gosain Thakurs, are Vaishnab in religion. There are many other Vaishnabs in the village and they belong to various castes—such as the Sadgops, the Gops, the Bagdis, the Kotals and so on. In fact, the Vaishnabs do not form a caste. On the other hand they cut across the divisions of caste. Sri Chaitanya, the great religious reformer of Bengal of the sixteenth century, spread Vaishnavism to save the then Hindu society from the corroding forces of "casteism". The Bengal Vaishnabs are followers of Shri Chaitanya, and the region around Kanchanpur is a stronghold of Vaishnavism.

The Vaishnab group is not a caste but there is a Vaishnab character and the people well know what traits of character they should seek in a Vaishnab. "I had a great desire in my mind" runs a popular saying "to lead the life of a Vaishnab; but I failed to cross the very fast hurdle: Lowlier than the leaves of grass". This refers to the neatly defined creed of the Vaishnabs: "Lowlier than the leaves of grass, more patient than the standing tree, honoring the dishonored brethren, the Vaishnab should ever sing the glories of the Lord".

The Kayastha and the Napit are said to be very quick-witted and shrewd and are often referred to as the jackal and the crow of village society. One sometimes hears such remarks from other castes: "Oh you son of a Napit, you are very clever. When your mouth says 'brother, brother', something else moves your bones at the same time". Or a villager, while referring to the cunning behavior of a Kayastha, may be heard to cite an oft-quoted saying:

> The dead body of a Kayastha
> Floats still on water;
> But the crow says, what is he feigning for?

> (*Kayeth more jale bhase*
> *Kak bale kon chhale achhe*).

Of the agricultural castes in the middle group, the Sadgops are noted for their submissive attitude and are said to have no capacity to imbibe culture. According to a village saying a chasa (a cultivator) cannot be made to imbibe culture!

The Ugra-Kshatriyas, on the other hand, are noted for their courage and independence. The Rev. Day in his book gives a delineation of their character which corresponds well with the popular estimation in our villages. He writes, "They are known to be a bold and somewhat fierce race, and less patient of any injustice or oppression than the ordinary Bengali raiyat." The phrase "Aguri gonar" or the "Aguri bully" which has passed into a proverb, indicates that the Aguris are, in the estimation of their countrymen, a hot-blooded class; that they are fearless and determined in their character, and that they resent the slightest insult that is offered them.

The Tanti (weaver) and the Gop (milkman) are said to be the dolts of the society. The Bengali word boka (stupid) is an adjective which is proverbially associated with a Tanti, and a popular saying fixes eighty years as the age of maturity for a Goala (i.e. Gop). As regards the traditional character of the Tanti, I again quote the following from the book of the Rev. Day:

Lancashire weavers are, we believe, very sharp—some say a little too sharp in their dealings; but we know not how it is that the Bengal weaver has, from time out of mind, been noted for his stupidity. In point of mental acuteness he is the very antipodes of the barber. Bokaram did no discredit to his caste, as he possessed no ordinary degree of stupidity. His friends used to say that providence had meant to make him an ass, but through inadvertence made him into a man.

Thak Tamli, bhisan Tili
Sonar Bener lathe path na chali
Jadi chalbi pathe, paysa nibi gnete.

The Tamulis (a trading class absent at Kanchanpur) are cheats and dangerously so are the Tilis. You should never walk in company with a Sonar Bene (i.e. Subarnabanik) on the road. If you happen to do so, you should keep your purse safe in the waist-knot of the cloth you wear.

The Sunris as sellers of country wine come in contact mainly with the low caste men addicted to drinking. Not only the Sunris' occupation considered degrading, but his character too is deemed to be void of any honor and integrity. "The drunkard as a witness to the Sunri" is a phrase that has passed into a proverb, and indicates the low estimation in which a Sunri is held in village society. But now that the Sunris of Kanchanpur have turned into an agricultural caste, the stigma on their character is slowly vanishing.

Among the exterior castes, the Bagdis, who style themselves as Byagra-Kshatriyas, are known to be a bold and fierce race like the Ugra-Kshatriyas. Possibly at one time the Bagdis formed a martial tribe and their racial ferocity has given birth to such saying as

Bagh, Bagdi, Mos,
Lathi thanga cchara, kachh na hos

This is, "You should not come near a tiger, a Bagdi or a buffalo, without a club or a weapon in hand!"

All the exterior castes are summarily termed "chhoto-loks", i.e. the "small or debased men". As "chhoto-loks", they are necessarily devoid of all good qualities. Unclean in mind and body, they pollute the respectable castes with their touch, and so they must go to live in segregated wards. As their services are useful, they must he settled on the village borders but kept under constant discipline. As regards these castes, a village proverb says:

> Keep them by the side of the village.
> And show them the clenched fists every now and then.

2.5—LIVING TOGETHER

The people of Kanchanpur have been described above on the basis of the caste system, as it still determines to a very large extent the behavior pattern of our village community. Each caste has its social status in regard to other castes, and a person in our village world is invariably seen as a member of a particular caste. The birth of a person in a caste, therefore, is still a potent factor in the villager's life.

But the villagers do not see the caste as a menace to their life. On the other hand they have accepted it as the very basis of their life, and their pattern of living is molded accordingly.

On the caste system, the Rev. Day wrote as follows:

> The system of caste prevents the different classes of Hindus from full social intercourse with one another. Aguris will not eat and intermarry with any that do not belong to that caste and the same is true of the thirty-six castes in which the whole Hindu community in Bengal is said to be divided; but short of eating, drinking and intermarrying, there is a good deal of intercourse and kindly feeling between members of different castes.

And again:

> Though the system of caste does not allow a blacksmith to dine with a carpenter, it does not seem to us to impede the flow of brotherly kindliness between members of the two different guilds. There is no country in the world where the spirit of caste is not to be found in some shape or other. In India, caste is practically based on occupations, people who pursue the same trade forming one caste by themselves; in England, it is based chiefly on money, the richer class forming the Brahmins and the poorer, the chandalas of English society. In its practical working, though not in its theory, the Indian system of caste is hardly worse than the English system. In England, though a rich goldsmith

dines with a rich cotton spinner, he does not admit to his table a very poor member of his own guild; in India, a rich goldsmith does not dine in the company of a rich cotton-spinner, but cheerfully admits to his a very poor goldsmith. In our opinion, this particular phase of the English system of caste is a great deal worse than that of the Hindu system.

The fact is that in spite of the restrictions on commensality and intermarriage, and in spite of the order of precedence and graded hierarchy amongst the different castes, the villagers live together more with a sense of community than of cleavage. The villagers do not see the caste as an outsider does. They are born in the caste system which provides them a fixed social milieu, and they live there as freely as fish grow and move in water. They accept the distinctions which birth in a particular caste has brought for them, and live and work for themselves and others as well. The priests, the baniks, the smiths, the barbers, the cultivators, the gops, the dais and all other occupationists do not work exclusively for their castes but for others as well. The relations of masters and servants, or creditors and debtors, patrons and clients cut across the divisions of castes. All the castes join the community festivals and rituals, and they belong to the village community as much as an individual as a member of a caste.

The village schism that was observed in 1933 is still there, but the group conflict then as now is more regional between the north side and the south side, and even this has softened down to a great extent in these years. It may be that "the spirit of caste" sometimes rises to spoil human relationships, but on the whole Kanchanpur lives, as said above, more with a sense of solidarity than of split.

CHAPTER 3

▼

THE CONTOURS OF CASTE

The preceding chapter presented the cultural pattern as inherited from the past. In this chapter I shall try to present the same pattern in terms of existing contours based on numbers and proportions which appear to change from time to time.

3.1—INCREASING POPULATION AND CHANGING RATIOS

The numerous large tanks and decorated temples, some even bearing the dates of their construction, indicate the prosperity of Kanchanpur in the eighteenth century. Even the picture of rural life in the mid-nineteenth century, as given by Lal Behari Day, depicts a fairly high degree of prosperous living at that period.

In the seventies of the last century, the Rev. Day had written that Kanchanpur had "a population of about fifteen hundred souls belonging to most of the thirty-six castes into which the Hindus of Bengal are generally divided; the predominating caste in the village was the Sadgops of the agricultural class". The Ugra-Kshatriyas, or Aguris, were also engaged in agricultural pursuits, and, though less numerous than the Sadgops, were an influential class in the village. It appears therefore that in the socioeconomic structure of the mid-nineteenth century the Zamindar dominated the scene while the agricultural castes, the Sadgops and the Aguris, formed the economic backbone of the village. There was also a considerable Brahmin population. The Kayasthas were few in number while there was the usual complement of Vaidyas (the medical caste), of Blacksmiths, Barbers, Weavers, Spice sellers, Oil men, and castes such as Bagdis, Doms, Haris, and so on. "Strange to say", remarked the Reverend Day, "there is hardly a single Muhamedan family in the village, the votaries of that faith being less numerous in western than in eastern Bengal."

In *Kanchanpur Revisited* (1933), the present writer had indicated the group composition of the village population from certain census data for 1931 obtained from the Supervisor's copy in the village. That data showed the total population of the village to consist of only 812 persons distributed among 270 households comprising different castes and caste groups. Unfortunately the number of people in each caste group was not ascertainable at that time. Dividing the figure for the total population with the number of households the average number of persons per household worked out to only 3.2. Evidently the decay, begun in the 1870's, had continued over the next sixty years and the population of Kanchanpur had been reduced to half of what it was when the Rev. Day had written about the village.

The next point of time at which we can get any information about the population of Kanchanpur is the Census year of 1951. The Census Handbook for Burdwan District gives some data for each mouza from which one gathers that the total population of Shona Palasi in that year was 1,101. This figure, compared with that for 1931, indicates an increase of 21% over the preceding twenty years, or, roughly, 1% per year.

In our present survey, however, some of the village young men themselves prepared a house to house list which showed the total population of Kanchanpur in 1959 to be no less than 1466—an increase of 33% in eight years, or 4% per year. In other words what Kanchanpur had lost by way of population in six decades, 1874 to 1933, it has regained in one decade of Independence. The opening of the canal and more facilities of cultivating land serve as partial explanation, but it needs to be noted that this rate of increase is double that of what we found in the neighbouring District of Birbhum, where the steady increase of population was 2% over the past thirty years. Perhaps Kanchanpur's having lagged behind until recently accounts for the more sudden spurt.

And yet the net change in the number of households over the past three decades is not conspicuous. The number of Brahmin households has decreased from 60 to 50 representing a loss of nearly 20%. The number of Bagdi households has increased from 27 to 49, an addition of 40%, while the increase in the total number of exterior caste households amounts to 25%. One is led to surmise that the Brahmins, now getting more income from the land cultivated by tenants, have a tendency to move over to the town and the city while more intensive agriculture is drawing more and more of the landless labouring castes to the village to cultivate the land either on wage or share basis. But this is a mere surmise suggested by the population figures. A special study devoted to emigration and immigration during the last nine years would have to be instituted for getting a dear picture of such movements and this is beyond the scope of our present general analysis.

3.2—PROPORTIONAL REPRESENTATION OF GROUP

In the preceding chapter it was suggested that the most significant method of classifying the village population would be to divide them into four groups, the High Castes, the Jal-Chals, the Jal-Achals, and the Exterior Castes. It was also there suggested that their respective positions in the village can best be pictured in the form of concentric circles. Let us here see how these suggestion can be translated into numbers and whether we can get an adequately clear picture of the relations through graphic presentation. In Table 1, column 2 gives the number of people in each of the four groups as found in 1959; in column 3 the figures represent percentages of the total village population.

TABLE 1—*The Four Groups of Kanchanpur Population-1959*

group	actual number	%
high caste	362	25
jal-chal castes	265	18
jal-achal castes	272	18
exterior castes	567	39
total	1,466	100

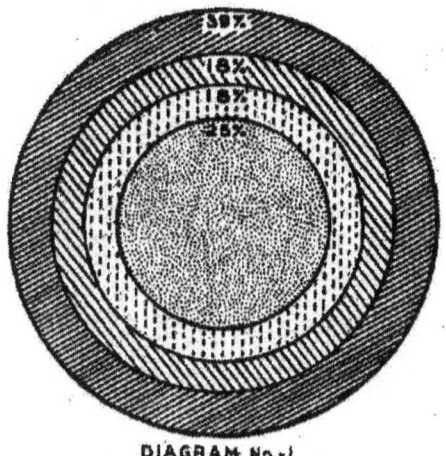

DIAGRAM No.-1

CONTOURS OF CASTE

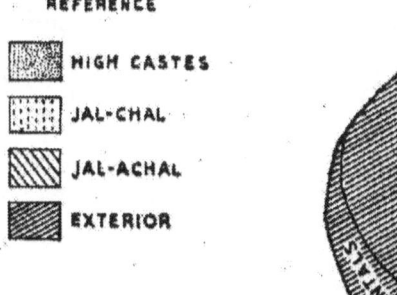

REFERENCE

HIGH CASTES

JAL-CHAL

JAL-ACHAL

EXTERIOR

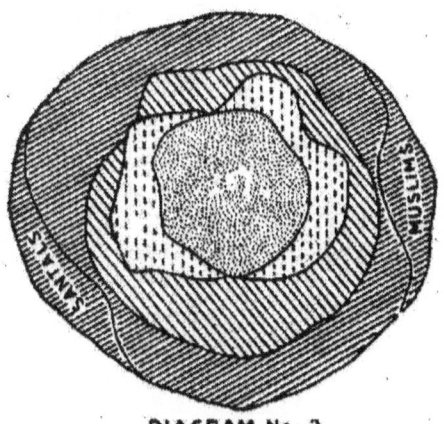

DIAGRAM No.- 2

Social layout and topography, like physical topography, can be best represented not by perfect circles but by irregular contours with bulges and depres-
sions, intersections and overlappings, which give individuality to the social
structure of each village. The irregular and elastic nature of the concentric divisions representing social stratification of castes groups in Kanchanpur, for exam-

ple, conform more realistically perhaps to the pattern shown in the third part of Figure 6. Contrary to the exact concentric rings whose boundaries would never intermingle, this pattern suggests certain contacts between the three inner caste groups but hardly any between these three and the outer or exterior castes. The only exception to this rule is perhaps that of the negligible number of Muslims even in Kanchanpur; for all practical purposes they are a part of the exterior castes, but in one or two minor aspects their status touches that of the jal-achals not beyond.

3.3—AGE AND SEX DISTRIBUTION ACCORDING TO CASTE GROUPS

Some light can be thrown on the distinguishing characteristics of the four groups of the population by the percent proportions representing the different age groups as seen in Table 2 and the sex ratios given in Table 3.

TABLE 2.—Age Distribution According to Caste Group

Group	infants below 6	children 6–12	adolesc. 13–21	Adults	total
high caste	90	37	70	165	362
jal-chal caste	69	30	52	114	26
jal-achal caste	38	44	49	121	272
exterior caste	149	62	87	269	567
total	366	173	258	669	1466
percentages					
high caste	25	10	19	46	100
jal-chal caste	26	11	20	43	100
jal-achal caste	21	16	18	45	100

exterior caste	26	11	15	48	100
all	25	12	17	46	100

TABLE 3—Sex Ratios (Females per 100 Males) According to age and Caste
Groups

Group	infants below 6	children 6–12	adolesc. 13–21	Adults	total
high castes	88	68	106	106	97
jal-chal castes	123	100	117	84	101
jal-achal castes	113	173	104	78	101
exterior castes	144	63	142	83	101
ulterior group					
total	119	90	119	87	100

The first of these shows that the different groups show no striking deviation from the normals of the village as a whole. Kanchanpur as a whole contains 25% toddlers below the age of 6 years; 12% of children between 6 and 12 years age; 17% adolescents between 13 and 21 years while the remaining 46% are adults above the age of 21. Even the deviations from this norm, which are noticeable, are only in cases where the actual numbers they represent are comparatively small.

The sex ratios too as shown in Table 3 present a few abnormalities. Out of the total population of 1466, exactly half the number, 733 are males and 733 are females. In the first and third age group there are 119 females to every 100 males; in the second and fourth age groups this relation is reversed and there are only 90 and 87 females respectively for every 100 males. The two figures representing extremes are those for the 6 to 12 age group of children in the jal-achal and the exterior castes; in the one it is 175 to 100 and in the other only 63 females to every 100 males; but it must be noted that the actual figures consist of only 44 children in the first and only 62 children in the second sub-group.

A numerical preponderance of one sex as against the other denotes certain characteristics of a given population. An excess of males suggests comparatively recent immigration, an adequacy of labour and a greater expectancy of change. Kanchanpur, evidently, is not conspicuous for any of these situations one way or the other.

3.4—MARITAL CONDITION ACCORDING TO CASTE GROUPS

Taking the village population as a whole, 57% of the males and 44% of the females are unmarried; the proportions of the married are more or less equal— 39% of the males and 38% of the females falling in that category. In the widowed class, females preponderate; while among males only 4 out of every hundred are widowers, the proportion of widows in the female population is no less than 18%. In 1933 a survey in the neighbouring District of Birbhum had shown that one out of every four females was a widow; the figures of Kanchanpur today show that the proportion here is now one widow out of every five females.

It is apparent that the high castes marry late, while the exterior castes go for early marriage. This is true for both males and females, 64% of the high caste males against 51% of the exterior caste males are found to be unmarried. Similarly 44% of the high caste females as against 40% of the exterior caste women are found to be unmarried. A good number of Subarnabanik men and girls, like the high caste group, are still unmarried. This condition has raised the percent figures for the unmarried in the jal-achal group.

Six amongst the boys of 12 to 21 age group are married, the adolescent girls for the corresponding age are mostly married. Still there are 44 amongst the 140 girls of this age group who are yet to be married. Here again the number of the unmarried is higher in case of the upper castes, and smaller for the exterior castes. The Subarnabaniks' conditions in this respect are similar to the high castes. Of the 11 unmarried adolescent girls in the jal-achal group, 10 belong to the Subarnabaniks. The more advanced a community is in education and culture, the higher, it seems, is the age of marriage. Consequently, in such a community there is a greater percentage of unmarried girls. Of the growing young women, 58% of the high castes as against only 10% of exterior castes have not yet been provided with their mates in life.

3.5—LITERACY

How Kanchanpur trains the young is a subject to which will be given more attention later; but in the meantime it is desirable to get an idea of the extent of literacy and education in our community in general.

The Subarnabanik community has got the lead with 73% and 61% of literacy for its males and females respectively. These figures exceed even those for the high castes. The position of the exterior castes in this respect is still very unhappy and the lack of progress in spite of governmental efforts for the group is remarkable.

Even in this exterior group, however, the Kotals or Namasudras are somewhat advanced. As owners of land they are better off than the other castes of this group and are taking interest in the matter of education as well. Against these the position of the Gops may be contrasted; they remain educationally behind the Kotals although the Gops have a superior caste status and a higher average of land ownership in Kanchanpur.

Of the total 33% of literates in the village, 21% have completed only the primary classes; 11% have completed the secondary school and only 1% of the persons have received college educations. The actual number of the persons who have gone up to the college standard is only ten. Five amongst them belong to the Subarnabanik community, and the other five come from the high castes—3 Brahmins and 2 Kayasthas. All these persons are males. Amongst the females, few have read even up to the secondary classes. In fact the girls of the village do not go even for secondary education. There is only one Brahmin girl of the village who is reading in a secondary school at Burdwan. Eight more females in the village are found to have gone higher than the primary standard—and they are the daughters-in-law of the high castes brought to the village through marriage. These nine girls constitute roughly 1% of the total female population.

CHAPTER 4

▼

LAND AND LIVELIHOOD

4.1—WHO OWNS THE LAND AT KANCHANPUR?

Now and then a villager is heard to say that all his life is spent in running after "ghee, salt and rice". In fact getting the material necessities of food, clothing and shelter occupies a major aspect of living at Kanchanpur, as elsewhere. In the round of life's activities, economic pursuits, therefore, deserve our first attention.

As agriculture is the mainstay of the village, land is seen to be the chief and almost only means of production. It is highly prized, and all savings are invested in land. In our village, the size of a person's agricultural holding is a true index of his economic status. There is only one exception. A Subarnabanik householder has a good income from service, but his surplus after expenses goes to increase his deposits in the banks. He holds no agricultural land, and is the only person in the village whose status does not depend on land ownership. He is one of the well-to-do families of the village, but excepting this person, it is land-ownership that determines class in our village.

According to village standards the families which own no land or less than 5 bighas of land are considered poor. Households that have 5 to 20 bighas of land are deemed to form the lower middle class group; those owning 21 to 50 bighas are the upper middle class of the village society and those who possess 50 bighas and more are classed as rich.

Generally speaking, the high castes are the rich class, and the exterior castes form the poor class. But not all high castes are rich nor all exterior castes poor. No less than 31.7% of the high castes are classed as poor, while only 6.3% are said to be rich. That is to say, speaking on the averages amongst the four caste groups, the high castes may be the richest, but a majority amongst the high caste themselves form the poor or the lower middle class. The jal-achal castes, though they are inferior in social position to the jal-chal castes, have better economic status as a group. It is because of the Subarnabaniks and the Sunris who are economically (and educationally as well) much better off than others in our village community.

In 1933-34, a rough and ready attempt was made to show the economic divisions of the village. It was done on the basis of the assessment list without an actual survey. If we bring those figures here, an apparently comparative table could then be produced.

Table 4—Economic Groupings

1933–34		1958–59	
class	no. of households	class	no. of households
in poverty	72	poor	177
above poverty	152	lower middle	77
below comfort	34	upper middle	28
in comfort	12	rich	5
total	270	total	287

From the above it would seem that the number of rich and fairly well-to-do households has decreased from 46 to 33 whereas the number of poor household has increased from 72 to 177 with also a proportionate decrease in the lower middle class. But it should be noted that actually the figures are not comparable at all. The criteria for the economic standard in 1933-34 were the amounts of U.B. rates payable by the different households. It is unfortunate that the amount of tax which served as a criterion for grouping a household in one or other class is not recorded. However, it is clear that in the 1933-34 standard if a family was exempted from payment of U.B. tax it was considered to "in poverty" level. That year there were 72 such families, but in 1958-59, it was found that less than 40 families were exempted from such payments. The total assessment of the village was found to be on an upward curve. On the whole I am inclined to believe—and this is also the feeling of the villagers themselves—that the general economic conditions of the village have improved since 1934.

Approximately speaking, 40% of the village lands are held by the Brahmins and 20% are in the hands of the Subarnabaniks. Next come the Sadgops who hold only 10% of the lands. The rest of the land consisting of about 30% of the arable area is distributed among all the other castes.

The high castes and the Baniks, the priestly, learned, and the merchant classes of the society, constituting 31% of the village population, are prevented by social custom from engaging in agricultural operations with their own hands. But, as seen in Table below it is these 31% who together hold 68% of the total lands.

Nowadays, ownership of land pays good dividend to villagers. A person simply by owning land gets his 50% share of produce from his bargadar.

Table 5—Land Owned by the Dominant Classes

group	no. of households	% to total no. of households	area of land in bighas	% of total village lands
Brahmin	52	18.1	761.5	38.5
Vaidya	4	1.4	78.0	4.0
Kayastha	7	2.4	88.5	4.5
Subarnabanik	23	8.0	373.3	18.3
Gandhabanik	5	1.7	50.0	2.5
Total	91	31.6	1351.3	68.0

In 1933 and the preceding years, when price of paddy was low and agriculture was a "gamble in rain", investment in land was not attractive. It had been difficult to meet the rents due to the Zamindars. Since those days, there is a negligible increase in rent, but the price of paddy has gone up higher and higher. The coming of the canal in our area, has also made agriculture no longer a gamble in rain. So land gets gradually concentrated in the hands of the investors, and the prices

demanded for land phenomenally increase. In 1933 it was difficult to get a purchaser for land or a cultivating tenant to till the lands on share or rent. The tenants found it hard to meet the rental dues of the Zamindars who had often to
excuse them from payment of dues instead of accepting their surrender of land.
Speaking of those days, an old peasant told me the origin of the name of a few
bighas of land in the southwestern part of our village. That land is known in the
locality as the "earpullets field", (kanmalar math). The cultivator of those lands,
in the times of the Zamindar, approached him and submitted that it would not
be possible for him to pay the arrears plus current rents and he would like to surrender those lands to the Zamindar. The Zamindar excused him from payment
of the rents but as a chastisement caused the cultivator's ears to be pulled by his
men. Without accepting the surrender, the Zamindar sent the cultivator back to
till those lands. Since then those fields came to be known to the people of Kanchanpur as the kanmalar math, as they came in lieu of a pull of the ears!

The Rev. Day observed that the Sadgops were the predominating caste and
the Ugra-Kshatriyas were also influential in those times. These two cultivating
classes, therefore, practically formed the bulk of Kanchanpur peasantry in his
time. After the lapse of a century or so there is a changed picture. These two
classes now hold only 10% of the land. The number of Sadgop households has
fallen to only 19, while the Ugra-Kshatriyas have all but vanished. There are only
three of their families in this village, and of them one is landless; the other two
households jointly own less than 10 bighas of land for cultivation.

Not the agricultural castes, but the priestly, learned, and the merchant classes
constituting 31.6% of the families, hold 68% of the village lands. As a consequence, there is a large growth in the population of the Harijan class, who are
mainly field labourers in our village community, and during the last twenty-five
years, the high caste men have encouraged the settlement of several Bagdi and
Santhal families on the village outskirts.

In addition to the above 68% owned by non-cultivating castes, another 21%
is held by caste groups for whom cultivation is not a traditional occupation but
who have taken to it instead of, or in addition to, their caste occupation. The distribution of this 21% is given in the Table on the next page.

Members of even labour castes are sometimes debarred from cultivation by the
dignity of a subsidiary occupation they may have taken up. For example, a Kar-

makar owns 8 bighas of land. He is a teacher in a primary school in the neighbouring village. He has given up his traditional occupation, and does not even help his hired labourers in his own land.

To be considered as landowning, a caste should have at least two thirds of its households as land owning, and should also hold at least 5 bighas of land for its average cultivator. On the basis of this test, the castes of Kanchanpur may be grouped as landowning and landless, and in this view the Ugra-Kshatriyas are no longer a land-owning caste so far as Kanchanpur is concerned.

Table 6—Land Held by Non-Cultivating Middle Castes and the Kotals

caste	no. of households	% of total	area in bighas	% of total land
Pallav Gop (milk-man)	15	5.2	144	7.2
Sunri (liquor seller)	9	3.2	103	5.2
Kotal (constabulary)	15	5.2	102	5.1
Kaibarta (fisherman)	5	1.7	30	1.5
Napit (barber)	2	0.7	23	1.2
Modak (confectioner)	1	0.4	10	0.5
Tili (oil dealer)	1	0.4	6	0.3
Total	48	16.8	418	21.0

Table 7 shows area of land held by different caste groups and number of landowning families in each and illustrates the extent of landlessness in each of the groups.

Table 7—Area of Land Held by Different Caste-Groups
and Number of Landowning Families in each

castes	# of house-holds	holdings			households	
		bigas	%	per hshld.	owning Land	%
high caste	63	928.0	47	14.7	57	90
jal-chal caste	48	435.5	22	9.1	43	90
jal-achal caste	45	508.8	25	11.3	36	80
exterior caste	131	122.0	6	0.9	20	15
Total	287	1994.3	100	6.9	156	54

Table 8 shows the percentage distribution of the households of the major castes into economic classes of land-holding groups. These castes have 15 or more households in their communities and are therefore considered as major. Among them the Subarnabaniks show the greatest average holding per household and only 22% amongst them own less than 5 bighas or no land at all. Next to them is the position of the Brahmins, and the Sadgops come third. The Gops and Kotals may be considered as land-holding communities, but it should be noted that 53% of each are in the poor class group, that is, they are landless or hold less than 5 bighas of land. Of these two castes, the position of the Gops is comparatively good, as their average holding is higher than that of the Kotals, and only 13% of them are landless as against 20% among the Kotals. The Kotals, however, are an exterior caste, and it should be pointed out that it is the only caste amongst the exterior group which may be classed with the land-owning castes. There is only one Bagdi family which owns more than 5 bighas of land; 2 Bagdi, one Hari and 1 Bauri household have lands less than 5 bighas each. The rest of them are landless.

Table 8

% Distribution of Households of Major Castes Into Economic Classes
(of the Land-Holding Group)

	Rich	upper middle > 20b.	lower middle > 5b.	poor	poor no
	>50b.	<50b.	<20b.	<5b.	land
Brahmin	8	17	44	21	10
Sadgop	-	11	58	26	5
Gop	7	7	33	40	31
Subarnabanik	-	35	43	9	13
Kotal	-	7	40	33	20
Bagdi	-	-	2	6	92
Hari	-	-	-	5	95
Bauri	-	-	-	5	59

Hitherto we have been trying to answer the question as to who owns how much land in our village community. But whatever land an individual owns is not held in a compact block, and this is a feature that is quite familiar to our rural economists. Figure 7 below illustrates how lands belonging to two culti-vating families of our village are scattered and fragmented. Both these families reside in the northwestern part of the village, and it will be seen that most of their land, though scattered, falls into that part of the mouza. The raiyats prefer to hold lands near to their homestead. Also, lands by the sides of the canal are prized. But the above two cultivators, who helped us with necessary informa-tion, explained that they would prefer the "near-village" lands close to their habitation it, the northwest, rather than to hold a "canal-side" plot in the extreme south or east of the village. Of course the canal-lands have improved because of the proximity of water, but since their own lands near the village also do not remain unirrigated they would prefer those closer to their homes if they have any choice in the matter.

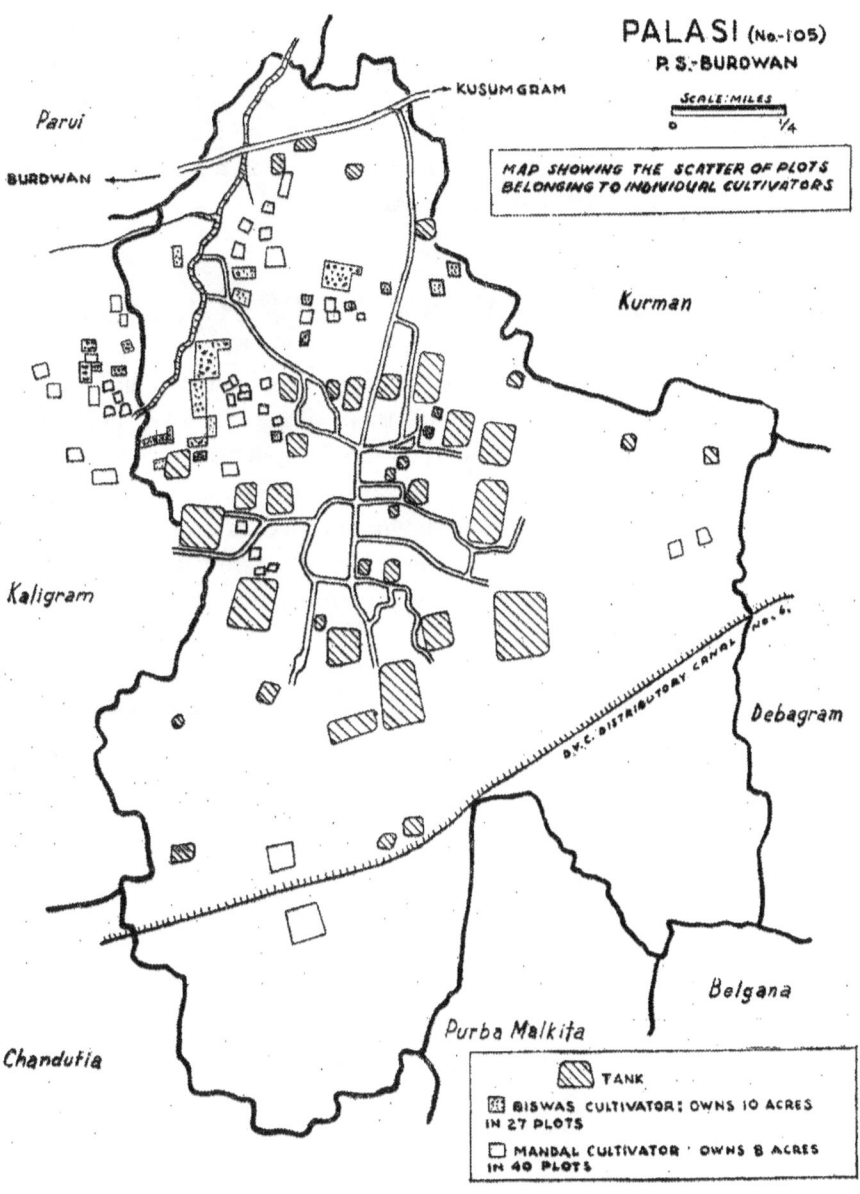

PALASI (No.-105)
P. S.-BURDWAN

SCALE: MILES
0   1/4

MAP SHOWING THE SCATTER OF PLOTS
BELONGING TO INDIVIDUAL CULTIVATORS

Parui

BURDWAN

KUSUMGRAM

Kurman

Kaligram

DV.C. DISTRIBUTORY CANAL   No-6.

Debagram

Chandutia

Purba Malkita

Belgana

TANK

BISWAS CULTIVATOR: OWNS 10 ACRES
IN 27 PLOTS

MANDAL CULTIVATOR · OWNS 8 ACRES
IN 40 PLOTS

Be that as it may, let us look at the present position of their lands. One of the households, Biswas, owns 10 acres of land consisting of 27 plots. These plots range from 2 cottas to 2 bighas and 5 of these fall within the adjoining mouza

Kaligram. The other cultivator Mandal owns 8 acres of land consisting of 40 plots varying from 1 cotta to 2 bighas and 12 of these plots fall in mouza Kaligram. It may be noted that cultivator (B) has two isolated plots in the northeast of the village and the cultivator (M) has 4 plots by the canal in the south and east. The rest of their lands, though not consolidated, fall in a compact area close to their houses marked (B) and (M) on the map.

4.2—WHAT KANCHANPUR DOES FOR ITS LIVING

The productive efforts and the aspirations of the people of Kanchanpur are centered over the arable area spread round their village. 82% of the households spend their working hours on the fields of Kanchanpur and another 4% depend on agriculture as their subsidiary source of living. The function of the rest of the workers of the village (excepting a lawyer who practices as a mukhtar at Burdwan, a teacher who goes to work in a neighbouring village, and a few salary earners who live in Burdwan or Calcutta) is to serve directly these 86% constituting the agricultural community of Kanchanpur.

For purposes of comparison the broad occupational patterns for 1933 and 1959 are given below.

Table 9—Occupational patterns (1933-1959)

	# of households		percentage	
	1933	1959	1933	1959
depending on agriculture	217	235	80	82
rent receiving class	20	-	7	-
non-cultivating owner	16	18	6	6
peasant proprietor and farmer	57	94	21	33
(field) labourer	124	123	46	43
depending on other occupations	53	52	20	18
doctor and kaviraj	9	1	-	-
trade	8	1	-	-

artisan and profession	5	5	-	-
service	31	15	-	-
brittibhogi	7	7	-	-
beggar	-	7	-	-
milk-man	-	5	-	-
paddy husker	-	5	-	-
chowkidar	-	1	-	-
all	270	287	100	100

It will be noticed that in 1959 even more people depended on agriculture than in 1933 (80 and 82%), but there is a socially favorable increase in the proprietors and managing farmers (21 to 33%). The 20 rent-receiving families have disappeared, probably accounting for the growth of the cultivating families. It may well be that as agriculture grew to be profitable, the owners took over the lands from the tenants for their own cultivation, and later the programme of estates acquisition by the State threatening abolition of all intermediary interests might have accelerated the process. (The 1951 census data indicate that 99% of the people of Palashi depend on agriculture.)

Again it seems from the above table that there is a slight decrease in field labourers (46 to 43%). But we have noted earlier that there has been a comparative growth in the landless working class in our village society. Here is then an anomaly that needs to be explained. In 1933 no house-to-house enquiry was made, and the occupational distribution of families was roughly worked out from U.B. Assessment list for 1940 B.S. There were 72 families that were then exempted from payment of U.B. rates, and they were presumed to be labourers and grouped in that class. But this presumption can not be justified. Herein lies the apparent contradiction in the fact that, although the village seems wealthier now, there are no fewer than 7 beggar families. In the 1933 Table no beggar was shown to live in the village. Nor are we justified in holding that other occupationists such as brittibhogis, milkmen, paddy huskers and chowkidars were not present on the village scene at that point of time. As to the decline in the number of services (31 to 15%), it is not now possible, without any detailed information for 1933, to indicate what services have been abolished and what are still being rendered.

Before we close this section, we should mention here a very significant change in the disappearance of the Kaviraj from the village scene. The Kaviraj it is said, derives his medical knowledge and insight from Sanskrit treatises that are believed to have been composed by divine inspiration, indeed to have been written by the finger of the great god Mahadeva himself. The Kaviruja usually belongs to the Vaidya i.e., the physician caste of Bengal. In Kanchanpur there were several families of this caste, "the male members of which" wrote the Rev. Day, "had in succession been practicing medicine, from time out of mind."

It was noted in *Kanchanpur Revisited* (1933–34):

> 17 Kavirajs (indigenous doctors) of the village have fallen on evil days. One part of the village is known as Kavirajpara, or the ward of the Kaviraj. But most of the families have now given up their hereditary occupations and only two still practice Kaviraji. One of them again has been trained in Ayurvedic science in a Calcutta institution but the other has inherited his profession from his father who, be it noticed, was one of the greatest Kavirajs in this locality.

Now, in 1959, there is none in the village to practice "Kaviraji". In the long-drawn battle with Western medicine, the latter completely triumphed. In the last century the Rev. Day wrote:

> For modern medicine, and especially European medicine, he (the village Kaviraj) had a perfect contempt and it was one of, his constant sayings that European doctors did not at all understand the treatment of Indian fever. He admitted the superiority of English to native doctors in surgery, but then it was his opinion that surgery formed no part of the functions of a medical man, as surgical operations belonged, properly speaking, to the province of the barber.

The present descendants of the Kavirajs have all taken to other occupations, but they cherish in their memory the proud traditions of their forebears. The grandson of "the greatest Kaviraj of the locality" of two generations ago, still relates many stories of the wonderful medical insight of his grandfather. He has carefully preserved a manuscript of medical writings left by his said grandfather as a valuable treasure in his family. The writing is in Sanskrit and is endorsed on "tulot" (a kind of indigenous yellowish paper). The book is crumbling into pieces, and the meaning of the writings could not be properly understood. He had shown it to many Sanskrit knowing Kavirajs—but none could properly grasp the formulas of medicine noted there and discovered by his grandfather in the vast medical experience of his life. "Woe to us that we have lost that science" regretted the grandson of the great Vaidya physician, whenever he used to relate such stories of his illustrious grandfather.

4.3—PADDY

The Rev. Day, in narrating the authentic history of the Bengal peasant had realized the importance of rice for the life of the people he was portraying and had, therefore, thought it proper to tell his readers all about it. From philology and history, the learned author sought justification for his inference that rice used to be grown in India before its conquest by the Aryans. But the author himself remarked "What has the petty trader in ginger to do with the news of ships?" Leaving philology, therefore, to the learned men, he spoke of paddy as it grew in the plains of Bengal.

How paddy came to be grown in this region may not be clearly known to the learned, but the villagers, specially the women of Kanchanpur, know quite well that the Goddess Lakshmi herself brought it down on earth for cultivation. In fact, paddy represents Lakshmi herself and the katha—a corn-measure filled with paddy—is the Bengal raiyat's sacred symbol for the Goddess.

In the good old times there lived a very poor cowherd in this land of Bharata (India). As it happened one day, the lamentations of the boy reached the ears of Lakshmi and Narayan while they were making a journey through the sky overhead. Mother Lakshmi's soft heart melted in pity, and she requested Narayan to remove the sufferings of the cowherd. God Narayan smilingly replied: "Lakshmi, I have nothing to do in the matter, and it is you who have the power to help him." Thus permitted by Narayan, Lakshmi came down on the earth, and handed over the seeds of paddy to the per cow boy. "Take these", said Lakshmi to him, "and poverty and sorrow will remain away from you. When the rains set in, go and sow these seeds in your fields. The plants will grow up and bear numerous fruits. When they take on the colour of gold like that of my body and a sweet smelling odour, as if of my person, comes out of them, you reap the fruits and bring them home."

The poor cow-boy did as instructed, and one day in the early winter in the month of Pous, he was delighted to see his fields filled up with a heavenly fragrance and lit with the colour of gold, as if Lakshmi herself made her presence felt there in her person.

The above folk story illustrates the importance given to paddy in the prosperity and culture of the villages of Bengal, which mainly depend on rice economy. But leaving folk-stories to our village people, let us add a few words more about how paddy is now grown in our village.

Viewed from the standpoint of the seasons in which it is grown, paddy is of three kinds—aus, aman, and boro. Correspondingly, one for each kind, there are three harvest months—the Bhadra (August-September), the Pous (December-January), and the Chaitra (March-April) of the Bengali year. These three months are also known in popular parlance as the months of Lakshmi and she is worshiped during these months by every peasant household with due rites.

At Kanchanpur, and in the district of Vardhamana, little of boro dhan is grown because the lands are, for the most part, high and dry. The cultivation of aus paddy, too, has diminished due to the coming of the canal. As most of the lands can now be irrigated, the peasants now prefer the aman crop which gives a much higher yield per bigha than aus. The aman has become, therefore, the most important crop in the village.

The canal has benefited the peasants in three principal ways. First, it is a safeguard against failure of the annual harvest as agriculture is no longer a gamble in rain. The heavens may be shut up, but cusecs of water are released from the great reservoir, a part of it eventually reaching the fields of Palashi. If "the sky is brass", and "the earth is flint", still there is hope that some harvest may yet be reaped.

Second, as the canal waters flow through the fields, the ponds and tanks which usually become dried up in the summer are filled up with water. Third, as irrigation is assured, the peasants apply a larger quantity of manure than they formerly did, and consequently the yield per bigha has also been appreciably increased.

Use of fertilizers (chiefly ammonium sulphate) and bone-dust is a significant introduction in the present-day cultivation of paddy, as compared to former times, when only cow dung, earth of crumbling walls, mud from tanks, and mustard oil-cakes were used as manure. But so far as the agricultural processes and the use of implements are concerned there appears to be little change in the practices; the traditional methods of ploughing, sowing, transplanting, weeding, hoeing and harvesting still prevail and the good old wooden plough and harrow, spade and sickle are still the peasants' valued tools.

But there is a remarkable change in the varieties of aman rice that are produced in the fields of Kanchanpur. The old kinds, except one or two mentioned by the Rev. Day, are no longer grown in our village. "Round about Khanchanpur, and in the district of Vardhamana generally," wrote the Rev. Day, "the following varieties are usually cultivated: (1) Nono, (2) Bangota, (3) Kalia, (4) Bangota, (5) Ramshali, (6) Chini Sarkara, (7) Suryamukhi, (8) Dadkhani, (9) Alam-Badshashi, and (10) Radhuni-Pagel, and the last one (Radhuni-Pagal, that is, cook-maddening) is so fine and fragrant that, while boiling it, the cook becomes mad with joy."

These names are met with no longer—except perhaps for Ramsali and Badshabhog which may be a transformation for Alam Badshahi, both being fine varieties, the latter being used for pilau. Other names now common are as following:

(a) Superfine—Kanakchur (used for puffed rice).

(b) Fine—Sitasal; Gobindabhog (used for payesh); Chatuinakhi (small as the nail of the sparrow); Nagra; Bakchur.

(c) Medium—Jhingashal

(d) Red—Sindur topor (vermilion topped), a red and coarse variety.

(e) Coarse—Bansnagra, Dudkalma, Dhali Kalma, Shuyo Kalma, Ghorasal, and Hatisal.

Whether these names represent newly introduced varieties or mere changes in nomenclature brought about by time it was not possible to ascertain.

4.4—SUGARCANE

Next in importance to the cultivation of paddy was the sugarcane plantation in the economy of Kanchanpur of the nineteenth century. It was at that time such a valuable crop to the Bengal raiyat that the Rev. Day devoted a separate chapter to the description of this crop also.

Now-a-days paddy forms not merely the staple produce of Kanchanpur, it is practically its only product. The cultivation of potato or winter vegetables or any other crops is on such small scale as scarcely to deserve mention. As regards the one time important sugarcane cultivation, there is hardly more than one acre of land under it at present. But since the coming of the canal is likely to bring the cultivation of this crop into prominence again and the acreage is likely to increase, it may not be out of place to add a few words on sugarcane as well.

Pandasur, the mighty demon, thus runs the village fable, started the plantation of sugarcane on this land of fair Bengal. The asura had been newly married, and naturally desired to spend a few days with his new bride then staying in her father's place. But as he had to prepare his land for sugarcane, he deferred his visit to the in-law's house. Now the mode of cultivating sugarcane is not only labourious, it is also continuous throughout the year. Lest his fields go unattended, Pandasur, time after time, deferred his visit to the in-law's place.

When, however, the sugarcane was cut, there was hardly any time for planting the next crop. The tops had been cut and preserved in nurseries which were to be again transplanted in the field, when the soil should be made ready to receive them. The process of tending the plants started again. Thus entangled in the plantation of the sugarcane, Pandasur could never manage to go to his father-in-law's place.

This village fable jocularly points to the continuous labour and pains with which the cultivation of sugarcane is attended. There is another village saying which states: "when the soil for sugarcane is ready for preparation, there is no time to eat even the served dinner". The Rev. Day had described in some details the processes in the cultivation of sugarcane in the village. There appears little change in them excepting the introduction of the chemical fertilizers.

As lands came into the hands of the non-cultivating castes like the Brahmins and the Subarnabaniks who have to depend on hired labour for cultivation, sugarcane plantation, involving a great amount of labour, was found to be commercially unattractive. This is perhaps the main reason why acreage under sugarcane fell. As the area under it diminished, the setting up of the sugarcane press also became a vexed problem. The Rev. Day described the sugarcane house and press as an affair of a joint stock company of the husband-men of Kanchanpur. Such houses were set up—one for those who grew sugarcane in the northern and the eastern divisions, and the other for the benefit of the cane growers of the southern and western divisions. In 1959 there was only one plot, less than 3 cottas, under sugarcane in the northern side of the village, and the cut sugarcane of the field had to be carried by carts to the southern outskirts at a distance of nearly a mile, where the only press was set up for the village this year.

Like paddy, Kanchanpur has changed the kinds of sugarcane to be produced, and is paying attention to cultivation of other varieties, however little the area for plantation may be. The Rev. Day mentioned that in the village there were three varieties of sugarcane, namely, the Puri, the Kajule, and the Bombai. But these are no longer grown in the village. The two kinds that are now found are the "Fati-Java" and the government variety No. 2222. It is claimed for the Fati-Java that it is a stout variety, and has a tough cover. The jackal and the children, both very fond of chewing the cane, find it hard to crack, and the plantation is thus saved from being robbed. For the Govt. 2222, it is claimed that it has the above quality of Fati-Java to some extent, and at the same time contains more saccharine batter. It should give, therefore, a higher yield in sugar, but the villagers who have been cultivating the variety are not yet satisfied with the result.

A technological improvement in the sugarcane-press used to crush the cane may be noted. The Rev. Day described the machine as consisting of two massive wooden cylinders, cut into notches all over, and furnished at both ends with wheels or rather simple spokes without a felloe. Two persons sitting opposite to each other inserted the cane between the cylinders which were kept in perpetual motion by four persons who worked at the spokes. Strong men were required to turn this mill, and describing one such working the machine, the Rev. Day said:

> There he was now, with his long legs placed firmly on opposite sides of the trench tugging away at the spokes with almost superhuman strength, now

pressing his lips together when making a grand pull and now hallooing his associates to excite them to get on briskly.

The press now consists of three closely set and grooved iron cylinders with teethed wheels on the top. A horizontal pole is fixed with the machine which is driven by a pair of bullocks or buffaloes. Even for the animals, it is not an easy task and they are changed for another fresh pair almost every hour.

With diminution in the acreage of plantation the village auksala (sugarcane house) has lost its importance, but has not yet ceased to be a scene of rural joy. When the sugarcane house is established, it is still duly consecrated with offerings to Brahma, the god of fire, and Viswakarma, the maker of the universe. But the Goddess Lakshmi is no longer associated there. Perhaps she has left the press of sugar, and has fixed her abode in the barnyard of paddy. The earthen image of the planter Pandasura, however, must invariably be installed at the auksala.

The press then moves, and the fire burns, and the auksala begins to operate. The little boys and girls still run to the place for obtaining cut pieces of sugarcane, which they get as a matter of course, as the belief and customs enjoin that they should not be turned away empty-handed. But the sugarcane house has lost its past glories, and no longer threatens the village primary school in the matter of attendance of the children.

4.5—LEVELS OF LIVING

It seems desirable to make a little more inquiry into the actual conditions of living of these socioeconomlc groups. An attempt has, therefore, been made below to ascertain the levels of living of these groups in terms of actual consumption of food, clothing and other necessaries of life, their use of semi-durable goods and conditions of housing.

4.5.1—The Rich Households

At the outset it maybe noted that the jal-achal and the exterior castes have no rich family amongst them. Of the five rich households in the village, four belong to the high castes and the fifth is a Gop family. While the four high caste families follow a similar pattern of living, the Gop household exhibits some significant differences.

Let us first take a Goswami Brahmin family, as representing the high caste rich group. The family holds about 53 bighas, i.e. about 18 acres of land and the head of the household is a pensioner receiving Rs. 150% p.m. The family consists of 13 members—3 male adults, 2 female adults, 4 male children and 4 female children.

> *Housing:* These members live in nine rooms which are inside an enclosed compound. Three of the rooms are made of mud wall and thatches of straw; the other six are semi-pucca.
>
> *Food:* The daily food taken by the family is usually as follows:
>
> Morning (7-8 am.)—Tea (for adults and the old only).
> Breakfast (9-10 am.)—Muri (puffed rice), milk, gur, and occasionally fried vegetables covered with powdered pulses.
> Mid-day meals (1-2 p.m.—Rice, dal, fish, hodgepodge of vegetables, tak (chutney) and milk.
> Evening tiffin (5-6 p.m.)—Tea (for adults & the old), muri, and biscuit.
> Night-meal (9-10 p.m.)—Items as in mid-day lunch, lurchi, or parata (bread fried in ghee) for the house-head and his eldest son.

It may be noted that the Goswamis are Vaisnabas and, therefore eat only fish but do not touch meat or eggs. Other well-to-do families, however, occasionally enrich their diet with such food.

> *Clothing:* The adult males wear dhotis, genjis (jerseys), fatuas and Punjabis. They also use either shoes or slippers. The family also possesses a coat, 3 chaddars, 2 pair of socks and 4 umbrellas. Gamchas are indispensable for males, females and children alike.

The female members wear saris, chemises, petticoats and blouses, and consume a greater yardage of cloth per head. The boys have pants (pantaloons), shirts and genjis to put on. For infants and smaller girls, pinnies and frocks are used.

The adult females do not use shoes, slippers or socks. There is, however, one lady's umbrella in the house. The children get shoes to cover their feet.

(The term "pinny" in Bengali is used to mean children's plain frocks. Apparently it is the English word "pinny"—a childish abbreviation of "pinafore". Here it may be of interest to point out that the terms coat, pantaloons, genji (for jersey) shirt, bodice, blouse, chemise, petticoat (saia), pinny and frock are all English words or have passed through the English language before they came to enrich the vocabulary of Bengali as and when the very costumes came in fashion under the English influence. "Saia", which is the same as petticoat, is a word of Portuguese origin.)

Domestic animals: The family has 10 cows, 4 buffaloes and 5 bullocks. There are three pet peacocks in the family.

Expenses: The family's expenses on items other than food and clothing stood in 1958 as follow:

Education	Rs. 436/-
(a) School fee	Rs. 96/-
(b) Private tuition	Rs. 240/-
(c) Others	Rs. 100/-
House repair	Rs. 20/-
Medical	Rs. 300/-
Taxes and rates	Rs. 225/-
functions and ceremonies	Rs. 60/-
Toilet	Rs. 50/-
Amusement	Rs. 50/-
Miscellaneous	Rs. 179/-
Total (excluding food & clothing)	Rs. 1500/-

Possessions:

The family's inventory of semi-durable foods in 1939, showed the following articles in its possession

Wooden cots	3
Wall-clock	1
Hurricane (lanterns)	6
Table	1
Time-piece	1
Crockery (set)	1
Chair	1
Watch	1
Almirah	4
Bell-metal thalas	10
Bell-metal batis	10
Alna	1 (a wooden frame for hanging clothes)
Bicycle	1
Torch	2
Aluminium handis	5
Petromax	1
Brass pitchers	5
Shelves	5

The rich Gop household consists of 6 members—3 males, 2 females and 1 child. They have 4 cottas of enclosed compound as their living space, on which stand 4 semi-pucca tin-thatched rooms and 1 mud walled straw-thatched hut.

So far as food habits are concerned this household is not accustomed to any wheat diet—and lurchis, paratas or biscuits are not at all consumed by this family. The adult males have no coats or socks, and the adult females do not use any foot-wear or umbrella.

The family owns 10 cows, 4 buffaloes and 2 bullocks. It maybe noted that like the other rich family in the high caste group, there is no peacock or any other domestic pet in the household.

In 1958 these Gops incurred expenditures of approximately Rs.200/-on taxes and rates, Rs.175/-on medicine, Rs.40/-on social function and ceremonies, Rs.1/-on toilet articles and Rs. 20/-on amusement—say Rs.500/-in all. As the family has no school-going children, it spent nothing on education. Of course most of the food comes from the land and cattle.

As regards the household goods, the Gop family has 1 wooden cot, 2 bicycles, 1 gun, 1 torch, 3 lanterns, 1 crockery set, 10 thalas, 12 batis and 5 handis. It may be noted that there is no table, chair, almirah, nor any clock, time-piece or watches in the family. The family can easily afford to own these things but there is no need felt for them. The household is situated a little towards the outskirts in the south-west, and last year it fell victim to a raid by dacoits. Thereafter the family purchased the gun which cost them nearly Rs.2000/-.

4.5.2—The Upper Middle-Class Households

As compared to rich households, milk, fish, meat or eggs are not taken daily, but only three or four days a week. Products made of ghee are seldom consumed.

Kinds of food in different caste groups are substantially alike. But in the diet of the Kotal household, the single one in this class amongst the exterior castes, there is practically no element of wheat.

In the consumption pattern of clothing, the differences are not striking. Indeed, our rural households, whether rich or of the upper middle class, do not use any great quantity of clothing. On the average, 3 pieces of dhutis (each of 5 yds. length), a couple of Punjabis or shirts, a gamcha, and sometimes a coat and a chaddar are all the apparels required by a male adult. The women's attire consists, in the average, of 4 saris (5 yds. each), 4 blouses and 4 petticoats and a gamcha. The boys wear pants (pantaloons), shirt and genjis (jersey), and the girls and infants use pinnies and frocks. The adult males use foot-wear and umbrellas, but the adult females excepting a few high caste and Subarnabanik women are not used to them.

Generally speaking, the houses of this group, like those of the rich ones, are usually either mud-made or semi-pucca. There are however six pucca buildings belonging to the Subarnabanik caste. As compared to the rich, this group as a whole spends less on education, house repair, medicine, taxes and rates, social functions, toilet and amusement.

The inventory of the semi-durable goods for the Kotal family reads as follows: 1 wooden cot, 1 chair, 1 shelf, 1 watch, 1 bicycle, 1 torch, 1 petromax, 3 lanterns, 1 crockery set, 8 thalas, 10 batis, 5 handis, 5 brass pitchers. A Brahmin or a Subarnabanik family may own a table or a chair more, but substantially they have the same kinds of articles in their houses.

4.5.3—Lower Middle Class

In our village community there are 77 families of this category spread in the different caste groups. The upper caste families and some among the exterior castes in this class are used to tea both morning and evening. For breakfast there is muri and gur for all the groups. Occasionally, for breakfast there is hand-made bread for the high caste group, and hot boiled rice for the exterior castes. Ordinary bhat, dal, tarkari, "posta" (poppy seeds), bans, (a dainty prepared from dal, pasted, spiced and sunned), tak, (chutney) etc., form the big meals of the day. For them, fish is a rare dish, and unless there is a milk cow at home, milk also does not form any part in the regular diet. The Kaibartas, however, as fishermen in the village regularly take good quantities of fish with rice. The exterior castes also usually have fish in their meals, as their womenfolk go out in the morning to get a catch of fish with their homely nets.

As compared with higher groups, there is seen a shrinkage in the yardage of cloth consumed, and especially so in the lower caste groups. A male adult or a widow of the latter group, has only 2 pieces of dhutis per head. The female adult has three or four saris and as undergarments she may have 2 blouses and a couple of petticoats. The adult males wear sandals and there may be 1 or 2 umbrellas in the upper caste families. For the females, there are neither sandals nor umbrellas in any of the groups.

All the families of the exterior castes and most of the families of the other groups in their lower middle class category spend practically nothing for the education of their children. They cannot afford to keep private tutors for them, and so far as institutional education up to the upper primary is concerned the Government now provides it free. Only the fees of their boys who are studying in the Kaligram or Kurman schools are to be paid. The exterior castes do not send any such pupils, and therefore, do not have to incur any sum at all as school fees for their children. Miscellaneous expenses spent on education are too insignificant an amount to be recorded.

Compared to the upper two economic classes, this group shows considerably less expenditure on other items: the ratio of expenditure between the rich and this class being approximately 4 to 1. The exterior castes show practically no expenditure on toilets and amusements.

4.5.4—Poor Households

An aged Brahmin widow is found to live on begging. She has one mud-walled straw-thatched room as her shelter. Muri and gur form her breakfast and night meal as well. Rice, dal, and a hodge-podge of vegetables constitute her day meals. She has two pieces of cloth to wear, and owns a heifer valued at Rs.25/-only. Her expenses on education, taxes, social functions, toilet and amusement are nil. In 1958, she spent Rs.25/-on house repair and Rs.51/-for medical treatment She owns one wooden cot, 1 alna, 1 shelf, 2 lanterns, 3 thalas, 3 bans, 1 handi and 1 pitcher.

A Gop family of two members has no land and maintains itself on animal husbandry. It lives in a mud-walled room. Tea is taken in the morning. Fish is rarely taken with rice. Muri, gur, and milk usually serve as breakfast. As producers of milk, they retain a certain quantity of this valuable food for their own consumption. Excepting these Gops, there is little milk in the poor men's diet. But most of the households have a fish diet, as the women of the exterior castes who form the bulk of the poor class and the Kaibartas are of piscatorial habits, and they supplement the diet with their catches.

Few of the exterior caste people take tea in the morning. As morning breakfast they usually take cold rice soaked overnight in water, with salt, chilies and onions. There is no element of wheat in their diet. Most of the men of this group are accustomed to take country-made liquor. For them, a jar of wine and meat are essential on occasions of banquets and feasts. The Bainris, the Haris and the Santhals keep pigs and eat pork occasionally. For all other castes and the Muslims, the pigs are considered unclean and their meat is detested.

The men and women of this class use a minimum of clothing, and the children have no clothing of any sort. In addition to dhutis and gamchas (napkins), the men now use a punjabi or a shirt, a pair of shoes or a piece of chaddar if, of course, their means permit. The women are also seen to use blouses, and petticoats as well, if there is some surplus money for such purchases. But none of the men has any coat nor any women a pair of shoes.

This class has nothing to spend on education, and little on house repairs and medicine. Few of the families have to pay any land tax as most of them are landless. There are families who are also exempted from payment of even the few annas of the anchal rates. Little sums are spent on social functions and amusements. No expenses were said to have been incurred on toilet by any of these poor families in 1958.

Though our village community has been grouped into four economic classes, it should be remembered that there are always variations within each group. Such are to be found in the poor class as well. Thus the share-cultivators, or able-bodied workers, may live in better houses or have a better share of food and clothing etc., whereas an old forlorn decrepit woman or a delinquent half cracked lonely young man may be found to go hungry without rice on many days and live in rejected rags and tottering shelters.

CHAPTER 5

▼

MARRIAGE AND HOME

5.1—THE HOUSES IN WHICH KANCHANPUR LIVES

In discussing the levels of living of the different classes of our village community we have described to some extent its housing conditions as well. Coming from the bus stop on the main road, you enter the village with your face to the south; just at the entrance on the right side of the road, a cluster of huts will come to your sight. If you are acquainted with a few Bengal villages, no body need tell you that it is one of the Harijan pallis of the village—a Bagdipara, a Bayenpara, a Bauripara or the like. As it is, it is one of the Hariparas of the village of Kanchanpur. The mud cottages stand there all exposed to the visitor's eyes, their privacy not guarded by any enclosure or walls. There are a few better looking huts, but a majority of them have a ragged appearance. Some of the huts stand without repairs, and their thatches are quite inadequate to prevent cold and rains from coming in. Perhaps you may find that there is no door in a hut, and in its stead is hung a cheap frame made of cut pieces of bamboo. If it is winter, that frame may be seen to be covered with torn gunny bags so as to oppose as best as they can the entry of the unkind cold wind.

In 1872 the Rev. Day wrote: "The bulk of the houses are mud cottages thatched with the straw of paddy, though there is considerable number of brick houses owned for the most part by the Kayasthas and the Banker caste." But no Kayastha has a brick-built house at present, and besides the ex-Zamindar's house, there are only six brick-built houses, all belonging to the middle class Subarna-baniks. The rest of the houses are all built of mud.

Here you see is a rich household consisting of mud huts. It has a compound enclosed with mud walls, over which there is a running thatch to protect the mud walls from damages of rain. You enter the inner yard through a door facing the south. On the right stands a newly built south facing two-storied mud building. The ground floor is cemented, while the first floor is made of wooden planks. The roof is thatched with corrugated tins.

The first floor room is occupied by the owner of the house. At right angles to this structure, there stand in a line three big rooms of mud walls and straw thatch, with their faces to the east. Beyond these rooms to the north is the kitchen, and further beyond the dug-well latrine which is used only by the old Karat (head) of the family. Persuaded by the Community Development people, some of the rich and upper class households had made such latrines in their houses, but in no time their use was abandoned and the inmates of the house returned to their habit of using the fields which they consider as more healthy and clean. Only the aged may require latrines at home. The only sanitary privy of the village has recently been constructed by the ex-zamindar, mainly because of his sufferings from gout which made his walks to the fields painful, and as the ex-zamindar commented, if latrines are to be constructed on the homestead, they should be of the sanitary type.

You will find in the inner courtyard of any rich household, as in this particular one, a row of mamis, that is, thatched rice granaries made of ropes of twisted straw and cylindrical in shape. These contain hundreds of maunds of paddy and where paddy is stored, so it is said, Sri (i.e., Goddess) Lakshmi herself resides. Outside this residential area, there is another enclosed area where stand two sheds and a couple of big paluis i.e., straw stacks. In one of the sheds the cows are tied, the other is meant for the bullocks and buffaloes of the household.

After you have glimpsed through the poor and the rich cottage, you may feel curious to have a cursory look into a house in which a middle class family resides. Haply you may be invited there say for a dinner with the family. You enter the front room, where on the mud floor is spread a sitalpati (a cane woven mat), and you are requested to sit down. This room is a part of a long shed which is parti-tioned in the middle by a wall.

The front portion serves as the room where visitors are accepted, and the inner portion is used as a bedroom. The floor and the walls are of mud and the room is supported on a structure of palmyra beams and rafters. The interstices of the framework are filled with alternate plain and colored Sara reeds and the roof is thatched with a thick layer of straw. Inside the room, there is no furniture but an old wooden shelf which contains some old school textbooks that once formed the subjects of study of the now grown-up sons of the family. On the walls are hung some photographs of the family members, and some cheap pictures of Hindu gods and goddesses. A relief map of India prepared by the second son of the family while he had been a student of the primary teachers' training institute at Burdwan along with a group photo of his classmates and teachers of the year are also hung on the walls there. There too appears a handiwork of a female member of the house which exhibits two devotional lines woven in wool on a carpet and runs as follows: "Thou art the hope in despair. The anchor in a shoreless ocean."

Knowing that you are interested to have a look at the house, your new friend takes you inside. The bara ghar (the big hut), of which the visitors' room is a part, faces to the east and has all open verandah in front of it Beyond to the east is the inner court-yard where the marais of the house stand neat and graceful. To the south of the yard is the tube well of the household in a little enclosure. To the north stands another big hut with its face to the south, and it is used by the householder as his bedroom. To the west there are also a small sleeping room and the kitchen, both of which face east

It may be pointed out that, in our villages, the people invariably build their best rooms to face either south or east, as this is the saying of Khana (a great astrologer-woman of traditional fame): "*dakshin dwari gharer raja, pub-duari tar praja*", i.e., south facing room is the king of huts, and the east facing one is his tenant. Construction of huts facing otherwise is not worth any consideration.

You enter the sleeping room of your friend, that is the inside portion of the big hut. The space there is almost entirely occupied by a big wooden cot. There are several trunks of the family. These are all tied together in an iron chain and by a knot with a foot of the big taktaposh (wooden cot) on which the elder son and his wife and children go for sleep. In a corner you find spears and a bow with a set of steel-headed arrows. As it is difficult for a villager to own a gun, these country weapons are kept for purposes of resisting the robbers, if such need arises. There are a couple of cycles which are used by the two elder sons of the family. A nice little dome of glass in the wall shelf may attract your notice, and on enquiry you learn that it is a table lamp with a bed switch, and is worked by electrically charged cells.

5.2—THE KINS OF THE KANCHANPUR HOUSEHOLDS

The 285 families living at Kanchanpur have been classified as incomplete, conjugal, extended and irregular. A household uninhabited by any married couple has been classed as "incomplete". A family of husband and wife with or without children belong to the "conjugal" type. When two or more conjugal families, related lineally, collaterally or otherwise, live in the same household it makes "extended" or "joint" family. A household inhabited by a man and woman, not in wedlock, is described here "as "irregular".

There are 58 households at Kanchanpur which are found to belong to the incomplete type. The householder in these is either a bachelor, a widow, a widower or a deserted spouse. Three households are irregular in the sense that the man and the woman here live together out of wedlock. All these incomplete or irregular households cannot be considered to present any family life in the proper sense of the term.

The rest of the households of Kanchanpur, numbering 224, have been classed as of two main types—(i) the conjugal and (ii) the joint. In our village community there are altogether 113 conjugal and 111 joint households. But it maybe noted that there is a higher proportion of joint families in the high castes, and a larger number of conjugal families in the exterior castes.

The extended (or joint) families are seen to be mainly of the linear type i.e., the parents and the sons' family living together. It is still considered a breach of filial duty to leave one's parents in their old days, and social opinion also discourages break-up of the family so long as the parents are alive. The father's ownership of the family lands also works as a deterrent to the splitting up of the family. All these factors are seen to work more strongly in the high caste groups. Amongst the exterior castes the sons do not feel obligations to the parents so binding, and as they mainly depend on their income from labour and have no expectation of property from their fathers in the future, the joint family type has lost much of its sanctity and young married couples go off to live separately. But such behavior is not possible for a high caste couple living in the group environment of Kanchanpur. "A son who separates himself from his mother in order to live with his wife, does not deserve to live; and when he dies the durra grass will sprout in his bones, and his soul will go to hell." Again, D.C., a son of a well-to-do Brahmin family, is a partner in some business firm at Calcutta, and lives there singly as he has kept his wife and children in the village with his aged parents. He does not even think of taking his wife and children to the city as that means his parents would be left alone in the village without proper care and attention. To quote his words: "I was brought up to my manhood by my parents, and now if they have to burn their hands for cooking their own food at their old age, it will be a great dereliction of my duty, and I shall have no place even in hell."

But the attitudes and values for joint families extended through collateral relationship are different. The accepted social code is that brothers should and do separate. If they are bound to live together for a long time, they become the subject of discussion, and instead of the family being praised some one or the other amongst the brothers is regarded a fool and as one being cheated of his legitimate share by the other more clever brothers. However, a certain percentage of such collaterally joint families exists in all the caste groups in the village.

There are four compound families in the sense that a householder has a second or third wife who is living with her stepchildren born of the earlier marriage of the man. In three cases, the previous wives had died, but in the case of M., a Kaibarta householder, both his wives are living with their husband in our village. As it happened the first wife did not come "to take rice" into her husband's house for years. Thereupon M's father got for his son a second wife. This led his first wife to file a maintenance suit in the courts of Burdwan. M. was ever willing to give her food and clothing if she came to live with him. Ultimately, however, matters got settled, and the first wife came to take her rice in the husband's home. M.'s father on his death gifted his property to the second wife of his son, but the first wife came to secure greater favor from the husband. It can be presumed that the relations between the co-wives are very strained and they live in separate parts of the house, but troubles frequently arise as there is only one man in the household.

There are three families in the village each of which is joint with another simple related family of a married couple or sister. Of these three households, two belong to the Brahmins and the third to the Sadgops. In one, a daughter deserted by her husband has come with her children to live under the roof of the father. In the second case, a sister gone insane is staying with her children in her brother's house. Her husband, however, sends regular support. The third is the case of a widower and his son in whose house a widowed sister of the householder's deceased wife has come with her children to live.

The three irregular families are not recognized as proper societal units, but their existence is a fact which cannot be overlooked. A Kayastha man is living with a Dom woman, and though he is held in low esteem by his caste brethren and others, no formal punishment has been enforced on him, and he has not been excluded from communion with his fellow caste-men. It is so because there are only a few Kayastha households in the village, and considering prudence to be the better part of valor, they did not formally excommunicate the degenerate. As one said, his services would be required by the community when the dead body of a Kayastha is to be carried to the crematory for burning. However, the man has left the Kayastha palii, and is living apart with his woman at a distance. Another such household consists of an Ugra-Kshatriya man and a Bagdi woman; and the third is a union of a Kotal man and a Gop woman. The Ugra-Kshatriyas and the Gops are supposed to possess higher social position, but in these cases their association with lowborn mates degraded their status, and the couples had to take their residence in the habitats of the exterior castes.

Apart from the above instances of man and woman living in overt illicit relations, there are in the village, so I was told, a few concubines in the keep of even "respectable" Brahmins. There are also, I heard it said, many hidden affairs as well, and the words of the Rev. Day may even now be repeated: "Of dishonorable criminal love there is no lack, but I do not intend to pollute the pages with its description".

In describing the family pattern of Kanchanpur, we have been viewing the matter from the standpoint of kinship structure, and the size of the family has been so long overlooked. The average size of family for the exterior castes is the lowest amongst the different social groups and is 4.3 only. The modal size for them is also a 4 member household. The upper caste households, which are more extended in their relationships, show, on the other hand, a higher figure as the mean side of the families, and the variation in the aggregate of members in each family ranges from 1 to 21 persons per household.

But the household cannot be reduced to a mere aggregate of persons. It is rather a complex of human relations in which the connected persons stand to each other and behave according to certain socially recognized rules. Describing the infra-familial relationships of a family, the Rev. Day wrote:

> Alanga, forty-six years old was the grihini or mistress of the household. Her son Badan paid her boundless respect, and always agreed to every domestic arrangement she made. Nor were her other sons and her daughters-in-law less obedient to her. Badan's wife Sundari, might be expected according to English notions, as the wife of the head of the family, to feel aggrieved at her being deprived of her rightful authority as the mistress of the house. But such a notion is never entertained by a Bengali wife while her mother-in-law is living. And the idea never occurred to Sundari; she deemed it her duty, and esteemed it a privilege to be under the guardianship of her husband's mother. She was thankful that all domestic affairs were under the management of one so much older, wiser and more experienced than she.

We have seen, so far as the upper castes are concerned, that the lineally extended family with the parents or any one of them as head, is the dominant type of household. The praise of filial piety in Hindu culture, and the persisting group habits of thoughts and behaviors have still retained for the mother the place of superiority and command over her sons and daughters-in-law. The components of such an extended village family are: (i) Parents, (ii) Married sons with wives and children, and (iii) Unmarried sons and unmarried daughters. The daughters go off to live with their husbands' people after marriage and they are not considered real kins of the family. They are brought up to be keepers of others' houses, and it is considered extremely unfortunate if a daughter or a sister, in widowhood or otherwise, comes back to live with her father or brother.

In purely conjugal relations, usually the male has the dominance and control. It is the husband's duty to maintain his wife—to provide her with food and clothing. The wife on her part should follow the path of her husband and be of one mind with her husband's. The man must feed, and the wife must submit—this is the broad conception of rights and duties in our rural couple. A person who tries to exercise control without rendering any good is often jeered with the

saying: "Not a husband to provide rice, but a Gosain (master) to use cuffs."
("*bhat debar bhatar nai, kil marbar gosain*")

The mother-in-law in our rural joint families still enjoys a privileged position, and the daughters-in-law are given a place of subordination. The village daughters are allowed greater liberties and are free in their movements. But a bou (daughter-in-law) of the family, usually from another village, has to go about her housework or elsewhere with her face completely veiled. It is indecent for her to speak with her husband's father or elder brothers. She cannot even pronounce the name of her husband or his elder relations. She is not supposed to violate this rule even when adherence to it may cause inconvenience or difficulty. The taboo applies equally to the women of the exterior castes. Thus one of them was seen to come to the president of the Panchayat for a ration card but she could not tell him whose wife she was. She tried to indicate it in various ways and finally referred to her husband as "the bird that sings in the spring". The president and all others who were assembled there then understood that she was the wife of the person named Kotil (the cuckoo), and the ration card was duly issued with the name of her husband recorded therein.

The village bou lives under the guardianship and control of the husband's mother. The harmony of family life is not lost so long as the silken ties of love bind the members of the family. But often there is seen less love and more dominance—as is brought out in the familiar village saying: "*dhane jabda sile, bou jabda kile*" i.e., "*The coriander seeds are ground when the entry stone is used; and the daughters-in-law are held in check when the clenched fists are shown.*"

5.3—MARRIAGE—A THING OF FATE

The ideal of the romantic love leading to marriage is not yet to be expected in our village community. It is true that now-a-days the girls of the upper castes are seldom married off before they are twelve years old and many of them now exceed even their teens before marriages can be arranged for them by their parents. But courtship is an idea foreign to the culture of rural Bengal. Often boys and girls grow up together in the village and it might well be that wishes of the parents and tender feelings between the playmates sometimes bring into existence a warm friendship and mutual interest between a boy and a girl. But marriages are always to be arranged in old fashioned ways and the warmth in the two adolescent hearts never inspires them to make love in the western sense with a view to marriage. It is for their elders either to make or wreck their marriage proposals.

Here is a true story from the mouth of a young man of our village:

> We knew from our childhood, both she and I, that we would be life mates to each other in future. Such was our hearts' desire and the wishes of my mother and her father. She was a girl of a neighbouring family, but she was more dear to me than my sister. We were inwardly interested in each other; but we never talked of it as that would be unbecoming and indecent.
>
> Both of us reached our respective marriageable age, and negotiations for our marriages were started. I had lost my father in my boyhood, and my mother was my guardian. She was fond of our neighbour's girl and wanted to see her as a bou in the family. The girl's father and brother were also desirous to give her in marriage to me. But the girl's mother, for reasons best known to her, was opposed to the alliance. Theirs was one of the dominant families in the village, and they considered themselves higher in status to ours. Still, the girl's father did not give up hopes, and though he did not bring any proposal to my mother for giving his daughter in marriage to me, he was wishing it and was expecting the proposal to come from my mother's side. Once my mother deputed him on her behalf to see a bride for me in another village. He came back and reported that the other party was seeking a better placed bride-groom, and the negotiations naturally fell through for the time being. But as luck would have it, the father of that girl in the neighbouring village, anxious as he was to get his daughter married, reproached my mother, and finally we were betrothed, and an auspicious date for the marriage was fixed.
>
> It was then that our neighbour, the father of my beloved girl, accosted my mother and said that marriage between his daughter and me had all along been intended by both the families. My mother replied that it was not for her, as a mother of a bridegroom, to bring the formal proposal first in the matter, and then it was too late as she was promise-bound and could not back out. The family pride of my neighbour, and my mother's independence not to stoop, wrecked our adolescent dreams. I was married to the other girl, and she to another man in the village of…Possibly I did not act very manly, but you see—marriage after all, like birth and death, is a thing of fate.

5.4—KANCHANPUR CHOOSES A BRIDE

Rev. Day wrote in 1872:

> As in India young men and women do not themselves choose their partners in life, they have to depend on the good offices of this happy functionary (the

match maker), who, however, bears his commission not from the parties themselves, but from their parents and guardian. He has never been known to find any fault with any young man or young woman of marriageable age. The spinster may be as ugly as one of Shakespeare's witches, and the young man may he as deformed as deformity itself, the ghatak (the match-maker) sees no defect in either. They are, in his eyes, or at any rate in his mouth, as beautiful and gentle as Lakshmi, and the other as handsome and accomplished as Kartikeya.

But this very virtue of the ghatak proved to be his undoing, and disqualified him in the profession as decades passed on. The guardians and parents do no longer like to see through the eyes, or believe what they hear from the mouths of any professional matchmaker. With some undesirable matches to their discredit the ghatak had to leave his field, and nowadays, it is mainly the responsibilities of the parents and relations of the parties to arrange the marriages at Kanchanpur.

Nowadays a match is usually proposed through mutual friends and relatives of the parties. Thereafter, one day the young man's father in company of some close relatives or friends visits the place of the girl's father to see whether the bride will be a fit partner for their boy. The girl has to pass through a stiff examination, and the payment of dowry must be settled before the ceremony of betrothal takes place. There, to quote the Bengali couplet:

barer baba base achhe parish hajarer ase
leaner babar bhanga kapat choker jate bhase

That is, the bridegroom's father, expecting his five thousand, smiles, but the bride's father, with his furrowed brow, is prone to tears.

This is, of course, the monetary aspect of the marriage negotiations, but what about the choice of the bride herself?

Our village friend Sri Gnetoo Kumar Chatterjee was accompanying the father and uncle of a Kanchanpur boy on a bride-seeing visit to another village. He was requested by the present writer to bring a true description of all that took place and his experiences are related below in his own words as follows:

...Returning from my stroll through the village, I found that both my companions were up from their noon-day siesta. Two big sataranjis had been spread on the outer verandah, and there in the center two carpeted seats were placed one facing the other. In the verandah, and the open yard, there gathered about twenty to twenty-two persons, old and middle-aged men and children of the village. The old men were seated on the sataranjis. Some of them were smoking tobacco in hookah. Occasionally the middle-aged men timidly extended their hands to take the kalki (earthen pot containing tobacco) from their elder's. They puffed the tobacco a few times and then transferred the kalki to others.

As I entered the place of gathering, an old man of eighty years extended his greetings to me—"Come, my friend, and be seated." I bowed to him and enquired about his health. The old man jokingly replied: "Well, my friend, very well. I am excessively well."

Just then the prospective bride or candidate dressed in everyday clothing and with hair untied was led by an old woman into the sabha (gathering), with slow and soft steps.

Rishikumar, the uncle of the prospective bridegroom, had already taken his seat on the first carpeted seat with his face to the east The girl came near, made her bows to the respectables in the assembly, and then slowly sat down on the other carpeted seat in front of Rishikumar. Her head was bent low and she waited there in all modesty. Humbly the bride's father intimated that her daughter might he asked any questions thought desirable by the party.

Rishikumar had already made himself prepared for the situation, and he at once started the examination:

"Ma, (mother), what is your name?"

"My name is Prativarani Chattopadhyay," replied the girl in a rather timid voice.

"What is your father's name?"

"My father's name is Sanatan Chattopadhyay."

"Very good, very good! (Besh! Besh)"

"Ma, do you know lekhapara (to read and write)?"

"Yes, I know."

"How far and up to what class have you read?"

"I read up to class four."

"Do you know writing?"

"Yes, I know," was the reply.

Then Rishikumar looked to the girl's father and found that he had already brought the requisite things for the test-paper, ink pot and pen, etc. Rishikumar took the writing materials and handed them to the girl.

"Well, mother, now you write your name on this paper."

The girl correctly wrote out her name on the paper.

"Now, mother, write down again your father's name with his address in this village".

Silently the girl complied with the direction.

Kishikumar took the paper in hand and read aloud:

"Srimati Prativarani Chattopadhyay,
Father's name—Srijukta Sanatan Chattopadhyay,
Village—Adityapur"
Post Office—Adityapur,
District—Burdwan."

"Good. The handwriting is also excellent."

"Well, mother, are you skilled in the art of sewing and stitching?"
"Yes, I am."

"What do you know?"

"I know to weave carpets, knit sweaters, prepare papos (doormats) make designs etc."

"Well, mother, do you know how to laugh? Let us see how you laugh".

As the bride was too strained to laugh, her father told her not to feel shy. He asked her to laugh and explained to her that she was asked to laugh so that her teeth might be inspected by the examining party.

But the bride still failed to laugh. In shame and fear she bent her head still lower and it seemed that she wanted to identify herself with the mother earth.

Then the old man of eighty years began to tell a story, and full of humor it was. Along with others, the young bride broke out in laughter, and the frolicsome nature of adolescence expressed itself.

Rishikumar keenly watched the teeth and laughter of the girl, and simultaneously remarked: "The girl's teeth are good. These are neither high nor low, neither long nor short. But Sir, I did not ask her to laugh only to see her teeth. When one laughs the cheeks unmistakably show signs—good as well as bad. It is one of the sayings of Khana (the great female astrologer of traditional fame):

hasyakale gandas kup hay jar,
sei nari bandhya babe janibek sar.

That is, "If a dimple is formed in the cheeks at the time of laughing, know it for certain that the woman is going to be sterile."

"Mother, lift the skirt of your sari from your ankle to the knee".

The girl blushed and grew crimson. But she must try to pass her examination as her father was being blamed for not getting her married as yet. Almost daily her father is running to distant villages in search of a bridegroom for her and for her sake he is undergoing many humiliations and troubles. She pondered and hesitated a little and then slowly drew up the ends of sari-skirt till both of her legs from the ankles to the kneel became visible to others eyes.

Rishikumar carefully examined the naked parts, and then asked the girl to drop the skirt and walk a bit.

The bride began to walk slowly.

"Quick! more quick!" and silently the girl obeyed the order.

"Now you see there is a brass jar underneath that pumpkin creeper in the yard. Go and fetch that pot on your waist, and then come here and sit down on your seat."

The girl did as she was directed. As she was coming with the pot on her waist, Rishikumar watched her gait with a fixed gaze to find out whether the fingers and soles of the feet were having their full press on the earth. Because, if it is not so, the girl does not possess good signs and therefore would be rejected.

When the girl was seated again Rishikumar asked her to turn round, so that he could examine the growth of her hair on the head. After such inspection, the girl was asked to extend her left hand towards him, which she did gracefully and then kept her eyes closed.

Rishikumar now began to carefully examine the lines on her palm. He spent some ten minutes over it, whispering at the same time his calculations in various indistinct sounds. Then he said: "No, the girl has very good lines! She has been born in all auspicious moment (lagna), and she owns good signs. My choice is made in favor of the girl."

But still the grind continued.

"Well, mother, do you know how to make tea and cook food?"

"Yes, I know."

"Do you know how to prepare offering for thakurpuja (i.e., worship of God)?"

"Yes, I do."

"Then tell me what are the things that are required in thakurpuja." "Flowers, durva grass, tulsi leaves, Ganges water, haritaki (myrobalan), black til (sesamum), sandalwood paste, incense, lamp, sun dried rice, sandesh or batasa."

But I was becoming restive and intervened saying: "Good, good, you need not tell any further". I then turned to speak to Rishikumar: "Well, Sir, just now you carefully examined the lines of her palms and gave us your judgment that she was born in an auspicious moment and she has very good marks to indicate that she would be happy and prosperous in life and make others so. When you have read all these on her palms, and when you are confident of your predictions, what good is there in further examination?"

Then, in order to prevent any altercation between us growing, the old man of eighty years spoke again. He thus addressed me: "No, my son, no. Allow him to go on with his questions. All these may be necessary, as you cannot see in the palm whether the girl is deaf or dumb!"

Thus stopped, I requested Rishi Babu to go on as he would like.

"Well", said Rishi Babu, "I need not ask any further questions. But I want to be supplied with a copy of the girl's thikuji (i.e., the paper recording the moment of birth with position of the sun, the moon, the planets and stars at that time). This is needed for a comparison with the boy's horoscope and to find whether the heavenly influences of the parties will be compatible in this marriage."

The bride's father promised to hand over the said birth-moment document immediately, and inquired whether he would like to ask any further question of the girl. Rishikumar turned to the bride and said: "Mother, I have given you much trouble, but Mother, I am your son. Now go and prepare tea with your own hands and see that you yourself serve us the cups."

The girl got up and left the place with soft steps and entered the kitchen of the house. A few minutes later she came again with ten cups of tea placed on a tray, served these to the guests one by one, and then stood still.

"Well, mother, you may go." said Rishikumar as he sipped the cup of tea. "You have prepared very good tea. It has excellent taste. Now, mother, you may go inside."

With the empty tray in hand, the bride turned towards the inner yard of the house with the same slow and soft steps with which she had entered at first.

When the bride had thus been chosen, the question of dowry arose. It was settled that the bridegroom would be presented with a cycle, a wrist-watch and a set of gold buttons. At sampradan (giving away ceremony) during marriage, the bride would be presented to the groom, with 25 tolas of gold ornaments on her body. Lastly, a sum of Rs. 500/in cash was to be paid to the bridegroom's father for meeting his part of the expenses.

Thus, it seems, was an old-fashioned marriage arranged. But forces of modernisation are also having their impact on our village community, and slow changes are coming. In the above matter, though everything was settled, I was told by Rishikumar himself that the bridegroom with his brother-in-law and a friend would be sent to have a look at the girl. It was out of question that the boy might reject the choice of his father and guardians. But still he must be sent, and his visit to the girl's place would at the same time give an opportunity to the bride and her people to have a look at the boy as well.

5.5—KANCHANPUR CELEBRATES A MARRIAGE

A.O.'s sister was going to be married. "Her real age" said J.B. to me, "was twenty-two, but what could we do but give out to the bridegroom's people that she was only seventeen? It was a great relief to the girls' relatives that the marriage could be arranged after all."

The auspicious moment for celebrating the marriage was fixed on the 11th Falgun. The bridegroom with his party entered Kanchanpur in the service bus, which on receipt of an extra 5 rupees drove up to the central Shivatala of the village, and dropped the passengers there. The marriage-party was cordially received by the bride's people and was led to an adjoining house where arrangements for seats of the bridegroom and the party had been made. There was no hookah to go round. But cigarettes and bidis in plates, and cups of tea were served off and on.

In the enclosed yard of the bride's house, under a canopy overhead, arrangements had been made for celebration of the marriage. In one corner of the yard was the chhatnatala where the ceremony of the striachar was to be performed. ("chhatna" is an indigenous word which means "to tie". Chhatnatala, therefore, literally means the place where the bridegroom is to be tied. The term, however, has acquired a generic sense and means the place where the striachar is to be performed.) The striachar literally means the female customs and forms the first part of the marriage to be performed by the women. In the center of the yard, arrangements had been made for the ceremony of sampradan (gift) which is performed according to Brahminic rite. There the priests and the napits of both the parties were waiting for the beginning of the ceremony, and the salgram, the oval black stone used as a symbol of God Narayana, was already placed on its throne in the central mandap (platform).

As the eminently auspicious hour arrived, which according to the calculations of the Hindu astrologers was the great moment for a man and a woman to be united as husband and wife, the uncle of the bride sought permission from the priests and the assembled gentlemen in the yard that the marriage ceremony might be started. All said: "Yes, yes, please begin the ceremony", and thereafter the bridegroom was led to the seat. As the bride had lost her father, her uncle would give her in sampradan (gift of the bride i.e., in marriage), and he was called upon by his priest to make the sankalpa (resolution before God) for the ceremony. The bridegroom was then honored and gifts of silken cloth, gold ring, a wrist-watch and other presents were made over to him. Thereafter, he was sent to the female department for performance of what is called the striachar.

A married grandmother of the bride, assisted by several other married women, first gave the bridegroom the ceremonial welcome (baran). But thereafter the bridegroom's plight began. His hands were tied by the women and he was asked to bleat or remain in bondage. On promise of payment of a fee, however, he was allowed to be free. Next came the burning of 28 sticks. The women, assisted by some men as well, took the burning sticks round and round the bride-groom and the heat and soot that came out in the process must have caused same pain and suffering to the would-be carrier-away of the bride. It was now time for the bride to be brought forward on the scene. The ceremony of satpak (seven binding) was started by carrying the bride seated on a wooden stool seven times round the bridegroom, and was completed by moving her seven times up and down in front of him. Then a veil was thrown over the heads of the couple and they are asked to make the subha-dristi (i.e., auspicious sight). After this came the exchange of flower garlands between the parties which, according to the female custom, completed the union.

During all the above processes, there were sounds of ulu and conch shells all around. Printed poems composed on the occasion were distributed by both the parties. When the striachar was declared to be over, the napit, who is an important functionary in all marriage ceremonies and stands next to the priest, came forward to recite some self-composed rhymes. First the napit of the bridegroom's party displayed his poetic skill, and then the bride's napit gave the reply. Both of them described in their own verses, the marriage ceremony between Ram and Sita and compared the present marriage to that of the great Hindu epic. Both of them glorified the traditional ideal of married womanhood as embodied in Sita:

> Here Sita stands, my daughter fair:
> The duties of thy life to share.
> Take from her father, take thy bride,
> Join hand to hand, the bliss betide.
> A faithful wife, most blest is she,
> And, as thy shade, will follow thee.

(Quoted by the Rev. Day from Griffith's *Ramayana*).

Now the couple were led to the asar (place for sampradan). Here now the marriage ceremony was to be performed according to Sanskritic rites. The bride's left hand was placed over the palm of the bridegroom's right hand and the function of sampradan (gift of the girl) was performed. After a brief respite the ceremony of kusandika began. Some sand was spread on the earth and a square was drawn on it by a straw of kasha grass. Inside the square of sand, a sacrificial fire was lit. After hom (offering in fire) of ghee and fried rice to God, such rites as panigrahan (i.e., taking of the bride's hand by the groom), saptapadi (i.e., walking seven steps together), dhruba darshan (seeing the pole star—so that the wife may remain fixed and true in her husband's family like the said star), arundhati darshan (so that the wife may remain chaste and pure like Arundhati, now a star in heaven but really the wife of the great sage Vasistha), sindurdan (giving the vermilion on the head), lajja-dan (bestowal of modesty in which rite the bridegroom draws the veil on the face of the bride) were performed one after another with citation of the holy Sanskrit mantras by the priests. Finally came the purnahuti (full offering in fire) after which the sacrificial fire was extinguished.

Thus the sacramental marriage came to an end and with their skirts tied to each other's clothes the married couple retired to the vasarghar (i.e., bedroom of the nuptial night) while other persons were served the dinner. The night at vasarghar, however, was not an exclusive affair for the couple, and the place was crowded with a number of young and old women on terms of jovial relation whose only purpose was to spend the night in getting amusement and teasing the pair, and especially the bridegroom.

The next day, the bridegroom and his party were to return with the bride to their own place. J.B. on behalf of the interested groups of the village approached the karta (the head) of the bridegroom's party and realized some Rs.16 as fees and subscriptions payable on such occasions. Rs.2 was levied as dagra-salami—the same as dhelabhan-gani mentioned by the Rev. Day—as payment to the adolescent boys as purchase price for abstention from stoning the marriage party while entering the village. Another Rs.2 were realized for untying the bridegroom's hands during striachar and also a further amount of Rs.7 was exacted for sayyato-lan, (i.e., allowing the bridegroom to get up from the nuptial bed). These six rupees were to be invested in sweets by the respective parties. The rest of the money was to be equally divided among the different village institution such as the Panchayat, the Old Siva, the F.P. School, the Memorial Library, and lastly the Dakshinpara Barwari, to which locality the bride's people belonged.

After the ceremony of asirbad (benedictions), the bride left the village in tears, with her husband and his friends and relatives. For the married couple, a palki (palanquin), the only one in the village, was requisitioned to carry them up to the bus-stand. The friends and relatives, however, walked down this little distance. Before leaving the village the palki was twice stopped before the temple of the Old Siva, and the place of the great mother, and the couple got down to pray so that they might receive the blessings of their gods in the beginning of their new life.

5.6—Household Duties at Kanchanpur

The days of Kanchanpur's women are full of work. The men of our village community do not share the burden of household duties. The old female values persist and the men are not even expected to cooperate with their women in the housework of the family. Rich or poor, of high or low caste, the village women have to work and attend to various domestic affairs from morn till night.

Getting out of bed early in the morning, the first duty which a housewife has to perform or have it performed is to sprinkle water on the door steps, and thereafter to scatter the solution of cow dung and water on the open yards and at the entrance of the front doors. These places are then swept by a broom and then polished by means of a piece of rag dipped in the solution of cow dung and water. All Kanchanpur women, whatever their class or caste may be, follow the above practice, as it is known to them:

> Where water is sprinkled, and sweeping is done before the rise of the sun,
> And where the lamps are lit as the sun sets,
> There I love to reside, says Mother Lakshmi.

Excepting a very limited number of rich and a few upper middle class households of the village, Kanchanpur women cannot afford to engage the service of maid-servants for their housework. But even those housewives are not very free or leisured, as there are spheres of work in which the maid-servants are not allowed to enter.

After the morning sprinkling of water and cow dung solution, the women begin the cleaning of the house. Beddings used at night are rolled up and stocked properly; ashes from ovens are taken out and thrown on the manure-heaps. The whole house is swept by a broom, and all earthen floors and yards are polished with cow dung solution. The maid-servants of the rich households perform the ordinary work of cleaning and washing, but they are not allowed to enter the thakurghar (the deity's room), the kitchen and some special rooms, and consequently those are to be cleansed by the women of the house.

For the rich the maid-servants boil paddy and dry it in the sun, but most of the housewives of the village do those duties themselves. Such boiled and sunned paddy is then usually sent to be turned into rice in the neighbouring hulling machines. But there are many families, especially amongst the poor and the exterior castes, who are still depending and working on their homely pedals.

Morning and evening, the cooking pots and pans, and the dishes, glasses and saucers etc., used during meals are taken to the nearest tank and scoured and cleansed there. In case of the rich households, it is the job of the maidservants, but they are not allowed to enter the kitchen; women of the house should take those outside the kitchen to be handed over to the maid-servant, and again arrange them inside when the cleansing has been done.

The upper-caste old ladies, especially the widows, take early baths and spend a part of their morning in regular prayers and pujas. Those who have daily worship of the deities in their houses, make arrangements for such worship, and thereafter they go to help in other domestic duties.

Drinking of tea has become a habit, especially with the upper classes. For such households, tea-making and serving have, therefore, come to be a part of the housewives' regular work. For all classes and castes, the care of the children is a necessary housework. But children belonging to the upper sections of the society usually get better food, clothings and home education, while those of the lower sections appear neglected.

The cleansing of the cowsheds is also a regular task of Kanchanpur women, and most of the households have cows. The making of the cow dung cakes and balls mixed with coal dust to be used as fuel, when dry, is also an art in which the Kanchanpur women are almost daily engaged.

When the house has been cleansed and fire has been given to the coke in the family oven, the Kanchanpur women should go to take their ablutions. After washing the used garments and clothings of the house members, they take their bath and hurry home as the fire has been ready for the most important part of their work, that it, cooking for the members of the family. It is their especial charge, and even the rich households of the village are not used to engaging the services of a cook. Drawing of water, cutting of vegetables, or making a paste of spices to be used in the curries are also activities usually done by the village women. The rich housewives, however, usually get the services of poor but high-caste women for bringing water from tube wells, or frying rice, or muri or pasting of spices for curries, in fact any such honorable tasks as cannot be left to maid-servant of the exterior castes. The daughters and housewives of other classes do these tasks for themselves, and moreover they have to fetch their cooking and drinking water usually from the nearest public tube well. A lady with a pitcher on the waist and a bucket in her right hand is a familiar sight in the streets of Kan-chanpur.

The exterior caste women, besides their household work, go out to catch fish with their homely nets. They and especially the poorer amongst them also collect cow dung from the streets and fields, and also dried twigs and sticks etc. to be used as their fuel.

The upper caste and the Subarnabanik women prepare boris and varieties of pickles. They also do a little bit of sewing and knitting after their noon-day meals. The exterior caste women do not generally know how to do such things.

Spinning has fallen into disuse and no longer the "ghhan ghanan ghanan" of the charka is heard in any of the houses of Kanchanpur.

Shopping is usually done by the children of the upper castes and the women of the lower castes.

When the afternoon comes, cleansing of the house is done a second time but not so thoroughly as was done in the morning. The dried up clothes are collected and kept in order on the alna for inmates of the house. The upper caste and the Subarnabanik bous and girls comb and tie their hair and go to the tanks for their evening washing of clothes and bodies. The low-caste women are not particular about this.

When the evening draws near, Kanchanpur's housewives light their oil lamps and sound their conchs. Then they go for preparation of the night meals for the family. When cooking is finished, it is for them to arrange the seats and plates and serve the courses of the dinner. When all others are fed, the housewives have their repast. It is already late at night and others have gone to bed. The house-wives get the doors of the house properly bolted or locked, and retire for the night as they will have to rise up early next morning which brings to them the usual round of duties.

Bringing water from the tank

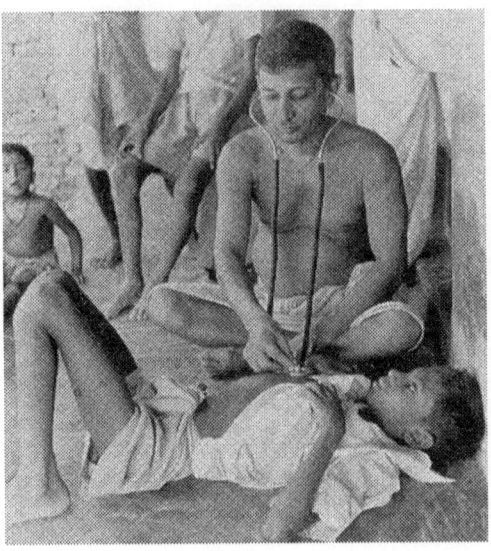

A visit to the doctor

The home of a middle-class Brahmin family

School time

CHAPTER 6

▼

EDUCATION

6.1—THE SCHOOL HOUSE OF KANCHANPUR

A modest, mud-walled hall partitioned into three class rooms under a general roof of corrugated sheets is the structure which houses the present free primary school of Kanchanpur. This school-house was built in 1935, and before that our village school had no separate building of its own.

In the times of the Rev. Day, the pathsala had been held in the open colonnade before the central Shivtala, and it continued to be so held when the village was first revisited by the present writer in 1933-34. The Rev. Day had also mentioned a second village pathsala under a Kayastha teacher who held his school in the yard at his house, in the shade of an umbrageous kantala tree (Jack tree), excepting in the rainy season, when he removed it to the verandah of his cottage. But the village pathsala, properly so called, had all along been held at the Shivtala—the multipurpose site of our village community. Besides, being the place of worship of the Old Shiva, and the seat of learning of the village children, it served as the venue of all community activities at Kanchanpur. The site had been requisitioned for Barwari and Panchayat sittings, for hearing complaints and proceedings of arbitrations, for fairs and festivals, for jatras and theaters, for kabis and tarjas, for thakas and chhabis, for meetings and receptions and what not. A separate school-house had been a "felt-need", and finally in 1935 Kanchanpur could boast of possessing one for its community.

The village elders selected for their school a site about a hundred yards to the west of the central-Shivtala, and the north of the Shiva's temple at goyla chatar (i.e., the milkmen's court). The hall faces to the east, with a running verandah in front and covers an area of about a thousand square feet. In front there is an unenclosed open space belonging to the school, in the north side of which is a small flower garden. A Laha family of Calcutta had kindly donated a tube well to the school. The school owns at present 0.27 acre of land, of which 0.21 acre was made over by the then zamindar of the village, and the rest 0.06 acre came from the local Hazra family.

The middle room of the hall is the biggest one, and accommodates the Class I students of the school. Next in size is the southern room where Classes II and III are jointly held. A fewer number of boys and girls go up to Class IV, which is run in the northern and the smallest room.

The teacher no longer sits on a mat, but has his chair, and the upper class pupils have their benches. The Class I boys and girls, however, have not yet been promoted to this honor. They still sit on the floor, or at best on gunny bags or woven palm leaves which served as seats for all our rural pupils even 25 years ago.

At present the school owns 4 chairs, 3 tables, 7 benches, 4 blackboards and one almirah. As there are three teachers, each of them may, therefore, use a chair and a table for himself. The fourth additional chair is presumably there for any visitor who may come to see the school. The school also has a table clock, which is daily removed to the headmaster's house after school hours for safe custody. The school had also a bell metal gong which struck the sound as period after period was over. Unfortunately the gong has very recently been stolen, and the school now loses its periodical resonant sounds which bring such a lively stir in the classes of any of our schools.

It need not be pointed out that any of the above furniture was unthought of in the old-fashioned orthodox village pathsala of the noineteenth century. In 1933-34, it had been noted that the only apparatus which the school possessed was its black-board which always hung on one of the columns of the verandah. But when the Rev. Day wrote, the blackboards were "as unknown in the path-salas as Babbages' Calculating Machine." Outwardly, therefore, the village school has changed, but has the content of school life changed?

6.2—THE SCHOOL LIFE OF KANCHANPUR

The Rev. Dais pathsala had four classes: (i) the floor class, (ii) the palm-leaf class, (iii) the plantain-leaf class, and lastly (iv) the paper-class. In the lowest class the beginner used to trace the Bengali alphabet on the ground with a chalk. After a few months the pupil exchanged the ground for the palmyra leaves, and chalk for some years on the mud floor, as palmyra leaves were ill adopted for such purpose. Higher than the palm-leaf stage was the plantain-leaf class. Palm leaves and plantain leaves cost nothing in the village, and working on them, when the pupil became somewhat adept in calligraphy, arithmetic and some correspondence, he baandoned the leaves for the costly paper. With practice on paper, his education at the pathsala came to a successful end.

In 1933-34, the village pathsala was an Upper Primary school with three forms. But the palm and plantain leaves of the old days had been replaced by the more "modern" slate and pencil.

The school was raised to the U.P. standard in 1935, and it became a free institution in 1948. At present the school is divided into four classes Class I, II, III and IV. A student is supposed to read in each of the classes for one year, but formerly there was no such annual session of classes. The pathsala was held twice a day first from early in the morning till about 11 o'clock, and again from three o'clock in the afternoon till candle light. At present the village school is held in the day time from 10:30 a.m. to 4:00 p.m. with a short recess at midday for lunch.

In the old fashioned village pathsala, the subjects to which greatest attention was paid were calligraphy, arithmetic and Bengali letter writing. In the present day curriculum, both calligraphy and letter writing are neglected, while the subject of arithmetic is not so diligently pursued as it was in the village pathsala. In those days the pupils of the pathsala seldom read a book, but at the end of their school career, they came out with an education quite useful to their practical life. They could write decently, calculate accurately and correspond properly. But now-a-days, a pupil leaves school usually with an awfully bad handwriting, which makes it difficult for others to follow his scribblings; he is weaker in arithmetic, and is practically incapable of making any epistolary address in the proper form. The system of the village pathsala aimed at the practical and the needful and was quite sensible. The subjects it taught were few; in fact these were only arithmetic and letter-writing, but the pupils were made to learn the two subjects assiduously, and knowledge about them proved quite useful in their future lives.

The school student has now-a-days to read so many books, and learn so many subjects. One really wonders at the attempt on the part of our planners, to fill so much knowledge in the little heads. The elders of the village are of opinion that their students' standard has gone down, and the performance of the pupils of the orthodox pathsala was much better. Besides arithmetic and mother language, the students of our village school are now required under the syllabus of the Education Directorate to learn history, geography, primary science, hygiene, social science, and various miscellaneous things, such as crafts, gardening, drill and sports, national song, religious stotras, practical social work, and what not. The curriculum is no doubt imposing, and if mere curriculum could make men, the finished products of the present village Free Primary School would turn out to be perfect citizens of the country. But both the village teachers and the guardians are apprehensive of the result of shoving too much knowledge in the little heads of children who usually belong to the age group of six to eleven years.

Further, the village guardians have their grievances against the teachers also. According to the present system of primary education, the teachers are paid by the District School Board out of funds raised by the State through taxation. It is said to be free primary education, as the village guardians are not required to pay any fee for their wards. The monthly salaries of the primary teachers are remitted to the village post office by the School Board, but there is practically no departmental supervision or inspection over the running of the school. True, there is an advisory committee from the village public, but it has no control over the affairs of the school, and its members complain that the teachers have slackened their efforts, as they are financially independent of the village public. Is it any wonder, they say, that the standard of village education has gone down?

Another remarkable feature in the modern primary education is the virtual abolition of the age-old system of disciplinary correction. Whether sparing of the rod is spoiling the child, or causing the standard to fall is a matter for our educationalists to decide; but the old faith in the rod has vanished. The village school-master of the Rev. Day was a strict disciplinarian. He constantly had by him a thin but longish twig of bamboo which often resounded, not only on the palms of his pupils' hands, but on their heads and backs. Sometimes too with cruel ingenuity he would strike their knuckles, their knee joints and their ankles.

He had also other ways of administering discipline. One famous mode of juvenile punishment was called Naru-Gopal, and another such was the application of the stinging bichhuti leaves to the skin. These disciplinary processes, however, were time-honoured institutions which had been handed down from generation to generation of Bengali village school masters. In *Kanchanpur Revisited* (1933-34), the present writer had remarked:

> Spare the rod and spoil the child, is still the principle by which a village pathsala is run; and all the ingenious methods of punishment are strictly followed. Oh yes, one change and that perhaps in deference to modern notions. The punishment of Naru Gopal (stooping in the posture of Shrikrishna with sweets in his hands, as shown in Hindu religious scriptures) has been supplanted by the "chair system" i.e., keeping the body in the shape of an armchair—quite an original invention. To develop the best in the child, says the modern educationist, the child should be given liberty and approached with reverence.
>
> The village gurumashai, rich with the experiences of fourteen generations, would surely be staggered by such an idea.

But with the disappearance of the old-fashioned orthodox pathsalas, the village gurumashai has also left the scene. The state-wide system of primary education has been introduced, and trained teachers are now being appointed in the upper Primary Schools. The principles of the modern educationalists are being honored by the new teachers, and though the juvenile penal code could not possibly be altogether abolished, the present teachers are no longer its advocates.

With the teachers relaxing and the rod vanishing, the school is no longer a dreadful place for our village children. They are coming to love it. If you happen to come over to their classes to see what the teachers and the pupils are engaged in doing—and as you are not a school inspector but a friendly visitor—you are sure to enjoy the lively atmosphere that prevails there. There is great jubilation in the whole school, classes are stopped, and all the three teachers come forward to welcome you. The senior boys run to find out the extra chair and place it for you. After ordinary greetings, you request the teachers to go on with their classes as usual, and yourself intend to accompany one of the teachers to his classroom. The students of other classes at once catch hold of you and try to drag you to their room. Assuring them that you would come to them by turn, you just enter one of the class rooms. The little boys and girls surround you and pull you towards the chair. They simply ask the class teacher—be he their headmaster, the second master or the young master—to take his leave for the period, and request you to take their lessons for the day. Or it may be that you are asked to act as their polling officer for the day as the date has been fixed for election of the health minister of the school. Instead of teaching them, you may want to learn what sort of health activities the minister will remain in charge of. You are told that the health minister is responsible for seeing that his schoolmates are following healthy habits and giving up the bad ones. It is his duty to see that the school house and the individual rooms are cleansed, and the school children are using washed clothing, and maintaining clean teeth, nails, hair etc. Thus instead of giving them any lessons, you try to learn from the pupils what they learn and do in their school. Particularly you are attracted to the social service program. On being asked what sorts of service they render to their village community, several boys and girls bring a few exercise books to you. You take up one such and read what is written on the coverage.

Shri Paresh Kumar Daw,
Village—Shona Palashi,
Class—IV,
Upakar Khata (Social Service Book),
1365 B.S.

Inside, you may be pleased to note such entries as

1365 B.S. 28th Tuesday, Month of Pous
I have lifted a load of straw off the head of Biswanath Daw.
I have driven off the cow of the Jhunus from eating paddy,
29th Pous, Wednesday, 1365 B. S.
The goats of the Kesavs had been eating paddy, and I drove them out.
1st Magh—The cow of the Khukus was running away, and I got her tied.
2nd Magh—I have bought Kerosene oil for the Bishis.

So ran the daily list of benefits rendered by our schoolboy servant of village society.

6.3—WHO GOES TO SCHOOL

The school is meant for all the children of the village community, usually belonging to the age group of six to eleven, irrespective of any caste or creed. The boy and girls of Barabagan, a hamlet close to our village in the West also attend this (Sona Palashi) F.P. School. Exclusively inhabited by a few Kotal households, the Barabagan is not an integral part of the village. Nevertheless, it depends on Kanchanpur for various social services, as in this matter of initiating their young in to the mysteries of lekhapara.

In the time of the Rev. Day, at the Shivtala pathsala sons of Brahmins, Kayasthas and wealthy bankers received instructions from a Brahmin gurumashai. The Kayastha pedagogue, having a far inferior social position to that of the Brahmin, obtained only a third part of the pupils of the other. Any day one might have seen in the school of the Brahmin gurumashai between sixty and seventy boys, whereas in the other school one seldom saw more than twenty students chiefly coming from the lower castes and poorer classes of the village.

The situation in 1933-34 is pictured in *Kanchanpur Revisited*. The then register of the Shivtala pathsala showed the number of students to be 48, of which ten were girls. There was no restriction as to the caste, but practically no pupil came from any of the depressed classes. At that time there was also a rival school, but three fourths of the village pupils took lessons at the Shivtala pathsala.

In the Kanchanpur of New India, primary education is said to be both free and compulsory, and yet only 40% of the boys and 35% of the girls of 6 to 11 years age-group are found to attend the school. The corresponding figures for the exterior castes are only 5% and 4% for their boys and girls respectively and indicate the slowness of progress in this respect. The Kaibartas and Chunaris of the jal-achal group, and the Hari, Bauri Muchi, Kora, Santal and the Muslim of the exterior group, are seen to have a fair number of children amongst them, but none are sent to the village school. Of 21 Bagdi boys and girls in our community, only one boy and one girl actually go to school.

There were in January 1959, 173 children of the age-group of 6 to 11 years. Of them only 98 were found to be enrolled in the school register, and amongst them only 74 were found to be actually attending the school. Of these 74 again, all were not regular. What if education is free, what even if education is compulsory, most of the girls of Kanchanpur, and the boys of its labouring classes, cannot be conveniently allowed to waste their time in the school by their parents and guardians. For them life brings another education quite different from that which is given in the schools; the girls are drawn to assist their mother and grandmother in the work of housewifery, and the boys take charge of cows and bullocks and begin their apprenticeship in the world of labour.

An inspection of the school register showed that 98 students had been enrolled, but a house to house enquiry brought out the fact that only 74 students were actually sent to school by the householders. That is to say there were found to be 24 children in the village, whose names were in the school rolls, but who did not at all join the school. As a matter of fact, they were caused to be enrolled, but not meant to be schooled. This is what leads to extension of our primary education on paper. As grants of the School Board for teachers depend on the roll-strength of the school and as some extension of education for the village— now within a compulsory area—is to be shown by our teachers to the higher authorities, the tendency is to send forth inflated statistics. One wonders how much is paper extension in the work of our various newly growing welfare agencies.

Now let us look to the distribution of the pupils in the four different classes as given in the school register.

Number of Students

Class I	48
Class II	28
Class III	21
Class 1V	11

Forty-eight students are seen in the first year of the school, and in Class IV there are only eleven. The roll strength falls year after year, and only a small percentage of the admitted students passes out of the final class. For the majority of them the school career is brought to a close much earlier. This year out of eleven students in Class IV only eight sat in the U.P. Examination held in March 1959, and neither of the two girls was amongst them. Of the eight examinees, seven passed out successfully, a performance of which the village teachers felt proud.

6.4—Education Abroad Kanchanpur

It is desirable here to make a little enquiry in respect of the students who go outside the village for education. There are 10 boys and 3 girls of the village who are being brought up in other places. Two of these girls are reading in the primary classes, while the third, a Brahmin, is studying in a secondary school at Burdwan, and is the only girl of the village who is pursuing her studies higher than the U.P. As a matter of fact the father of the girl, a qualified doctor, although claiming to belong to the joint family consisting of his father and brother in Kanchanpur, is himself settled at Burdwan. The education of his daughter, therefore, is to be taken as an exception from the village standard. (Since our inquiry and writing of these lines the girl was placed in marriage and discontinued her studies.).

To the Kaligram Junior High School, and the Kurman High School, Kanchanpur sends 9 and 13 boys respectively. All these students, excepting one Subarnabanik boy, take their big meals before 10 am. and plod their way to the neighbouring villages of Kaligram or Kurman as the case may be and return home after school hours. The Subarnabanik scholar, however, is a resident of the hostel attached to the Kaligram Junior High School. It is not the distance of the school from his house, which is hardly a couple of miles, but the distance between himself and his step-mother at home that has led to his sojourn in the school hostel.

Two of the young men of Kanchanpur are undergoing regular college education in Calcutta. One of them is a Brahmin boy and the other is a Subarnabanik. I also understand that another young man of the Vaidya caste, an employee in a Calcutta firm, has also begun to take his lessons in the evening classes in a college of the City.

6.5—THE TRAINING OF A GIRL

As no girl of Kanchanpur goes for higher education, and as most of its girls are not even allowed to go up to the U.P., it behooves us to inquire a little and see what sort of training Kanchanpur imparts to its girls.

> There is the beating of a broomstick waiting for you in the in-laws' house

is the oft-used reprimand of the village mother for her growing daughter. The most important thing in the life of a girl at Kanchanpur is to be skilled in housework so that she can render good account of herself when she goes to her in-laws' house after marriage.

Our inquiry has shown that out of 82 girl-children of 6-11 age group in the village, 37 were enrolled in the U.P. School although only 31 actually attended classes. The above 37 girls were distributed in the four classes as follows:

Class I	17
Class II	13
Class III	5
Class IV	2

When the U.P. examination was held, the two girls dropped out. In the value systems of Kanchanpur's culture, the passing of the school-examinations for a girl is not of any material importance. Of greater consequence to her is the passing of the bride selection test. Thereafter she has to take housewifery, and she is disciplined under her mother and other female guardians accordingly. If her housekeeping, her etiquette and behavior in the in-laws' place are not up to the standard, then it is her mother and those relatives who are to be blamed, and the girl herself would have to face a life of trial with her in-laws.

Before the days of childhood are over, the girl of Kanchanpur learns to assist her mother and grandmother in fifty little things in the house.

An increasing volume of work allotted to her seldom allows her to finish her four-year scholastic career in the village school. She looks after the new babies that are born in the household, goes on errands bringing from the village shops oil, salt, spices, etc. and gradually grows to a whole-time helper adept in all kinds of housework. Thus she becomes the assistant manager of her father's household, till she is taken away as a bou by another.

When in school in the early days of girlhood, she is taught along with others the Bengali alphabet, and thereafter something of the three R's., Reading, Writing and Arithmetic. But she is not supposed to keep any regular attendance, and off and on her mother asks her not to go to her classes for the day. Her services are then requisitioned for those days in the household. Any preferential interest shown by the girl for her school is sure to bring on her some gibe like this: "Do you think that you will get the honor of judgeship in future and will not have to take up housewifery in the in-law's house?"

Simultaneously with this practical training in household work the daughter is taught submission and endurance as she has to fit herself wherever her lot places her in life. She also learns to know from the beginning of her career that the males are the lords of creation and the lesson is brought home to her by the differential treatment in the family between herself and her brothers. Ah! The boy brings wealth, but the girl deserves the hanging rope.

In her training course, a girl of Kanchanpur has to perform a set of bratas in each annual cycle. A brata means a solemn vow. In practice, it is a sort of religious discipline in worship of one or the other god, observed in expectation of some material rewards or religious merits to follow. As a matter of fact Kanchanpur's women observe a lot of bratas, but there are some special ones for the unmarried girls of the village.

The bratas exert an influence in the molding of the girl-child's mind. When the god is worshiped, the brata verses are recited which describe the kinds of things which the praying girl has to desire in her life. The community faiths and values according to which our girl has to live are expressed in those verses, which you may hear repeated by the little girls in many a yard of Kanchanpur's houses in different times and seasons. Thus in the early mornings in the month of Baishakh, the village virgins may be seen engaged in the familiar Shiva puja, taken as a brata to be performed for the whole of the month. Simultaneously some other girls might be seen to observe the "vow" of punni-pikur, i.e. the Sacred Tank. In the yard a small tank measuring about one square foot has been dug, and it has also been fitted with four ghats (flights of steps) on four sides. The tank is filled with water, and inside the center is planted a twig of either the sacred tulsi (sanctum) or the bad (Aegle marmelos). After the sacred tulsi or the bael is worshiped with due rites, you may hear the praying girl repeat such brata verses as:

> In the Sacred Tank, with garlands of flowers who worships Thee at this morning hour?
> I am the girl Lilavati—the fortunate sister of seven brothers.
> What do I get in worshiping Thee?
> I shall get the treasure of a Yaksha
> I shall become pure as Savitri, and be beloved of my husband. I shall get ever living immortal sons, and the Yama (God of death) shall never send his sufferings to me. Leaving my sons here on earth, I shall end my life where the Ganges flows with my head on the breast of my husband.

Or you may see another group of girls engaged in the worship of Harircharan (i.e., The Lord's feet), and you hear their prayers recited:

"Lord's feet! 0, Lord's feet!
Who is the girl that worships Thee?
And what does she pray for?"

"She wants for herself a beauteous husband, a son as the light of the court, and a son-in-law as an ornament to any society. She likes to get for her a daughter of good qualities, and a daughter-in-law skilled in housewifery. Bright be the clothings in her alna; and the utensils in her room give shine. Her cowshed will be full of corns, and her granaries will remain stocked with paddy. She will ever have the vermilion on her head, and the betel leaf in her mouth. She will not see the death of her husband, sons or friends. She will die in the waters of the Ganges, and in the end she will get to Thy feet, O Lord."

Or, in the twilight in the early winter in the month of Agrahayan, you may watch some little girls engaged in the brata of sanjh puja (evening worship), otherwise called senjuti. Lamps are lit and worship is done. Then prayers go forth and gifts are asked: "Let families of my mother and father grow in wealth and lineage. O Hara, O Sankara, O Bholanath, do not place me in the hands of a fool."

In a village home the bovines are considered to form no less a part of the household as the humans. The growing girl is also trained to love and respect the inmates of the cowshed. For her there are a few bratas for cow-worship as well. Thus in the brata of gokal (cow-serving period), in Baishakh you may see a little girl paint the hooves, horn, and the forehead of a cow with vermilion and worship her with reverence. You may also hear the brata verses repeated: "This period of my cow-serving is my period in gokul (heaven). As I feed the cow with grass, so my place is assured in Baikuntha (The heavenly abode of Vishnu)." Or in the winter evening you may hear some girls pray with offerings of cow dung and husk and repeat their brata verses: "With these flowers of cow dung, we pay our homage to our three ancestral lines."

To build up a happy home in abundance, with her husband and sons, relatives and friends, "with cows in the shed and paddy in the granary", is all that the village girl prays for and her desires and values are still cherished in the traditional culture of Kanchanpur.

CHAPTER 7

▼

COMMUNITY ACTIVITIES

7.1—THE NEW PANCHAYAT

The governmental pattern of rural democracy in West Bengal has been set up by the West Bengal Panchayat Act, 1956. On the base are the Gram-Sabhas who elect the Gram-Panchayats. These Gram-Panchayats send their representative to the Anchal, but a member of the Anchal Panchayat cannot at the same time function as a member of the Gram-Panchayat.

An anchal means in English a region, and several such regions go to the formation of a "Block". The Development Officer at the Block, working under the Community Projects Administrator, guides the activities of the Gram and Anchal Panchayats.

Kanchanpur and its neighbouring village Debagram together form a Gram-Sabha, for which there is one Gram-Panchayat. This is one of the six constituent Gram-Panchayats which go to the organization of the Kurman Anchal Panchayat. Besides Kanchanpur, the five other Gram-Panchayats are Kurman, Belgona (with Malkita), Sadya (with Sinhapara), Choto-Belun, and Burar (Ramchandrapur). Sri Khudiram Rai, a resident of Kurman, is the Pradhan (i.e., President) of our Anchal. The Gram-Panchayat of Kanchanpur and Debagram has returned four members to the Anchal Panchayat. Of these four sabhyas (members), three are Brahmins and natives of Kanchanpur, the fourth is an inhabitant of Debagram and is an Ugra-Kshatriyas by caste.

At present there are thirteen members of the Gram-Panchayat, and all of them are appointed by the B.D.O. (i.e., the Block Development Officer). In 1956, it was decided by the State Government to organize the village Panchayats on an experimental basis. Accordingly, on an appointed day, a general meeting of the Gram-Sabha was called for election of members of the Panchayat. This Gram-Sabha consisted of all the persons of these two villages enlisted as voters in the state. They organized themselves into two parties, and wanted to contend for the seats in the Gram-Panchayat. But ultimately through the mediation of the polling officer, who came down from the Block, it was decided to avoid the contest and with it all those divisions and tensions and counting of hands. The compromise between the parties was to empower five elders in the village in whom all expressed confidence, and to them was entrusted the task of selecting, from amongst the candidates, a representative body of workers to sit on the Gram-Panchayat. Thus a coalition Panchayat was set up in our villages with 10 members from Kanchanpur and 5 from Debagram. Their caste-wise distribution was as follows:

Brahmin	7	Ugra Kshatriya	4
Vaidya	1	Sadgop	1
Kayastha	1	Bagdi	1

All the 4 Ugra-Kshatriyas in the holy companionship of a Brahmin came from Debagram. The rest of the members belonged to Kanchanpur. Later on it was found that names of two amongst the selected had not been included in the voters' list, and thereon those persons, one a Kanchanpur Brahmin and the other Bagdi were unseated. The remaining members of the Panchayat Board, unaware of the "thirteen" superstition, are still functioning as the village fathers, and in 1958, instead of holding a fresh election the B.D.Q. of the area got them reappointed. The present Panchayat has a Kayastha young man as its Adhyaksha (President), and an elderly Brahmin as the Upadhyaksha (Vice-President), and both of them belong to Kanchanpur.

In the community development program of India, it is the intention of the Government to execute all works and schemes with the help of and through the medium of the Gram-Panchayat. They have already been invested with certain powers and duties which are defined in the said West Bengal Panchayat Act The Panchayat also receives minor complaints and tries to settle them amicably within the village. A few specimen of cases dealt with by the Panchayat may be of interest to the readers and are therefore, translated below from the Bengali records of the Panchayat:

Case No. 1

To The respected Adhyaksha,
Shona Palashi Gram Panchayat

Sir,
As the culvert at the back of Sri Indra Mandal's house has subsided, the waters of the south side village which formerly used to pass through it, find no outlet at present As a result, my tank has overflown, and I have suffered loss to the extent of rupees three hundred. At the same time there is an apprehension that my house will collapse. Under these circumstances, it is humbly prayed that you and your Committee be pleased to make a spot enquiry, and thereafter kindly arrange for the outlet of the waters. Please save me from this danger, or I shall become houseless.

With these humble submissions,
Yours
A. Laha

Dated, Shona Palashi,?t1-7-1958.

The matter was duly enquired into by the Adhyaksha and the members. It was decided that Sri N.G., a member of that locality, be entrusted with the work of repair of the culvert, and an amount of Rs. 4/-was sanctioned from the village Road Development Fund.

Case No. 5

To The Adhyaksha,
Shona Palashi Gram Panchayat

Sir,
We, the inhabitants of Debagram, humbly state as follows: That on plot no. 931 of the mouza Debagram we have been playing football and other games for the last 35 years. It is true that the field is also a pasture ground. But the cows graze there up to 3 p.m. and thereafter we play football there. It is on this ground that we were engaged in various competitive and tournament games with different football teams of different villages. Now Sri D. K., son of late U.K., Sri KS., son of late AS., Sri D.S., son of late S.S., M/s. D.S. and M.S.,

sons of late S.S., all of village Debagram. have combined together, and have declared that no football play could be allowed on that ground. Under these circumstances, there is a sure apprehension of breach of peace. We, therefore, request you to enquire whether we have been all along playing games there and also to make sufficient arrangements that no breach of peace occurs. With these submissions on this date of 28th Aswin, 1365, B.S. (Eng.15-10-58).

On behalf of the residents of Debagram, K.R., S.G., S.M., AD. and sons.

The matter was enquired into and a compromise was effected between the parties so that there would not be any opposition to the playing of games.

The following is a copy of a notice issued by the Adhyaksha, Gram-Panchayat and it speaks for itself.

Notice to the members of the Shona Palashi Gram-Panchayat, and to the resident members of the Anchal Panchayat

Sirs,
We were elected by the public for advancing peace and development of our community, and all of us are responsible for any good or harm that may befall our village. It was usually seen that some troubles and breaches of peace happen every year on the last day of the festival of Badhai and such occurrences endanger our community sense and safety. My earnest request to you, therefore, is that you should realize your responsibilities and duties and remain present at the festival till the end on the last date the 3rd Aswin, Saturday, being the 20th of September 1958 of the English year. It lies on you to see that the function is performed in a disciplined manner, and that no such incidents occur as may create cleavage or embitter human relations in our village. This is my humble request Yours J. B. Adhyaksha 19-9-58

The members of the Gram-Panchayat and the Anchal abhyas' made their presence felt, and the Badhai festival was peacefully performed. The concerned circles are of opinion that never in the last forty years was the Badhai so peacefully observed.

7.2—THE OLD "BARWARI"

The Barwari is the indigenous institution for the welfare of our village community. But at Kanchanpur there are two locality groups and for each such group there is a separate Barwari.

The Barwari as an organization for the common good is not a creature of any statute. The village community, living in comparative isolation, had to organize itself for some common purposes, and the Barwari grew up accordingly. It had no defined rights and obligations. The organization took up powers and duties as the village needed it. On occasions when any question sprang up which affected the common weal, the villagers were called to an assembly for discussion and decision. Such an assembly is known in Bengal as the Barwari which comes from the term Bar-O-Pakari (i.e., the institution which works for the common weal). Usually the trusted leaders of the village guide the destinies of such assemblies. For working convenience, a cabinet of the Barwari also grew up, consisting of leaders who were trusted.

The basis of the Barwari has all along been voluntary cooperation and not any law of the State. For past decades, the persuasion of State powers in our villages and the growing consciousness of legal right of the individuals are weakening the organization of the Barwari. The Union Boards had come into existence, and now the Panchayats have been ushered in and these bodies had and have official origin and support The Union Board, however, did not affect the functioning of the Barwari in its local field. The Union Board represented a group of villages, and for any particular village its working was rather formal and distant. But the Barwari functioned in an intimate face-to-face relationship, and it continued to live.

Now that the Gram-Panchayats have been brought into existence, there is at present a sort of diarchy in the village affairs. The Panchayat is set up in a legal framework, while the Bawari lives on traditions. Again the jurisdiction of our Panchayat is much wider. It represents the two sister villages of Kanchanpur and Debagram. But the Barwari represents a smaller locality group, and Kanchanpur itself has two such—one for the north side and the other for the south side. The Bawaris are dominated by the traditional leaders, who, with the approval of the general Barwari, function as the high-powered committee of the public.

Various affairs affecting community life such as organization of festivals and ceremonies on community basis, dealing out of village justice, discussion and decision on any common problem—all these come up to the Barwari for consideration. It is inevitable that some of the powers and duties of the Barwaris would be gradually taken over by the Panchayat. But the Barwaris are still now functioning bodies, and some recent instances are related below to illustrate their present position in the village.

P.B. is a Bauri of some means but unfortunately he came in conflict with an influential Brahmin of the Dakshinpara. The Brahmin took up the matter in the Barwari Committee. This caste-ridden body sent for the Bauri accused who could not refuse to come. After a hearing, a fine was imposed on the latter and, worst of all, he was dishonored as he was forced to rub his nose on the ground before the assembly.

P.B., infuriated with the insult, went to Burdwan, and on advice of a lawyer filed a criminal complaint against some leaders of the Dakshinpara Barwari. The O.C. (Officer-in-charge) of the Burdwan P.S. (Police station) came on enquiry, and there was a great commotion in the village, as seldom in the history of the Barwari had any one from the depressed castes ventured to bring such a case against the members of the upper castes. P.B. was, of course, too weak to sustain the prosecution for any length of time, and the opposite party also did not like to be dragged into the courts. As the heat of the moment subsided, the matter was soon compromised, but in the meantime the hands of the police had to be sufficiently oiled by both the parties.

Here is told another incident brought before the Barwari of the North side. It had been announced by beat of drums that picking of jhoro (falling) paddy was prohibited this season, and anybody found guilty would be punished by the Barwari. Now jhoro is a kind of spurious paddy that falls to the ground before the ears are ripe. The jhoro seeds remain in the cracks of the earth, and their plants again shoot up next year and get mixed with the good varieties of paddy in the fields. If the jhoro is picked up before it falls down, the farmers are profited thereby. The poor people were used to collect jhoro before the harvest, and this practice grew up as an accepted custom in the village. But for several years, in the process and pretext of collecting jhoro, good paddy was being stolen, and the sympathy of the cultivators was alienated from the pickers. The matter was therefore discussed in the Barwari, and the services of the village drummer were requisitioned to proclaim that the picking of jhoro would be penalized thenceforth.

But the poor, accustomed to collect jhoro for years, did not, or could not, pay any heed to the declaration made through the drummer. As the harvest was approaching, they went on to gather the jhoro as before. A few Santal girls were caught in the act, and the executive committee of the north Barwari took disciplinary measures against them. The culprits were given mild beatings and their baskets containing jhoro were confiscated. They were further asked to pay a fine.

The above action of the Barwari caused great indignation amongst the Santals, and a group of them left the village with the chastised girls. At Burdwan they were advised by a friend to lodge an application to the Tribal Welfare Officer. The said Officer came to the village to make an enquiry and dealt some reprimand to the overbearing leaders. They were asked to settle the matter with the aggrieved Santals. Otherwise official wrath would fall on them. Needless to say, the visit and rebukes of the Welfare Officer had a sobering effect on the Barwari executive.

Here I relate another problem brought before the Barwari in a new context. It also illustrates the varied nature of questions that a Barwari executive may be called upon to answer. This time when I spent a few weeks in the village and had made as many friends as I could and had grown confident of my position in the village, I launched my schedules and questionnaires to my village world. But, never in the long history of Kanchanpur had such an inquiry been seen or heard of. Instantly the instinct of self-protection, especially of the village "haves" was aroused. Surely, the investigation would bring them to ruin, but what could be done as the enemy was being assisted in his inquiry by some of the young leaders of their own village? In such circumstances, the investigator could neither be deceived nor denied, and so the executive committees of the village Barwari sat to discuss the situation and chalk out a course of common policy in the matter.

What could be the real purpose of this inquiry? That question was vehemently discussed. As the investigator was presumably a man of the Government he should not be trusted. His assessment of their conditions was bound to lead to fresh taxation. The friendly leaders explained that the investigator was not a man of the Government; his only purpose was to make a sociological study of their village, made famous by their own Rev. Lal Behari Day, and the new study would not cause any harm, but might bring some good to them. Thus debates for and against the investigation went on, and finally the Committee expressed its view that information should not be withheld to the investigator, but the interviewees were cautioned to make very guarded statements so that those might not be used to their disadvantage in future. It may be added here that we also, on our part, revised the schedules and questionnaires and made them as innocuous as possible.

7.3—THE INTERESTS OF THE EXTERIOR CASTES

"We must work on as we have to live, and the bhadraloks (the gentlemen folk) do not tell us anything", H.P., (a Kora labourer), remarked to me, when enquiries were made of him with regard to the activities of the Panchayat in the village. K.P., a Bauri householder, said that he had no idea what was happening with it. When some Panchayat work was pointed out to be in his ken, his first attitude of ignorance was changed to apathy and then to negative criticism. Yes, he had known the existence of the Panchayat and was under the impression that it was doing something. He also knew that it had a member, a Tentule Bagdi on the Board, to represent their caste group. (This man however, was disqualified to function as a member of the Panchayat as his name was not included in the voters' list). But still K.P. was sure that the institution of the Panchayat was not for their welfare; it was meant for the Babus of the upper castes. The idea of the Panchayat, its aims and objects were not clear to him at all. But his strong feeling was that it was not meant for them.

Reference was made to the night school in the village, which had been organized as a Social Education Center with some help from the Block. K.P. felt that the night school was being neglected—it remained practically closed. Yes, he had joined the school and there had been many students like him, but the school did not continue. But I found K.P. quite conscious of the prestige which education meant, and I heard him say in answer to a woman of the family—"I know it, Oh woman! I read it in the school."

H.P. on the other hand felt that the school was of no use to them. As for himself, he said: "Three loads of wood had already been sent (to the crematory where a Hindu is burned), and only the fourth load remains. What is the good of getting any outside information to persons like us who must work on as we have to live." Indeed, the exterior castes, furnishing the backbone of agricultural labour in our village community are still victims of an agrestic and social serfdom. In spite of the constitutional rights and other benign new laws, in spite of the State given educational facilities and benefits of representative institutions, in spite of various attempts on the part of the Government and private welfare agencies, there is but negligible change in their position, especially in villages such as Kanchanpur.

7.4—A THREE DAYS TRAINING CAMP

For improvement of agriculture and for making the community development programs effective, a three days camp for training the village leaders was organized at Kaligram. Sri D.S., of the said village Kaligram, had been shown to be the convener, but Sri B.M., the Village Level Worker of the Anchal, appeared to be very busy. He explained to me that it was really the Block that was organizing the camp, but it was their method to do things in the names of the people.

It is said that the fundamental principle of the community development work is that it should not be the Government's program but the "people's program". Unfortunately it is not yet a "people's program", and our Development Officers are merely trying to make it look like a people's program.

They made arrangements for fifty trainees, but on the appointed day hardly twenty turned up as there was a general apathy. The B.D.O. himself had requested the Adhyaksha of our village to join the camp, but he could not possibly manage to attend. He, however, tried to send others. R.D. a younger man, was asked to join. He said that on enquiry he had found out that the matter was but a farce. It was only the Block peoples' stunt so that they could get their lifts and increment. Even if they took those three days' trouble, there would be no certificate for them for this training. But B.M., the Village Level Worker, repeatedly assured that the trainees could surely be granted certificates and those would be seen then to bear signatures of quite distinguished persons of the Rajbhavan.

On the evening previous to the training days, Charan Das, the village Muchi, came out in the streets of Kanchanpur and proclaimed by beat of his drum that there would be a meeting of the agriculturists at Kaligram hattola from next day. Free show of "talkies" would be arranged. "Come and see, come and see".

R.D. and another young man joined the camp from Kanchanpur. But after a few hours R.D. was seen to be on the way back to the village. He had been sent on deputation to recruit further trainees. As highly placed officers would visit the camp during these three days, the organizers were trying their best to "keep their face" to the honorable visitors.

R.D. returned to the camp with three more trainees from Kanchanpur and Debagram. And lo! forty-eight hours later all of them came back with the treasured certificates in their hands.

7.5—THE SUNRIPARA GETS A TUBE WELL

The V.L.W. brought the news to our Adhyaksha that the Block was going to make several grants for sinking of tube wells in the Anchal. This village too might get one, and the V.L.W. was also trying for it.

Our Adkyaksha was thinking of the Sunris of the village. Year after year, they had been suffering from lack of good drinking water. They lived in the eastern wing of the village in a separate para quite apart from the central cluster of houses of the village. It was not convenient for their women to come to such distance for taking drinking water from tube wells situated in the middle of the village. Tank water was liable to be polluted and poisoned, and its use was often followed by breaking out of epidemic diseases. A tube well at the Sunripara was therefore, a "felt need".

Next morning, as our Adhyaksha was going to the Sunripara, I came out to accompany him. The purpose of his visit had already been communicated to the few householders of the locality on the previous day. It was harvest season, and most of them were threshing paddy in their own barnyards. A couple of householders were away to their fields on some work.

We arrived and went to the house of A.S., an elderly cultivator and the leader amongst the Sunris of the village. Common greetings were exchanged, and in the meantime a rough blanket was brought from inside and spread on the earthen floor of the verandah, when we were requested to sit.

All the Sunri householders were called to the place. They gathered there excepting one who could not come. Then an informal meeting was held and discussions were started. The Adhyaksha explained that if any of them gave a few square feet of land to the public for installation of the tube well and they together raised subscription amongst themselves towards 50% of the costs, the other 50% would come as a grant from the Block. They should combine to make this little joint effort, and take the opportunity now given to them by the Block; if they failed to do so, the opportunity would slip away, and it would be even more difficult for them to install a tube well in their ward, the need of which had all along been so keenly felt

All the householders present agreed at once that they should take the opportunity and bring the tube well in their ward. But details could not be so easily agreed to. Whose land should be taken? What should be the exact site of the tube well that might bring the greatest possible convenience to the householders? How much subscription would each pay? Over all these points there arose differences, and hours passed on. As it was getting late we expressed our intention to get up. The elderly leader and his friends assured the Adhyaksha that they would settle these little differences between themselves and requested him to proceed in the matter with diligence. The Adhyaksha took his pen and brought out a piece of paper from his pocket He then wrote out an application, on behalf of the inhabitants of Sunripara, and addressed it to the B.D.O. of the area. He handed over the application to the elderly leader and told him to get the signatures or thumb impressions of all the householders, and as many adults as possible. He addressed the assembly and told them to settle the matter after mutual discussion, and he expressed the hope that he would get back the signed application in a day or two. Thereafter both of us returned.

The Sunripara of Kanchanpur got its tube well after a couple of months.

7.6—Public Demands and Private Loans

When the threshing of the paddy crop is over, then it is time for our village creditors to make a drive for realization of their dues. The debtors, on the other hand, sell away their share of produce to clear those dues. The indebted agricultural labourers, however, usually pay back in kind, as they are used to take advances of paddy from their employers earlier in the year.

N.B., the Tax collector of the Anchal, comes with his register and the receipt book, and he requisitions the services of both the Chowkidars of the village to assist him in the collection. He takes his seat in some central part of the village and sends the Chowkidar to the defaulters in that locality for bringing money for payment of their dues both current and arrears. But the response is poor as usual and N.B. moves from one part of the village to another with both the Chowkidars accompanying him.

After the collection of this particular day is over, N.B. returns, crying that he does not come in the village for begging. He will come next on such and such a date, and if anybody still remains a defaulter, he will cause the distress warrant to be issued and take away the front door of his house for sale. Thus week after week the collection of the taxes goes on, and on each occasion, the above threat is held out, but no action is ever taken.

This is also the time when the village post office frequently brings the demand notices to the villagers to pay their outstanding canal rates to the Government. Occasionally a court peon comes with a notice of certificate for proclaiming attachment for sale on a piece of land of some defaulting owner who had not yet paid his rents or rates due to the Government. The debtors then hurry up, sell some portions of their paddy stock, and run to Burdwan to make the necessary tadbirs (arrangements) and payments.

The Block loans and also the Cooperative loan are to be paid back. On appointed dates, a departmental man comes from the Block to the Anchal headquarters at Kurman and the debtors go there to pay up their outstanding loans, so that when need arises, fresh loans may be obtained next year for agricultural purposes. Often the manager of the Co-operative (Kurman Union Cooperative Agricultural Credit Society Ltd.) is seen on his bicycle come to realize the loans due to his Society. It was stipulated in the bonds that the loans would be paid up by 30th Falgun of the year. But many debtors did not pay in time. If the Manager pressed for payment, the debtors simply refused, saying that they could not sell their paddy at a loss at the low price fixed by the Government. They would like to defer payment of their loans and count interest thereon rather than dispose of their stock at present. The Government would certainly fail to keep the price at that level, and it is bound to rise, and then it will be time for them to sell their stocks and pay up the loans.

7.7—ON THE ZAMINDAR'S EXIT

In the Bengal of the nineteenth century the Zamindar had an influential place in the rural economy of the country. The Rev. Day devoted several chapters in describing the relation between the landlord and the tenant of those days. He presented to his readers two contrasting types of Bengal Zamindars—one an oppressor and the other a benefactor:

> The Zamindar of Kanchanpur was strictly speaking not a Zamindar, but a middle-man; for he only held a pattani Taluk under His Highness the Maharaja of Vardhamana, but though he was only a pattanidar, he was usually called the Zamindar of Kanchanpur and of scores of other villages lying round about. He paid 2,000 rupees a year to the Maharaja for the village of Kanchanpur, but it was generally believed that he himself realized in rents three times that amount. For the whole of his Zamindari or rather pattani, he gave eighty thousand rupees to the Raja, but he himself admitted that after paying the radar jama his own net profit amounted to the round sum of two lakhs a year. Such immense profit could only be obtained by a system of rack renting, of illegal extortion and of cruel oppression; and it must be admitted that Jayachand (for such was the name of the Zamindar of Kanchanpur) belonged to the class of Zamindars who were the greatest curses to their country. Unscrupulous in his character, he did not hesitate to have recourse to any means, however illegal or dishonorable to screw out of his raiyats as much money as he could…

Of the Zamindar of Durganagar he wrote:

> This Zamindar was determined, according to his means and ability, to promote the welfare of his tenant. He fought against the oppression of the influential British indigo planters for justice to the poor and ill-treated raiyats of his Zamindari.
>
> Nor was he unaware of the oppressive conduct of several Zamindars. He regretted this for the sake of the poor peasantry, and for the sake of the class to which he belonged, as he looked upon these Zamindars as a disgrace to their order. Nava Krishna (for such was the name of this Zamindar) was, it thus appears, one of those few Zamindars, who knew the duties attached to their station, who was actuated by Public spirit, who was inspired by liberal and patriotic sentiments, who had sympathy with the down-trodden raiyats, and who was honorable in all actions.

The Zamindars of Bengal, both the oppressive and the benevolent, ceased to be Zamindars with the passing of the West Bengal Estates Acquisition Act of

1953. The well-known Permanent Settlement, equally maligned and praised, vanished and the curtain was hung down on the scene with which Bengal was familiar for the last one hundred and fifty years.

Along with his class, the Zamindar of Kanchanpur lost his official position but the person who had last occupied that position still lives. The Zamindari system was abolished peacefully with payment of compensation for the rights now acquired by the State. But the vestige of social prestige that was once enjoyed by our Zamindar of Kanchanpur is still left with the same person and he still continues to be known as the Zamindar of the village.

This Zamindar without the Zamindari is still the biggest landowner and the owner of the best building in the village. With an aggressive personality, he still plays a important role in the affairs of Kanchanpur. He is the permanent president of the village Barwari, the school committee and the theater party. He is not a member of the Gram-Panchayat itself, but the Gram-Panchayat has returned him to the Anchal Board. It is his eldest son who has been appointed by the Government as the Tahsildar, and the peasants still visit his Kachheri for payment of the rents. The Tahsildar, however, does not credit the receipts in the account of his father, but sends them to the big absentee landlord, the Government itself at the Rajbhavan of Calcutta. But the Kachheri and the house as well are still called as the Zamindar's Kachheri and the Zamindar's house.

When marriages are celebrated by the middle caste and the Kotals and the Bagdis of the village, they still show their honor to the Zamindar and send a sida (gift of rice, pulses, vegetables, etc.) to his house. When sacrifices are received at the Manasa puja, Rakshakali puja, Kshetrapul puja or such community puja, a share of the sacrifice is still sent to our Zamindar of Kanchanpur as his due. In the Old Shiva annual ganjan, undoubtedly the greatest ritual function of the village, the head sannyasi himself marches in procession amidst bell-gongs and drum-beats to bring the offering of our Zamindar to Old Siva, and returns the same to him after worship. And when any great puja is finished, and time comes for the priest to put the sacrificial charrings on the foreheads of the party, it is the Zamindar who must first receive it. If he is not present at the time, he must be sent for, and until he receives the sacred charrings, others must wait for the same. Thus even with his Zamindari gone, the Zamindar still lives in the traditions of Kanchanpur.

7.8—The Impact of Land Reforms

The abolition of the estates and the intermediary rights is supposed to be an *a priori* measure that will lead to beneficial land reforms. Talks on such reforms have been loudly going on since Independence, and the legislature of West Bengal, consequent on the acquisition of the large estates and rights of the intermediaries, also passed in the sixth year of the Republic of India, the West Bengal Land Reforms Act of 1955. The Act provides that "no raiyat should be entitled to own more than 25 acres of land excluding homestead." In the whole village of Kanchanpur, none but the ex-zamindar could have come within the purview of the Act, but he had already got a portion of his lands transferred in the names of his sons to avoid the coming law as regard fixation of ceiling. Barring this instance, there was not a single householder who owned more than the fixed ceiling. The village has no surplus lands and the real malady here, as in most of India's villages, is that there are too many people on too little land.

The Act also aims at consolidation by providing for acquisition of holdings and redistribution of land thereafter. But the cultivators do not care to take advantage of these sections and consequently they are but a dead letter till now. There is another provision to encourage consolidation. The Act has given a preferential right for purchase of land to a co-sharer or a continuous tenant. Such a party has been invested with the right to get the land reconveyed through court in his favor from any other purchaser, provided he deposits the consideration money together with a further sum of 10% of the purchase price paid for the land. Usually after the harvests are reaped and before the next sowing season comes, Kanchanpur sees a few transactions of land sales every year. The rising peasant families like to add a bigha or two to their holdings, while there are families who may be pressed to sell a portion of their lands. The seller expects that he should get the bet price for his land, which does not necessarily come from his co-sharer or the owner of a contiguous plot. The purchaser who pays the best price does not like to face the possibility of losing the land after purchase and as a precaution he makes the seller agree to overvalue the deed of sale, showing the passing of much higher consideration money than is actually paid. This device frustrates the policy of the legislators and acts as a deterrent to the retransfer of the land a contemplated in the Act.

In Kanchanpur's agrarian system, there is a large number of persons who depend on bhagchar, that is, cultivation of other's land on share basis. The Land

Reforms Act (1955) fixed the proportions in which the produce of the land is to be shared between the owner and the cultivator. If plow, cattle, manure and seeds are supplied by the persons holding the land, the produce is to be shared on a 50-50 basis. In all other cases, the proportion is 60-40, the bagadar getting the major share. At Kanchanpur, the owner and the bhagachasi still go on sharing the produce on a 50-50 basis, though the latter continues to supply the plow, cattle, manure, and seeds. The owners do not voluntarily accept less share as prescribed in law; and the bargadars are too poor and unorganized to claim their rights under the law. If they insist on the higher proportion, they may not get any lands for cultivation at all, though the Act intends to protect the bargadar from unjust eviction.

It was further provided that the provisions in respect of the bhagachasis will apply so long as cultivation by a bargadar continues. It was suggested during discussions that the system of share cultivation was to be abolished in ten years. This, however, was not incorporated in the body of the Act. The attitude of the reformers, however, had already created an apprehension in the minds of the landholders, that rights to land may ultimately be transferred to the tillers, and the rights of the non-cultivating owners may vanish like those of the Zamindars and intermediaries. As a result, many bhagachasis were evicted, and lands were brought under personal cultivation. Many small landholders got together and began cultivating their lands under some kind of joint partnership. Indeed, the bargadars had to face a hard situation, and as a result "land to the tillers" attitude was restrained for the time being.

Instead of seeing the ownership and control of their lands going to the hands of the bargadars or actual tillers of the soil, the landholders would rather get their lands vested in the cooperative to which the Government has promised so many concessions and facilities—such as reduction in land revenue, financial assistance, free technical advice, better marketing arrangement, cheap seeds and manures etc. A few years ago these considerations mainly led to the formation of a cooperative farming society at Sadya, a sister village within the Anchal. By banding themselves under the cooperative banner, the landholders not only saved themselves from the menace of the tillers of the soil, they were at the same time considered to perform a very meritorious act and became a favorite of the Government.

It is more than half a century since the cooperative movement came to be started in our country, but the peasants' desire to hold their lands in individual proprietorship is so strong that the pace of cooperation could not be forced at all. In recent days, in our political world emphasis is being laid on "service co-operatives" and "farming cooperatives" with new force as keys to our agrarian problem. The Congress in its Nagpur Session (1959) has given a "spurt" to the movement.

If the proprietary instinct is a strong part of peasant nature (in fact of human nature), the instinct of self-protection is stronger still. The land owners of Sadya parted with their individual rights, but through the co-operative they managed to hold joint control over their lands. This was a lesser evil to them than yielding to the legislators' demand for vesting the tillers with rights in their land.

No landless person was allowed to join the cooperative. It was quite natural that a group of land owners, who had come together for their own interests, would not like to share the management of their lands with any of the landless. In pooling their lands and resources together, the land owners could introduce tractors and other machines. Consequently they required less labour. The members provided in their bylaws that one third of the produce of the lands would be taken as ownership dividend which would remain the first charge on the cooperative. On winding up the cooperative, the lands would, after meeting all liabilities, be redistributed to original owners on a pro-rata basis.

Thus the cooperative organization was used to their advantage by the Sadya land-owning cultivators. But the Agricultural Income Tax people had an eye on them and demanded a portion of their profits as the proper share of the State. Now a co-operative farming Society was entitled to get various concessions and facilities from the State, but nowhere did the law provide any relief or reduction in the payment of the agricultural income tax. An individual owner was allowed in law to hold land to the limit of 95 acres, and such holding was exempted from assessment of income tax; but the cooperative holding much exceeded the taxable limit, and the society became liable to payment of the income tax. The Sadya cooperative refused to pay the tax, and the members passed a resolution of dissolution rather than pay the tax. But they are at the same time hoping that the Government may change the law to give to the cooperative farming societies relief from payment of income tax. It is also significant to note that as soon as the Income Tax people have come to the scene, the cooperative management is showing lesser yields and higher costs, and therefore consequent losses in the working of the farm.

The example of the Sadya cooperative teaches several lessons:

(i) Both as a measure of self protection, and for sharing the advantages of better farming, the landholders may organize themselves into co-operatives.

(ii) The landless and near-landless labourer will be excluded from the cooperative organization. Further, they will be put to additional difficulties, as with cooperatives certain amounts of mechanization will be introduced in our agriculture. A good many labourers will be weaned away from land, and to find alternative employment for them will become a more difficult problem to Government.

(iii) A greater amount of agricultural production is expected, but the State's attempt to take a share of it may be resisted.

Our "spurt" to the cooperative movement defeats those who want to give land to the tillers. It also defeats those who want to give land to the State. But the specters haunt, and our "Kulaks" may, for their own self preservation, come forward to join the new cooperatives. It may bring for the country an era of agricultural prosperity; but the State's right to have a share of it for the general good and the interest of the vast number of agricultural labourers must always be kept in mind whenever a reform is attempted in the rural setup.

7.9—Politics at the Shivtala

Kanchanpur is growing politically conscious. It now gets more information, and speaks more freely on public affairs.

Twenty-five years ago it was written:

> Few and far between are the echoes that come to our village from the outside world, and life flows here in its narrow restricted channels. Movements may come and movements may go, but Kanchanpur goes on without change.
>
> The Congress programs did not affect the village. Even news of any important event that happens outside has no attraction for the people of Kanchanpur. They do not see a single newspaper or magazine even in these modern days. Only on each Friday one or two of the more interested villagers may get a newspaper, because on that day the post office receives a Bengali Weekly Basumati, addressed to a resident of a neighbouring village. The newspaper is kept for the day and next morning is handed over to the peon for delivery to the proper address."

At present the post office receives the following newspaper and reports for the village:

1. *Jugantar* (one)—a daily newspaper in Bengali published at Calcutta,

2. *Varahaman* (two)—a weekly magazine published by a Congress organization at Burdwan.

3. *Nutan Patrika* (one)—a weekly organ of the Communist party—published at Burdwan.

4. *Shiksha-Samachar* (one)—a fortnightly educational magazine from Calcutta.

5. *American Reporter* (eight)—a fortnightly report published by U.S.I.S. from Calcutta.

The daily *Jugantar*, a weekly *Vardhaman* and also the *American Reporter* are subscribed by the "Sakti-Sangha"—a young men's association in the village. Another copy of *Vardhaman* comes to the Secretary, Social Education Center. The Free Primary School receives the *Shikslta Samachar* and an *American Reporter*. The *Nutian Patrika* and other *American Reporters* are subscribed for by individuals.

As soon as the post office opens at about 11 am., a group of young men take out the *Jugantar* and for a couple of hours it is read and discussed amongst them. When they leave for their bath and meals, the newspaper finds its place either in the shop or the house of B.C., whose son generously pays up the monthly bill for the newspaper, on behalf of the Sakti-Sangha. When the afternoon comes, KG., an old and almost sightless pensioner slowly comes with his stick in hand and takes his seat on the verandah of a shop at the tri-junctional road of the north side. Then it is the duty of B.M., the village postmaster himself, to bring the newspaper out and read it aloud to his aged listener. As the reading proceeds, an audience surrounds them, and comments and discussions spring up. The weekly *Vardhaman* is also perused with interest by several persons in the village, but its reading clientele is not so wide as that of the daily *Jugantar*.

Besides the above newspaper and periodicals, three householders keep bat-
tery-charged radio sets which regularly bring the entertainments and news of the
broadcasting stations to our village world.

In 1933-34 when India was following Gandhi in his fight for freedom, of
Kanchanpur it was written thus:

> Here are no high discussions on politics—national or international—the
> burning topics of the day. Kanchanpur, like so many other villages in India, is
> indifferent to such matters. The peasantry, and not even all of them, know
> that their king is someone called George V, the lord of the whole world, and
> that he lives in a land called Bilat (England), a distant country beyond the
> seven seas and thirteen rivers. He has maintained here his two employees—
> Baralat, the Viceroy (literally, the greater lord) and Chhotatal, the Governor
> of Bengal (literally, the lesser lord) to rule over them. Beyond this they do not
> know anything of the governmental hierarchy or of the parliamentary assem-
> blies under the governor's tutelage. Gandhi? They know him as the great
> national hero who is fighting the British raj to win Swaraj for the country. But
> they have only the vaguest idea as to what Swaraj may be.

In this eleventh year of India's Independence, with the troubling consciousness of political freedom after centuries of bondage, with adult franchise and
newspapers in the village, Kanchanpur is now found to be no longer indifferent
to any discussion in politics. It often participates in political meetings and does
not hesitate to make adverse criticism of the Government.

The central Shivtala is the rendezvous for the political meetings of Kanchanpur. There one day you may see a communist leader, the president of the Vardhaman District Krishak Samity or the like, come and address the village public on
the anti-krishak policy of the present Congress Government. He receives hearty
commendation from his rustic audience, and he goes on in a tune such as this:

> The agriculturists are being deprived of the just price of their crops; and the
> canal rate has been unduly increased. At the present rate for paddy fixed by the
> Government the peasants may not find any profits after meeting the expenses
> of cultivation. The Government has failed to bring down the prices of all
> other commodities, and the peasants find it difficult to meet their costs while
> they have now been asked to sell their products at a "lower-than-just" price.
> The Food Minister Sri Sen, with his characteristic negligence, had said that
> only one million out of 6.2 million householders of Bengal have any surplus
> for sale. The Government has to think more of the other five millions and two

lacs of families who are deficit or non growing in respect of rice production. The policy of the Government is bound to prejudice agricultural production, and consequently it will affect not only the interests of the peasantry but the nation as a whole. It is for the peasants to organize themselves and fight for an increase in the controlled rate of paddy and a reduction of the canal rates, so unreasonably enhanced. At the same time the Government should be pressed to fix the prices of other necessary goods—such as oil, oil cake, chemical manures, clothes etc. proportionately in relation to price of paddy. The peasants must organize themselves to resist this anti-peasant and destructive policy of the Government. The Government must be made to yield. Long live revolution!...

In these days of democracy, the people know that the Government can be freely criticized, and there is no need of secrecy in the discussions over any public affairs. Often in group discussion you may hear an aged leader exclaim: "It was right that the British said that we are not fit for independence. See what a bad administration we are living under. On the one hand they are squeezing us with taxation, and with the money thus raised, they are playing ducks and drakes. Corruption is reigning in all the Government departments, and most of the top executives are expert thieves. Their bad deeds are being brought to light by the newspapers almost every day. What is left of a man if he is labeled a thief! But such things are destined to happen, and irresistible is the movement of Time! It is after all the Kaliyug!"

CHAPTER 8

▼

BELIEFS AND RITES

8.1—THE VILLAGE GODS

Nobody can fail to observe the dominance of religious practices in the life of Kanchanpur. Persisting through an unbroken tradition, the beliefs and rites have permeated the whole social life and play an important role in the round of activities in the village.

Kanchanpur has numerous gods and goddesses. The Brahmins of the north side are said to be devotees of Sakti, while the Goswamis and the Subarnabanik priests of the south side worship the god Vishnu. The Subarnabaniks and most of the middle and exterior castes are also known to be Vaishnabs. There is no Saiva sect in the village in the formal sense of the term but the Old Siva is the guardian deity of the village and throughout Kanchanpur are scattered numerous Siva temples. But truly speaking, the villagers are neither Saivas, nor Vaishnabs, nor Saktas. They believe in all the gods and goddesses of the Hindu pantheon; they believe in all the especial deities that reign in their own and neighbouring villages.

The great gods of the Hindus, the Vishnu, the Siva and the Sakti get their nit-yaseva (daily service) from their votaries of the upper castes. If the votary himself is a Brahmin, it is well and good; otherwise he has to commission the services of a pujari Brahmin, that is, he has to commission a professional Brahmin priest. It is said that each of the above god or goddess has one hundred and eight different names and forms. Thus Vishnu is known and worshiped as Narayan, Damodar,

Janardan, Gopinath, Shyamasundar, Sridhar, Gadadhar, Bansidhar and so on. For Siva also there are so many names—old Siva, Smasaneswar, Ishaneswar, Mahadeb, Kshetrapal and so on. Sakti also appears in different forms—Tarasundari, Sidheswari, Sinhabahim, Kali and so on. The usual symbol of Vishnu (more commonly called here as Narayan) is a black oval shaped stone, (the Narayan Sila or Salagram Sila), and that of Siva a black phallic stone (the Siva-linga). The mother goddess is usually represented through a brass female image, modeled according to description given in religious books of the Hindus. Similar brass idols are used for Sridhar, Bansidhar or Gadadhar or some other forms of Vishnu. The Kshetrapal and the Yogadya of the village are symbolized in ordinary crude stones.

Besides the above mentioned Vishnu, Siva and Kali, the three great gods of Hinduism, the upper castes here have also accepted Devi Manasa who is now used to getting her nitya-seva (daily service). She is the queen goddess of the snakes, and is worshiped in the form of a lady with ornaments of snakes round her. An image of a snake in an earthen pot also symbolizes this goddess, and it is in this shape that she is seen by the side of Lord Mahadeva in a couple of the Siva temples of Kanchanpur.

The Vaishnab Goswamis give daily service to Gouranga and Nityananda as well. Lord Gouranga, or Chaitanya Mahaprabhu, was a great man of religion of the sixteenth-century Bengal. Sri Mityananda was his disciple and associate.

Centering on Sri Chaitanya, there grew up in Bengal a great devotional literature of Vaishnava religion and philosophy. He was a great preacher and reformer, and his followers now worship him as a god or more strictly speaking as an atavar (incarnation) of Krishna. Along with him, his associate Nityananda has been raised to the status of godhead. Their images installed in a temple at Mahaprabhutala receive the daily adorations of the Goswami Brahmins of Dakshinpara. And often you may hear at Kanchanpur, on a sankranti or a full moon night or on any other special occasion, a party of devout Vaishnabs going round the streets of the village in nagar-sankirtan. With music of mridanga and kartal, the party sings and dances *"Haribol, Haribol bole, Gour Nitai neche jai"*, i.e. Gour and Nitai go round dancing and singing the name of Hari.

The Dharmaraj of Kanchanpur also gets his "daily service" which is offered by a priest of the Bagdi caste who is surnamed Pundit. The god is symbolized in a tortoise shaped stone and is seated on a wooden throne. It appears that while Devi Manasa has been able to find out her way to the temple of the Hindu upper castes and now receives daily service from them, Dharmaraj is still, to a certain extent, outside their walls. He is however revered by all the villagers of whatever caste or position they may be, as one of the great gods of their village.

The Bagdi priest offers daily worship to god Panchanan also who lives symbolized in several pieces of stones under the shade of a Krishnachuda tree by the side of the temple of Dharmaraj. He is the five-faced god whose malignant influence over village children was so nicely described by the Rev. Day. There is another god in the village—the Kai Bhairab. He is the all-destroying form of Lord Siva, and his place is under a palmyra tree, at the south end of the village, where he is worshiped in the shape of a rough black stone. He belongs especially to the Bauris, and a Bauri priest ministers to his daily worship. This god, like god Panchanan, is dreaded and respected by all the villagers as he not only destroys but also renders much good to the afflicted. Through his grace, barren women become prolific, the lame children learn to walk, and the deaf and dumb regain their hearing and power of speech.

8.2—THE GODS OF RECURRENT HONOR

Besides the above gods of daily worship, the god Satyanaryan and the goddesses Lakshmi and Shasthi receive their periodical offerings in a regular manner. These are usually done by the village women, and are perhaps the most important of the brata pujas that they are known to perform.

Satya-Narayan is worshiped usually on the full moon and sankranti days. His puja may be observed on any auspicious day. Satya-Narayan means that Truth and Narayana (God) are the same. It is also of interest to note that the brata-katha of this puja enjoins the votaries to bow to god Satya Pir (a folk god or some saint of the Muslims), and declares in course of the narrative that Pir and Narayan are the same god. Offerings of sweetmeats etc. given to Satya Narayan are known as sirni, a Persian word which has now passed to Bengali language and indicates the Muslim connection of this Hindu god. There is a peculiar list of articles for this puja, and specially there must be the ingredients of sirni which consists of flour, gur, and milk in fixed proportion. These materials are mixed together and often various fruits are superadded. When the puja is over and the

Brahmin priest gets his dakshina (fee), sirni has then to be distributed to the devotees present, and also to inmates of the household and the neighbours as well.

Lakshmi, as the goddess of prosperity, is regarded with peculiar veneration by all our village householders. Out of the churning of the ocean she arose from the depths of the seas, and Lord Vishnu himself took her for his own. It is through her auspicious influence that one becomes prosperous in life, and on her desertion one becomes lakshmichhada, i.e. wretched and poor. She is worshiped on each Thursday (which is also known in Bengal as the Lakshmi Day) in almost every household. The housewives believe that if Lakshmibrata is regularly observed the goddess will remain stationary in the house, and prosperity and peace are bound to follow wherever Lakshmi resides.

Apart from such weekly worship of Lakshmi, the goddess is to be offered ceremonial pujas, as noted earlier in our passage of Paddy, in the three months of Bhadra, Pous and Chaitra, also known to be the months of Lakshmi. It is so said, as asu dhanya ripens in Bhadra, haimanti in Pous and boro in Chaitra. Paddy symbolizes Lakshmi, and the three months, therefore, are considered to befit seasons for the worship of the goddess.

Later, in our description of annual festivals and pujas it will be seen that Lakshmi is also worshiped on other and different occasions in the year. In the meantime let us have a look at Shasthi who, as the goddess of fecundity and as the protectress of children, is held in no less peculiar veneration than Lakshmi, the goddess of wealth and harvest.

It is said that there are thirteen Shasthis in the twelve months of the year. The goddess is contemplated as a beautiful lady with vermilion on her forehead, a conch circlet on the wrist and turmeric toilet for the body. On the sixth lunar day of the full moon fortnight, she comes down from heaven to this earth to receive offerings and bestow favors to her worshipers. Besides these twelve Shasthis, there is another Shasthi, which is observed on the day previous to the Chaitra-sankranti, i.e. the last day of the Bengali year. According to the Hindu almanac, the day may not be the sixth day of the moon, but is the day of Nil-puja which celebrated the anniversary of the marriage of Lilavati (Goddess Durga) with Nilkantha (Lord Mahadev). Goddess Shasthi is also worshiped on the day which, therefore, is known Nil-shasthi of the year. Besides the above thirteen recognized Shasthis, the goddess is also worshiped on the sixth day after the birth of a child, and also on the day when the ceremonial uncleanness of the lying-in room is over for the mother on the eleventh, fifteenth, or twenty-first day after a child is born, according to the custom of the family. At the ceremony of annaprasan (ceremony of giving first rice to the child commonly termed the bhojan) Devi Shasthi is to be worshiped before rice may be given to the child.

At Kanchanpur the goddess Shasthi has a permanent place of residence, (called Shasthitala) under the neem tree in the northeast side of the village. There, in sunshine and rain, without a roof overhead, lives Mother Shasthi as symbolized in a few pieces of stones, besmeared in vermilion and turmeric. Whenever there is an occasion of Shasthi puja, women are seen to proceed there with offerings of rice, fruits and flowers, while the bell-gongs and drum-beats usually proclaim the occasion to the village world.

8.3—Epidemic Goddesses and the Raksha Kali

These are the goddesses who are dreaded and worshiped because of their power over disease and affliction.

One of them is the Didi-Thakrun, the presiding deity over cholera, and another is Basanta Chandi, the presiding deity over smallpox. Having power over these great epidemics which used to spread in the countryside each and every year, these goddesses, of all the deities in the village pantheon, are very much dreaded and worshiped more in appeasement than in veneration.

The goddess Didi-Thakrun especially belongs to the Bagdis of the village, and though she, in the shape of a stone, shares the temple hut of Dharma Thakur, her worship is done in the distant village of Bhatar. On a Saturday or a Tuesday in the month of Magh, the Bagdis of Dharmatala, accompanied by several of their women carrying basketfuls of offerings to the goddess, march out of the village in procession amidst drumbeats and bell gongs. As the puja is thus announced, offerings pour forth from each household and fill up the big baskets of the women carriers. At the same time sounds of ulu and conch shells celebrate the ceremonial march. Similar puja to Didi-Thakrun is sent in the month of Falgun as well.

Basanta Chandi is worshiped with proper offerings in a place in the southwest outside the village borders. No image of the goddess is made, nor is there any stone symbol. Her worshipers carry their offerings under a tree beyond the village boundary, where her presence is invoked in the ghat (a water jar in lieu of an idol and worshiped as the symbolic representation of the deity), and the necessary puja is made to propitiate her.

Often householders, afflicted with smallpox in their house, arrange for the worship of the goddess in their own yard or cowshed. This Basanta Chandi is also otherwise known to the people as Mother Sitala, and she too has no temple or abode of any sort in the village. But you may chance to see the goddess carried in a litter by some stranger on the streets of Kanchanpur. He announces with sounds of conch that the Mother herself has come down to the village to take her worship, and the inhabitants should propitiate her by their pujas. The man may be seen to be accompanied by an assistant whose business is to carry the load of offerings that pour in from every side. Curiosity may lead you to have a look at this mighty goddess, but your sight is obstructed by a heap of bael leaves which almost cover the august deity. With good care you notice however the reddish patch of vermilion paint on a stone with eruptions. You are told that the painted stone is no other than the goddess Sitala, and the eruptions represent the sixty four varieties of smallpox over which she presides. Instantly you hear again the words ring forth "Mother Sitala has come to the village far her puja". The doors of the neighbouring houses open, and women and children flock to make their bows and pour their offerings of rice and pice (small change) in the baskets of the stranger.

For the villagers in difficulty, there is another goddess—the Raksha-Kali, i.e. the Kali who protects. Goddess Kali is the terrible all-destroying form of Sakti, but here she is worshiped and propitiated so that she may forgive and protect. Her puja is held at the southern end of the village at Khirintala so called because of a pair of umbrageous Khirni trees standing there. In the current year 1959, the date of the puja of the goddess Rakshakali at Kanchanpur was fixed on the 26th of Falgun of 1365 B.S. (10th March 1959) and the decision was conveyed to the village community by beats of drum. An earthen image of the goddess was made, colored, dressed, worshiped and drowned on the very day of the puja. The goddess was shaped in the form of a four-armed naked black lady with a garland of human heads on her neck. Her feet were placed on the body of God Siva. With one of her left hands she held a severed blood-dropping human head, and in the other she held a curved sword. Her two right hands were, however, raised to bestow security and benedictions on her devotees.

The Rakshakali of Kanchanpur attracts devotees from other villages, far and near, and she is reputed to be a great "awake" goddess. Relations of the village people, mainly of the exterior castes, are seen to come to fulfill their vows, and bring with them the animals to be sacrificed as the offerings promised. On that night of worship, on the 26th of Falgun, twenty-five goats and many birds were sacrificed at the altar of the goddess. Indeed, as a savior in difficulties and fulfiller of human desires, great is the fame of the Rakshakali of Kanchanpur.

8.4—THE ANNUAL FESTIVALS AND PUJAS

The principal festivals of our village community are all based on its religious practices, and are generally held at the annual celebrations of the pujas of one or other of the village deities. Of these, two, however, are more secular in their nature, and may properly be looked at as harvest festivals. One is Navanna—the feast of new rice in early Agrahayan and the other is piths sankrati—the festival days of rice cakes, ending on the last day of Pous. But goddess Lakshmi is the presiding deity in both the festivals where she appears either as Navanna Lakshmi or Pous Lakshmi to receive the offerings from the peasantry of Bengal.

On the date fixed for the worship of Navanna Lakshmi, which usually falls early in the month of Agrahayan (late November), the villagers, especially women, boys and girls, take early baths to join the feast of new-rice. New rice is mixed in milk with all seasonal fruits and edible roots cut into small pieces. A dish of this magnificent food is sent by each householder to the Old Siva at his temple in the center of the village. Goddess Lakshmi is worshiped at home with navanna prepared as above. Then all the deities of the village and forebears of the family are offered the said grand dish. The bovines of the household, the beasts of the fields, the birds of the air, the fish in the tanks, the insects of the earth, in short, all living creatures are thereafter offered a portion of the said dainty. Men and children then partake of the new rice, and finally the women of the finally come in for their shares.

On the sankranti, that is, the last day of the month of Pous (middle of January), is held the worship of Goddess Lakshmi. On this occasion the villagers have a three days festival ending on the sankranti. This is the festival of cakes, the piths paraan, after the harvesting of paddy. Like narvanna this festival is greatly enjoyed by the people of Kanchanpur. On the evening of the first day of the festival, the harvest month is given a welcome address in a doggerel verse:

Pous, oh Golden Pous,
You are welcome—you should not go,
You should not leave us through different births;
Stay on, please stay on. Pous, Pous, oh Golden Pous.

For three days different varieties of rice cakes are prepared and eaten. On the last day Lakshmi, the goddess of harvest, especially known as Pous Lakshmi, is worshiped with due rites. Pous and Lakshmi seem to be the same.

Pour, Pous, oh Golden Pous, come and sit here on the floor of the big hut.

It has already been observed that the days of the annual celebrations of the village gods are also days of festivals and have both religious and recreational value. Most of them are common to all castes and are observed as community festivals.

There are some, however, which are distinctly observed by individual castes or by groups of castes. Thus the puja of Gandheswari is special to the Gandhabarnik caste. She is none but the Goddess Durga, seated on the lion, and is worshiped on the full moon day in the month of Baisakh, the very day on which the gajan of Dharmaraj is held at Kanchanpur. The votaries of Gandheswari offer their merchant's balance and the standard weights before the Goddess and, so far as Kanchanpur is concerned, they celebrate the puja in a quiet and simple manner. Goddess Jogadya is the special deity of the Ugra-Kshatriyas; Haris have their special Kali, the Bauris and the Bagdis their special Lakshmi, and the Koras their special Manasa. The Kotals too have their special deities, the grahas of the sky. Ministrations to the gods or goddesses of the exterior castes cannot, however, be offered by true Brahmins. The services of the patit (fallen) Brahmins, or the lowly esteemed Grahacharyas or Vaishnabs, are requisitioned for conducting the rituals of their pujas.

The merchant castes—the Subarnabaniks and the Gandhabaniks of the village have their special dinghi (a small boat) festival on the first of Magh of the Bengali year (February-March). A toy-ship is made of plantain leaf stalks and cut pieces of bamboos. The upper part of the ship is covered with thin red paper, and a scarlet flag is hoisted on the top. Idols prepared of thickened milk and cow dung are placed inside the ship. Oranges, plantains and other seasonal fruits are given as offerings to the deities Suo and Duo, i.e. Prosperity and Adversity. Both these goddesses are worshiped by the Hindu baruks—the former for securing favor and the latter perhaps for avoiding disfavor. As the evening falls, candles are lit and placed inside the toy ships. Bells toll, conchs sound and the ships are then launched in the tanks of the village.

The principal religious festivals of the village, however, are all observed on a community basis. All of these belong to the great tradition of India and Bengal, and are held in honor of the great gods, Siva, Dharma or Krishna or the goddesses Durga, Kali, lrakshmi, Saraswati or Manasa.

With whatever castes one or other of the above festivals originated, they have slowly spread from one caste to another. It is the argument of the sociologists that there is a continuous process of assimilation in an evolving culture. Accordingly, the high caste festivals show a tendency of gradually including the lower castes and their practices in their rituals, while the low caste festivals show a leaning for acceptance of the ritual traits of the high castes who also increasingly participate in those festivals. How this process of universalization is going on may be illustrated from the ganjans of Old Siva and Dharmaraj, the two great folk festivals in our village community.

But before we come to their description, let us shortly dispose of the other annual pujas at Kanchanpur. Here again, compared to the festivals of Kali, Krishna and Durga, those of Lakshmi, Saraswati and Manasa are of minor importance in the village.

The annual Kali puja is held both at the north side and the south side, but the north side Kali has acquired a preeminently superior status. She is the Great Mother of the village. Her site and tin shed temple is under a big peepal tree (said to be two hundred years old), near the ex-Zamindar's house at the western end of the Uttarpara (north side). There every year an imposing image of Goddess Kali, ten cubits in height, is raised at the appointed time and duly worshiped by the village community. This Kali has obtained the name of Great Mother of the village, not only because of her gigantic bodily frame, but also because she is supposed to he the most "awake" goddess of the village. I am told by several persons of the locality that at the dead of night, they never approach the place of this Kali, as from a distance they can see a halo-light and hear an awe-inspiring sound pervading the site of their Great Mother.

The Durga puja days (September-October) and the festal fortnight of Krishna and Radha known in the village as badhai festival, apart from their recreational and religious values, have a special significance in the life of our community. The period of badhai festival is from Krishnasfami (birthday of Lord Krishna) to Radhastami (birthday of Radha, the beloved of Krishna), and it usually falls in the month of Bhadra (August-September). During both of these festivals, and especially in the badhai, local group-feelings between the north side and the south side run high as one side tries to excel the other in performance. The very word badhai in Bengali means creating conflict, and possibly indicates the origin of the festival in the rivalry between the two groups, though it may well be that badhai is the changed form of bhadhai bhadui, i.e. the festival of the month of Bhadra, which is found in some of the districts of Bengal. When crops have been sown and seedlings are taking their roots in the month of Bhadra, it is natural that all agricultural community spend some time in festive activities and, as the period coincides with the days of birth of Krishna and Radha, the love play of this divine pair forms the subject matter of devotion and merriment in our village community. Children dressed as Radha and Krishna, or life like images of the deities, are placed in mobile revolving stages (known as thakas) to portray one or other scene of the lily (play) of the eternal lovers. Both the north and south sides bring their thakas in procession and strive with each other for excellence. This competitive mood reaches its climax on the last day of the festival.

The rivalry between the two local groups is manifest also at the time of the Durga Puja. In October, 1958, on the day of visarjan (i.e., immersion of the earthen image of the deity on the last day), the Dakshinpara people were jubilant over the fact that they had on the occasion a lighted gate and a band party from the town, to accompany the procession for bisarjan. Members of that hired body of musicians wore white uniforms with scarlet stripes, and their performance with their wind-instruments captivated the rustic hearts. But most of the hearts of the northern side smarted at the same sight, as the credit went to the people of Dakshinpara. It may, however, be noted here that the group tension between the two sides has considerably softened down as the present leaders of the Panchayat are working on a community basis, and are taking necessary steps to prevent the rise of any conflicting situation.

Brick relief—work on a village temple

The central Shivtala

Khirnitala

A child dressed as Krishna

8.5—Old Siva's Gajan

Gajan festivals are held in honor of Old Siva as well as the Dharmaraj of our village. Gajan is derived from the Bengali word garjan which means "roaring". Evidently it refers to the thundering sound caused by the big gathering of persons come together to celebrate the festival in honor of their deity. Gajan has, therefore, come to mean the folk-festival itself held in worship of such village gods as Siva and Dharmaraj.

Old Siva's gajan starts with the initiation of the mul sannyasi, i.e. the main or head ascetic and the two deulias, i.e. the temple bearers, seven days before the Chaitra sankranti which is the last day of the Bengali year (middle of April). The head ascetic is invested with his wand of office to lead the sannyasis of the gajan, while the temple bearers get the right to carry the palanquin of the Gajanesmr (lord of gajan) in his ceremonial march through the village streets. Gajaneswar is the Old Siva himself. But in the temple, he is represented by a phallic symbol, a black smooth stone fixed on the floor in brick and mortar, while in the procession of the gajan, the deity is represented by a big egg-like plain white stone, known as Gajaneswar to the votaries.

The sannyasis of Siva come from all castes. They have to purify their bodies by baths in the Ganges, shave themselves clean, and put on new clothes. Thereafter they are initiated to sannyasi-hood for the consecrated period of the gajan days. As an insignia of sannyasi-hood, the ascetics wear the utri (sacred threads) and all of them are then regarded to belong to saiva gotra (Siva's clan) above all earthly castes. The Brahmin and the Vaidya votaries, who already wear their sacred threads, throw away the old ones, and themselves take the utri. But devotees of other castes cannot take the same without the ministrations of a Brahmin. For them, a gajan Brahmin turns up—nobody knows from where—to officiate at the ceremony of handing utri. As most of the votaries come from low castes, the gajan Brahmin is considered to be degraded in ministering to them. The visitor Brahmin, therefore, prefers to remain incognito, but the villagers are sure that he would appear out of the blue at the proper time and place every year during the time of gajan. In case, however, the gajan Brahmin does not turn up, the head sannyasi has the right and duty to give the utri to those devotees. The head sannyasi himself along with the two temple bearers had already been initiated to asceticism on the first day by the Brahmin sevait of Old Siva.

In the April 1959 gajan, there were fifty-nine sannyasis, and their numerical strength from different castes stood as follows:

Caste	No.	Total
Brahmin	4	4
Sadgop	2	12
Tanti	2	
Karmakar	1	
Gop	7	
Sunri	4	8
Chunari	2	
Kaibatra	2	
Bagdi	8	33
Hari	6	
Kotal	8	
Muchi	1	
Bauri	9	
Kora	1	

The mul-sannyasi for 1959 was a Brahmin, the first in the history of Kanchanpur's gajan. Like all village functionaries the head sannyasi-hood was also a hereditary office, and a Sadgop family had hitherto held the honor. The last head sannyasi supported by the deulias refused to carry on the duties of their offices, unless some handsome payments were made to them. The work of the head sannyasi is a responsible and strenuous one, and this year he demanded a greater percentage of profits from the sevaits of Siva, who earn a good income from the gajan festival. The sevaits did not agree to the demand of the head sannyasi who consequently expressed his inability to lead the gajan for the year. A situation was created in which systematic celebration of the festival was threatened, and the sevaits placed the matter to the sixteen annas of the village public. The Sadgops made a united stand, and no person came forward from them to accept the office of the head ascetic. Some of the lower caste members offered to lend their services, but the leaders did not like that such a dignified office should be held by a person of the exterior castes. Finally, a Brahmin rose and volunteered to hold the office and the sevaits and a majority of the public accepted his proposal.

From the fourth day before the sankranti, i.e., the 26th or the 27th Chaitra of the Bengali era, the gajan of Kanchanpur takes its festive turn. The god Gajaneswar is carried in the palanquin with due ceremony with beats of drums and bell gongs. He is first taken to the ghat of the Dighi Tank wherefrom, it is said, Old Siva had arisen during excavation. There on a raised lime-washed earthen platform, the palanquin of the Gajaneswar is placed, and the god is duly worshiped. It is the closing date of taking vows and the last batch of devotees take their baths, offer prayers to the Sun-god and take the sacred utri from the gajan Brahmin.

Now it is time for the gajan party to start its trek with their Lord, singing and dancing through the streets of the village. The party is led by the head sannyasi who holds the wand of his office in one hand. With his other hand he holds on his shoulders an earthen pot which contains snanjal (ablution water of the Lord's body) that is otherwise known as charanamitra (i.e. nectarine water of the Lord's feet). The deulias (temple bearers) carry the palanquin of the Lord, and sets of drums and bells make a deafening music. Old Siva has his own drummer who had been settled with lands by the founder of the deity, for service to be rendered during the festivals. (Similarly all the functionaries of the gajan had been given some lands from the devottar endowment to the deity belonging to Old Siva for properly carrying out their duties to their god). The Pauls and Duttas of the village had also been giving annual drums to Old Siva at his gajan procession. People also promise to honor Old Siva with drum party, in fulfillment of their vows. The drums are covered with colored cloths, and are decorated with white feathers and black cowries. At different hours in the festival, the musical party make their beats, to make the villagers alert about the activities of the gajan, and children, men and women throng to the appointed places to join the function.

Merrily goes round the gajan, and now it comes to stop at the household of the Biswas. The open space lying between the outer room of the family and the two Siva temples, a little to the east, has been cleansed and polished with cow dung. As the palanquin of the Lord comes, two boys of the family lie prostrate at the verandah steps, and the bearers carry the conveyance of the God over the breasts of the boys and place the deity inside the room. There it is worshiped by the head sannyasi with due rites and prayers. Outside, the feet of the sannyasis are washed with water, and off and on sandal water is sprinkled on their heads and breasts. The party sings and dances in honor of Siva and to proclaim glory to the Lord and to praise to his servants "Siva, Sambhunath, Mahadeb,—victory to the Biswas barga (group)." As the puja is over, the customary dues to the gajan are paid by the family. To the assembly then are distributed the nectarine water of the Lord's feet and the leavings of food partaken of by the deity. Now the head sannyasi gives the signal and the drummers start their beats and the idol is brought out from the room. Immediately the two boys of the family lie prostrate at the steps, and the Lord's palanquin rides out over their breasts as it came in a few minutes ago. The procession then moves on to the Jogadya-talc at the eastern end, to the temple of Isaneswar on the bank of the Auddy's tank at the South-East, to the site of Dhanmaraj at the Bagdipara, to Khiniitala in the South, where a large crowd has already gathered to welcome the party. The sannyasis with their god stop there for a couple of hours and show various feats to the public—such as the head-dance, the lathi-dance, the "awakening" dance, the pedal-dance and so on. These displays are the most attractive features in the day's gajan which is therefore known to the villagers as the gajan of Khirnitala.

After the performances at Khirnitala the procession moves on and goes to different households in a traditional order, and finally retires to the colonnade of the Shivtala. At about midnight, the sannyasis make their obeisances to Lord Siva, and the gajan of the day is then closed. On the next day the gajan moves round the village in quick steps and returns to the colonnade of Siva before dusk, as the sannyasis have to receive there the devotees of sister villages of Parui and Kurman, who come to pay their respects to Old Siva of Palashi.

Carrying their idols in a palanquin, the sannyasis of the two neighbouring villages enter Palashi. Over the palanquin is a big umbrella of colored silk on a silver stick. The party is led by the head sannyasi, but the priest also accompanies it, as he has to offer ministrations to the devotees at Shivatala. The entrance roads have already been watered by the villagers, and the streets have been decorated with strings of green mango or neem leaves. As the procession comes, the inmates of the households come out to wash the feet of the sannyasis and give their offerings to the gajan god. Before the shrine of Siva the ascetics of Palashi are waiting in a line. As their brethren from Parui or Kurman approach, they come forward to embrace them and offer them cheering tobacco bidi or a kalki according to one's liking. Making obeisances to Old Siva, the guest sannyasis return to their respective villages, while the local ascetics go home for their maha-habisya.

The devotees have not as yet taken any food for the day. At night they boil two grains of sun-dried rice and some vegetables together for their meals. This dinner is spoiled if there is any sound heard at the time of eating, whether it be the voice of a man, or the barking of a dog or the chirping of a lizard. In the stillness of night, closing the doors and windows of his room, the devotee offers his prayers to his god and partakes of his food—the mahahabiya—in the silence of night. If any sound enters his ears by chance, he has to get up. Next day he has to live on fruits and the day after he has to fast.

At midnight the drum beats at the Shivtala announce the time for making obeisances to the Lord. The sannyasis gather there and make their bows to the deity in thirty-six different forms. The priest then distributes the nirmalya (i.e. cast off flowers of the god) to the votaries, and closes the gajan for the day.

Next day brings the great ritual in the worship of Siva as Smasaneswar, i.e. the Lord of the Crematories. It starts with the flower dropping ceremony at about mid-day, and culminates in the crematorium dance in the dusky dawn before another day breaks.

As the drum beats announce that the flower dropping ceremony has started, the ascetics and the villagers come in flocks to the shrine of the Old Siva. The priest presses a bunch of single-petaled tagar flowers, and places the same on the slightly curved head of the Siva. The resonant drum-beats go on and on, and the priest and the votaries pray, and behold a flower has been dropped by Lord Siva as a sign of his sanction for commencing the great rite smasanpuja.

Today is the day of the smasan-bhakta sannyasi, i.e. those ascetics who have vowed to make puja of the Siva of the crematoria. There is another class of devotees who are known as bola-bhaktas who do not participate in the smasanpuja of Siva. Be that as it may, the function starts as usual with the carrying of the Gajaneswar to Dighi Tank, but he is brought back to the original shrine in a short time.

The samasan-bhakta have to be dressed today. They scatter in the different households that take charge of attiring them as mimics of Siva. The householder offers his sannyasi a repast of fruits, and then the dressing begins. The face and body of the imitation Siva is chalked white, his beard, mustache, and eye-brows are all painted, and black and red spots are impressed on the body in oil color. Over his head he wears a tinsel crown, and on his neck is a garland of paper flowers and also of golancha and akanda (kinds of flowers neglected by other gods and men, but greatly liked by god Siva.) The Siva's mimic puts on ornaments of flowers over different parts of his body. Round his waist he wears a string of bells, and there is a jingling anklet on his feet. He wears a dyed cloth, usually of saffron color and the palms of his hands are tinged with lac. There is a china-rosebud in his lips, and in one of his hands there is in earthen cup. In the other hand he holds a sword and a green mango is fixed there on the pointed head. Before the sannyasi leaves the household of the dresser, he exchanges the green mango for another, and hands over the fruit to the mistress or the daughter-in-law of the household, and the said fruit is eaten with its cover and seed and all by the bous of the family in the belief that such partaking of the fruit will cause fertility in them. It is time for the mimic god to come out of the household. He worships his Lord, and drum-beats begin. The sannyasi moves in the rhythm of a dance, and he dances a dance that is not his own. It is said that he is but the medium through which the Nataraj (i.e. the great dancer, an epithet as well as another name of Siva) is making his dance. Thus dancing he comes out and goes to the site of the great mother and then to the temple of the Smasaneswar (the lord of the crematorium—another epithet as well as name of Siva), where all the sannyasis are to meet. Flocks of boys and girls, men and women stand in rows by the streets to see the party of these grotesquely dressed sannyasis dancing according to the beats of the drums.

At the temple of the village Smasaneswar, the sevait distributes the Lord's nirmalyas (cast off flowers) to the sannyasis, on receipt of which they run out of the village for their trek to Kunman and Parui.

On the way a chosen few perform a secret ritual, and what it is all others do not know. Prohibited is the path on which the chosen few pass, and other ascetics have to follow a different route till their merits and austerities qualify them to a knowledge of the secret rite. Those who know what the rite is have to keep the secret within themselves as the god's wrath will surely descend on them if they disclose it to others. It was told by several ascetics that they had been practicing austerities for years to find out the mystery of the secret rite but as yet they are not considered qualified to know the great secret. Before entering Kurman, the sannyasis enter a smasan (crematorium) and worship the Lord Siva there with proper rites. From Kurman the sannyasis march to Parui to pay their respects to Lord Siva there. On their return to the village about midnight, fruits are distributed to the ascetics at the ghat of the Dighi Tank, and then there is a recess for them for the night.

At an hour when the dawn is contending with the night for removing darkness from the face of the earth, beats of drums at the streets of Kanchanpur announce to the people that the time is come for the great crematorium dance of the sannyasis. The drum beats continue to sound and the ascetics singly or in batches run to the north end of the village on the main street, wherefrom the dance is to start. By the sides of the principal road, at the durga-mandap of the north side and at the central Shivtala onlookers stand to see this outlandish, terrible and mad dance of the ascetics with heads of human corpses in one hand and swords in the other. To counteract the loathsome odor of the putrefied human heads, a dhup-sannyasis (an incense burning ascetic) accompanies the dancing party with a censer on his head. There are heads of all sorts, of both sexes and different ages, and most of the heads are fresh with their eyes still glaring.

When children die in the villages their bodies are not buried. Also unclaimed bodies from the Burdwan hospital are often dumped under earth. Many of the poor exterior castes cannot afford to burn their dead, especially at a time when cholera or smallpox take a heavy toll. The ascetics have an active intelligence department. At the dead of night they move in a group, dig up the dead bodies front the earth, sever the heads with their swords and steal away with the precious treasurers. They visit even distant villages for this purpose.

Mimics of Shiva

Sannyasis at the Crematorium Dance

A dancing sannyasis with the corpse of a child

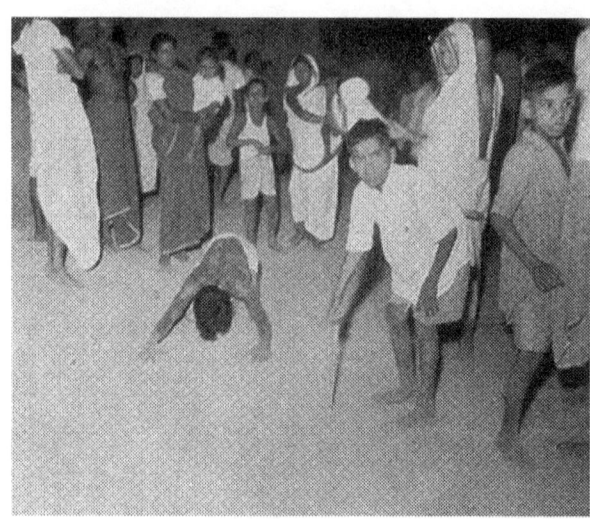

Digh Pranam

The tune of the skull-play dance is different Its postures and movements are also different In quick rhythm the drum beats sound, and the ascetics' steps fall quicker. The dancing procession moves on through the street, and stops at Shivtala for the final display. Surrounding the actors is a crowd of spectators who recede backwards in loath as any dancer moves towards them. But year after year the drama is enacted, and the villagers have become accustomed to the scene. But a stranger is bewildered! Is it heroic or cowardly? Is it terrible or ludicrous? Is it beautiful or ugly? Is it attractive or disgusting? Is it holy or profane? This mimicry of the death dance of Siva.

As the sun glides towards the west on the day of the fast, drum beats announce that the time is now come for the digh pranam, (i.e. the great obeisance) to be made by the ascetics to their god. Gajaneswar is carried to the ghat of the Dighi Tank where he receives the puja with due rites. The sannyasis then start their digh pranam, and along with them a few others many be seen who have come to make their long prostration in fulfillment of their vows.

The long prostration begins from the ghat of the Dighi-tank—in the north-east of the village, and ends at the shrine of the Old Siva. The distance is not less than half a mile, and the performance is an arduous and exhausting affair. With folded hands and bent head the devotee prays and calls his god—"*Tarakeswar*

Nath Mahadeb! Hara-Gourinath Mahadeb! Siva Sambhunath Mahadeb!" and the makes himself prostrate on the ground. His breast and face touch the earth, and his hands are outstretched in front. At the last reach a line is drawn, and the devotee gets up and walks up to the mark. Again he folds his hands and calls his Lord, and again he prostrates himself. Thus advancing, the whole ground is to be covered. If any one is forced to abandon this great obeisance, he remains a debtor to Lord Siva, and at one time or another in his life, he has to clear his dues to his god, lest there is no future for him in this life or in that after death.

Drum beats continue to sound, and the prostrating devotees, singly or in batches, slowly move on. Some seem to fall from the line, but no, they take a few minutes' rest and again drag their fatigued and unwilling bodies towards the their goal for the day. Silent and praying, the relatives and friends accompany the votaries, and do their best to give whatever relief they can to this toiling group. They mark the lines of advance on their behalf, they sprinkle water on their faces and fan them with the punkhas they carry with them. But even the longest road has its end; and the digh pranam too comes to its finish.

After a bath the ascetic returns again, and goes through a miniature ordeal of fire. He sits in "padmasan" and fire kept in three earthen cups is placed over his head and palms of hands. Incense is burned there for the god. After some time, he leaves the pots of fire, prays to Siva and retires to his bed for the night. It is only after the worshiping of Lilavati and Rudra next morning that the ascetic breaks his fast.

Possessing a more modern outlook on life, you may ask a village ascetic why he observes the austerities of the gajan. His answer is:

> Our austere living for the consecrated period—nay for the whole month of Chaitra keeps our body fit and active for the whole year. No disease can enter the body thus disciplined in the worship of the Lord. Prosperity also is bound to follow the worship of the Lord. The strict discipline, the different rites, the painstaking great pranam—all these have been transmitted to us from generation to generation, and who am I to break them? There must be something of value in them, otherwise why did our forebears follow them? Have not our scriptures also enjoined us to observe austerities? Have not they said that all may be accomplished by austerities. And lastly, when we make all these austerities for the sake of the Lord, His grace is bound to descend on us. How can He deny His favor when we are mortifying ourselves for Him?

The Manu Samhita says:

> Whatever is hard to be traversed,
> Whatever is hard to be attained,
> Whatever is hard to be reached,
> Whatever is hard to be performed,
> All may he accomplished by austerities.

> yad dustaram yad durapam yad durgamam yucca duskaram
> sarbantu tapasa, sadhayam rapo hi durartikamam.
> (Edited by Jogendra Chandra Vidyaratna, Chapter II)

On the evening of the Chaitra sankranti, the last day of the Bengali year, the Gajaneswar is led in procession to the Charnkatala at the south end of the village. But there is no erection of charak, no feats under penance. A portion of ground just outside the village is cleansed and polished with cow dung by the Kotals of that end. The palanquin of the Lord is placed there, and after His worship, the gajan functionaries and the sannyasis settle up their accounts. Soon after the gajan party returns to the shrine of Old Siva.

There, to the Charaktala, the Kotals come back with their newborn children and lay them on the earth where the Lord's palanquin was placed. They prostrate themselves on the ground, and scratch a little bit of the said earth and tie it carefully in a knot at the end of their cloths. After taking possession of this valuable treasure they take back the empty vessels in which offerings had been brought by them to the deity. The vessels, however, were not entirely empty as the head sannyasi had left there for them the nectarine water of the Lord's feet, a highly prized substance for the whole community.

The bells ring and the drum throbs in the new year of Kanchanpur and the Old Siva's gajan is to be officially closed on this first day of the month of Baisakh. The Napit shaves the ascetics, and a Dutta householder distributes mustard oil and turmeric paste to the party. The priest first takes some oil and a handful of turmeric paste from the lamp and touches the threshold of Old Siva. The ascetics then follow his example, and also touch the feet of the priest and the head sannyasi with oil and turmeric. Then the articles are freely distributed among the sannyasis for rubbing on their bodies. Great is the joy of the sannyasis who take as much oil and turmeric to besmear their own as others' bodies; and the floor of the colonnade of Shivatala takes the golden yellow colour of the turmeric. (Mustard oil and turmeric are used in various purificatory and propitious rites of the Hindus. I do not pretend to fathom the philosophy behind such use.)

Mustard oil is then distributed to the functionaries of the gajan. The old Siva has his quota which, of course, goes to the priest. The different share-holders of sevait-ship (office of priesthood), the gajan Brahmin, the head sannyasi, the deulias (temple-bearers), the dhup-sannyasi (censer carrying ascetic), the head sannyasi of Dharmaraj, the Napit, the Chaukidar, the cleaner of the human heads of the crematorium dance, the sweeper of Shivtala, the Modak distributor of oil and turmeric, and many others receive their quota of oil as a mark of honour for their services to the gajan.

After a bath the ascetics return to the Shivtala, and now the utris (sannyasis' sacred threads) are to be taken off so that the votaries may return to their normal life. The Brahmin ascetics change their utris for their ordinary sacred thread; and the head sannyasi helps the clean castes. But being a true Brahmin, he refuses to take off the threads from the ascetics of the exterior castes, and asks them to wait until the gajan Brahmin turns up. But as they become restive, a young Brahmin ascetic declares that he does not care for the age-long traditions and takes off the sannyasis' thread from the low caste votaries who rejoice in the action.

Old Siva is worshipped and it is now the occasion to call the sixteen annas Brahmins of the village for the touch of the sacred charrings. So the Napit is deputed for the job and the zamindar is first to be informed. The Zamindar's son, other Brahmins and the ascetics get the touch of the sacred charrings according to priority, and with it the gajan rituals for the year come to a close.

Now comes at last the feast of the devotees, known as bhakta-bhojan in the village. A Paul family of the Subarnabanik caste is the donor of the feast and it is now regarded as a necessary part of the year's gajan to which it gives the finishing touch. The banquet consists of ordinary courses—bhat, dal, hodge-podge of veg-etables, another hodge-podge with fish bones and oily substance of fish, and lastly tak mixed with fish. But, coming just after the days of scanty food and austere liv-ing of the consecrated period, the ascetics greatly enjoy the feast. Many others, especially of the poorer class freely take their lunch at the Shivtala where the feast is held and then take platefuls of rice and curry for their home. As the feast is over, the villagers say that the gajan has truly ended, but you may see about month later another gajan, that of Dhanmaraj of the Bagdis.

8.6—The Miracle of Dharmaraj

The gajan of Dhannaraj takes place on the Baisakhi purinama (the full moon day of the Bengali month of Baisakh—April-May). On the tenth lunar day, the initiation of the head sannyasi and the temple-bearers takes place. On the eleventh comes the function of the wearing of the utri (sanyassis' sacred thread) for the general body of ascetics. It may be noted that there comes no votary to Dharmaraj from amongst the high castes. In the 1959 gajan there were a few ascetics from the clean castes of the Nabasakh group, and the head sannyasi of the Dharmaraj of Kanchanpur has all along been a Sadgop. The total number of ascetics for the year is twenty-five. On the twelfth day of the lunar fortnight, the Gajaneswar is taken in procession to the neighbouring villages of Kurman and Debagram. Dharmaraj is represented as Gajaneswar in a black stone shaped like the Narayan-sila of the upper caste Hindus, and is carried in a palanquin like the Gajaneswar Old Siva. On the thirteenth lunar day—the day on which the ascetics have to live on fruits—the gajan of Palashi treks to Chandrahati, while the Kurman party pays their return visit to Palashi. On the fourteenth, i.e. the day before the purinama, the ascetics have to fast, and take their god in procession through the village streets to different households which contribute their customary stipends to the Gajeneswar Dharmaraj. At nightfall, a miracle is supposed to happen—a visible manifestation of Dharma Thakur on earth. But before we come to this, let us understand who this village god is.

Anukul Pandit, the Bagdi priest of Dharmaraj, cannot tell us who his Thakur is, and we do not expect him to be able to do so when the learned Pandits of Bengal's culture differ amongst themselves. At present the god is known as Dharmaraj or Dharma, evidently a Hindu or a Buddhist name. But originally it was one of the village gods whom the pre-Aryan inhabitants of Radh (i.e. the western part of Bengal beyond the Bhagirathi) used to worship. The Aryan influence could not penetrate in this country of Radh before the third century B.C., and the village gods retained their original characteristics till that date. They were the presiding deities of the village, to whom the inhabitants prayed in diseases and disasters. Usually they were considered to reside in some crude stone or a tree on the village border or beyond; they were almost always worshiped with animal sacrifices. Our present Dharmaraj is pre-Aryan to the core, though outwardly there is an influence of Buddhist or Hindu religion on him.

Dharmaraj, as we have seen, is the great god of the exterior castes, who were originally the pre-Aryan tribes of this eastern part of India. Even his priests belong to the exterior castes, and if a Brahmin happens to be his priest, he is considered a degraded Brahmin. When, in the reign of the Bauddha (Buddhist) Pals (eighth to twelfth centuries) Buddhism was spreading in the country of Radh, this pre-Aryan god, in order to save himself took the name of Dharma, a name from Buddhist literature and religion. Dharmaraj is also another name of Lord Buddha. From there also Dhannaraj came to be represented by a tortoise-shaped stone resembling a Buddhist stupa. The gajan festival of Dharmaraj is usually held at Baisakhi-Purnima which is otherwise known as Buddha-Purnima, as this particular day is taken to be the birth date of Lord Buddha. Further, the ascetics of Dharmaraj proclaim victory to Adi-deb Dharmaraj Niranjan at the time of the gajan. Adi-deb and Niranjan are both epithets as well as names of Lord Buddha.

On the ruins of Buddhism the Saivas raised their flags in Bengal. The old village god, already named Dharmaraj, then came to be marked with traits of Saivism and the gajans of both the deities were considerably influenced by each other. Later, in the sixteenth century, Raghunandab, the great juriconsult of Bengal, prescribed for Dharmaraj the code of rites of a Hindu God. Dharmaraj is now often identified as the Dharmaraj of the Hindu Pantheon, who is none other than Yama—the god of death. Or he is said to be the same as Vishnu—(the original god) of the Hindu. Thus we see Dharmaraj is a many-faced god; but let us now go back to the night of the fourteenth lunar day to see his manifestation on earth to receive the annual worship from his votaries of Kanchanpur.

You enter the site of the god Dharma. His temple is a south facing small hut built of mud walls and straw thatched with holes through which parts of the blue sky are visible. In front there is a stretch of land on which stand three big peepal trees and one krishna-chuda shrub.

Already an assemblage is thickening there.

With permission from the priest, and putting off your shoes, you enter the temple of the god. A strong smell of country liquor makes you look at one corner where you may find a couple of big earthen jars that you know later to be the "treasury" of Dharma (Dharma's bhandar). But you first approach the throne of the god and find the tortoise shaped idol no larger than a closed human fist. Surrounding him and his throne, you see a good many of the Hindu gods and goddesses in corresponding sizes as well as the village god Kalu Rai and goddess Didi-Thakrun. On the throne itself, by the side of Dharma, are Jagodya, Manasa and Kalu Rai. It is said that Kalu Rai is an old village god and is otherwise called Dharma Thakur in some parts of Bengal. Besides the throne the pancha-devata, that is, the five recognized deities (Vishnu, Siva, Sakti, Ganesh, and Surya) of the Hindus are also to be seen. The Pundits of Bengal's culture have described these gods as abaran-devata (encircling gods) who have been brought to the scene to give a cover of Hinduism to the pre-Aryan stone-god. Also in the puja rites next day, all the reputed gods of Hinduism, and those in the village as well, were called at the altar by the ascetics to receive their worship and obeisance.

Outside, a group of crude stones, representing the god Panchanan, occupies the earthen altar under the krishna-chuda tree. Two more earthen altars have been raised under two of the peepal trees. On one there has been planted an akanda shrub which is known to have won the favor of Lord Siva as well. This is the Akanda-tola where the Dharmaraj is to be worshiped next morning with due rites and sacrifices. On the third altar under another peepal tree, the Dharmaraj who is going to descend on earth as a wood-pole, is to be planted and worshiped.

The drummer

The God Dharmaraj amidst encircling gods and attended by a Bagdi
priest

Ganjaneswar Dharmaraj at the Panchanantala

The fourteenth lunar night arrives and the god becomes visible in the sacrificial vessel (koshakushi) of the worshiping priest at the temple but where a

hair-like shadow appears on the Ganges water of the pot. It is an indication that the god has come in the form of a pole and is to be found in the big Dutta's tank. The position of the shadow in the water vessel at the temple informs the priest of the exact position where the pole is to be searched for in the tank. The revelation does not come to a stranger like you, nor even to the eyes of the head ascetic, but the priest sees it and announces to the votaries and others the location of the god-pole in the tank. Drum-beats throb and the flower-dropping ceremony begins. As a flower is dropped from the convex head of the god, it is understood that sanction has been obtained to begin the rites for the year's puja. The Gajan-eswar god is carried in procession to the southern ghat (bathing place) of the big Dutta's tank, where the ghat-puja is done. Then the ascetics make their digh pranam (the long prostration) from the ghat of the said tank to the temple of the Dharmaraj.

Time has now come to fetch the god-pole from the tank and install him on the altar under the peepal tree.

Already men and women, boys and girls have come in flocks to the Dutta tank. There are vigilant visitors from nearby villages. All have thronged to the western embankment as the priest has said that the god is to rise at that end. Thousand eager eyes are fixed and happily the full moon is on her throne. Often the desecrating rays of electric torchlights flash, "Oh, there, there what is that small patch of a black shadow? Is it the head of the pole?"

The sannyasis headed by the priest have already jumped into the water and are swimming towards the place. Suddenly the priest is submerged, but he gets up again. Words ring forth from the audience "He has got it, he has got it". The priest gets under water and gets up, as if he is wrestling with his god to make him secure. Finally he triumphs, and the god-pole floats flat on the waters of the tank, and all the ascetics lay their hands on him.

In the meantime the god has been garlanded, and the sannyasis pull him up to the western ghat. There, before he is lifted, puja is offered with due rites, and a goat is sacrificed. As the priest sprinkles the blood over the head and body of the pole, the ascetics cry: "Glory to Adideb Dharmaraj Niranjan." He is then brought to the altar amidst shouts of such glories, and leans there on the trunk of the pee-pal tree. Thereafter the rite of mukta-dhowa is performed in which the brushings and washings of the temple are ceremonially thrown into the waters of the tank. It is already past midnight and the recess for the night begins.

The puja on the Purnima day begins with a ceremony at the rising dawn, and ends with bisarjan of the god-pole at the Chand Dutta's tank in the evening. We have already seen that in course of the puja of the Dharma god, honor is paid to all the great gods and goddesses of Hinduism. But the great feature in the worship of the day is the slaughter of a good number of goats as offerings to the deity. Sacrificial blood flows at the altar of the akanda shrub, at the altar of the god-pole, at the altar of God Panchanan under the krishna-chuda tree, in front of the temple door of Dharmaraj, and finally at the ghat when the god-pole is pushed to the tank in the act of bisarjan. The blood of the sacrificed animals is sprinkled over the fetish pole and stones—and all this in the name of Dharmaraj Niranjan, who is no other than Buddha, the great "Light of Asia".

Three days after the act of bisarjan, the god-pole vanishes from the surface of the water in the Chand Dutta's tank. I do not know nor have I seen how it vanishes, but the villagers say that it does. In this connection what was written twenty-five years ago in *Kanchanpur Revisited* may also be quoted here as the attitude and belief of the people remains substantially the same.

The people here believe that the appearances and disappearances of the pole are caused by the divine power of Dharmaraj. Despite repeated attempts to solve it, the mystery remains. Many traditions have now come to be associated with the incident. I have not met anyone who has himself kept watch; but they knew persons who did and who are now all dead. They once organized a strong party for the purpose, but towards the end of the night there came such a terrible storm with thunder and lightening that they were obliged to take shelter in a nearby house. But, wonder of wonders, in a minute or two the storm had subsided and returning to the sides of the tank, they no longer found any trace of the pole. I have heard this story from apparently trustworthy persons.

> There are even more stories connected with the matter. How people tied the god-pole to a tree and how, in the morning, they found the knots still tied and quite unchanged, but the pole had vanished. Some again carried the pole to their home on the third night, but in the morning it was to be found neither in the room nor outside it. It is superfluous to add that those activities enraged Dharmaraj and the families of those who thus defiled the god became extinct. Some even think—but they are the illiterate peasants—that their god had

given a pratyadesh (command given in a dream) to the first priest, that any-body who would spy on his going away would fall a victim to his anger and his family would be removed from the face of the earth. And they would point out to you the ruins of the houses of once flourishing families, like those of the Days Mandals, to whom our writer the Rev. Day belonged, who attempted the impossible and have consequently paid the price.

It is natural to doubt the authenticity of these statements, but the villagers contend that reason cannot explain the following events in this connection:

(1) How does the hair-like shadow appear in the priest's sacred pot of water?

(2) How is it that the pole is thrown into one tank and that it comes out in the other next year? Moreover, the people here are definite that the same pole does not appear every year, and that in all the villages in the vicinity there is not a single craftsman who is expert enough to make one like it.

(3) How is it that the pole appears in a vertical position and that when thrown into the water after the puja it floats quite flat?

(4) And lastly, but not least wonderful, how does it disappear always in the third night, and why has nobody ever been able to see it vanish?

If you, my gentle reader, do not believe these things, I invite you to come with me, for I too have been challenged by the people of Kanchanpur, to come to their village on the day previous to the Baisakhi purnima, to stay there for some four days in order to try and find out what takes place. The people are confident that I will fail for they believe most strongly that the mir-acle is wrought by the divinity of their god, Dharmaraj.

Twenty-five years later I come back to the village and describe what I see and feel in the ordinary course of things. If the mystery seems unresolved to you even now, I would like you, my gentle reader, to come to the village and look into the matter personally. Your diligence may possibly rip up the mystery but till then who is there so bold as not to believe in the annual miracle of Dharmaraj? The villagers continue to show an attitude as much as to say: "There are more things in heaven and earth, Horatio."

The altar at Dharmatala

The procession of Mukta-dhowa

The last flicker

8.7—Superstitions and Taboos

My American friend writes to me in a letter: "It is stated by the Rev. Day in his book that Bengali peasants would never answer a call at night unless three times repeated because of their fear of the goddess Nishi. Is that still so nowadays? Is it also even now usual for a married woman to wear an iron circlet around her wrist? Further, when the lizard chirps is it still regarded as a bad omen so much so that an important journey would be postponed?"

During my stay in Kanchanpur I tried to get answers to these questions.

"The belief in Nishi is fading," said an educated young man of the village, but his statement was immediately contradicted by others. Sri Ray, an elderly gentleman of the village, related how he had saved Patal Samanta from the clutches of a Nishi. N. Bauri, the village chowkidar, narrated his personal experience of how he was deluded by a Nishi one night in his young days. Hearing a call at night he came out and saw a clothed and veiled female person standing at a distance of a few steps.

The womanly figure moved and he followed it through the streets of the village beyond the human habitat and found himself standing in the fields of the southern end. But suddenly, through God's grace, he became aware of the situation, and turning back he made a run and did not stop till he reached his home.

Sri B.C., the head-master of the village school, then told several real stories of Nish-bhut and other village ghosts of whom he had personal experience. He related how Bhim Sardar of his native village, a man of prodigious strength and the leader of his caste, had been decoyed by Nishi, and found missing for several days. When all attempts to trace him failed, an ojha (exorcist) was consulted. He uttered his formula and made his calculation, and found out that Bhim had been confined by a Nishibhut on the top of a big simul (silk-cotton) tree about twelve miles south-east of the village. Agreeably to his findings Bhim's person was discovered and the ojha recovered him from the arrest of the Nishi. There was a heap of fish-bones beside him on a branch of the tree, and Bhim was till then alive. But his days were numbered as a man who is touched by Nishi cannot live much longer. The general opinion of the assembly was that Nishi does exist, and the best way to foil her malign action is not to respond to the first three calls at night. It is the belief that Nishi imitates the human voice to decoy her victims, but she calls only three times. If the voice is repeated for the fourth time, the inmates become sure that it is not ghostly and may then safely respond to the call. The belief is still quite strong amongst the illiterate working classes of the community.

A word maybe said in this connection as to the belief in the existence of ghosts in general. The general view is that there must be a bhut-yoni (ghost life), though the same is not visible to us in particular forms. The Narayan-sila, the village crematorium is believed to be inhabited by several village ghosts, and there are many stories of how they play tricks on persons who happen to pass by the place at dead of night. Ordinarily, the people will avoid that place after nightfall. The village ghosts are very fond of exercising their influence over young women, and last year two young girls, one a Gop daughter and the other a Goswami bou, were taken possession of by them. The ojhas (ghost-doctors), however, were quite competent to treat the cases and cured the victims of the demoniacal agency of the bhuts.

It is believed that people who die of accidents or resort to suicide become bhuts and their spirits hover in the air till they receive proper funeral cakes at the pret-sila—a mountain at Gaya where obsequial offerings are given to those who are supposed to have become evil spirits after death. I was told by some elderly persons that formerly there had been a good many ghosts at Kanchanpur. But now with the construction of the railways, Gaya can be easily reached and pindas (funeral cakes) can be duly offered at the pret-silo for the benefit of the tortured souls of the departed. When they receive the offerings they become free from the bondage of bhut-yoni (life of ghosts). As a result the bhuts have become very rare even in a village like Kanchanpur.

The answer to the second question of my American friend is a simple affirmative, as a married woman in the village invariably wears an iron circlet around her wrist even now. A woman may part with all her ornaments, but not the iron wristlet as long as her husband is alive. "Let the iron circlet on your hand be everlasting" is the most precious blessing that a married woman receives from her elders.

In reply to the third question of my friend it has to be observed that even now an important journey has to be postponed if a lizard chirps at the moment of start. It is said that the lizard had eaten up the cut-off tongue of Khans (the woman astrologer of traditional fame), and since then its chirpings reveal the past and the future of human life.

It is apparent from what has been said above that a villager's life is still hedged in by numerous restrictions and superstitions. Like the lizard's chirp, the sneezing of a human being is also considered a good or a bad omen according to the circumstances of the situation. Important journeys have also to be postponed, if, on the point of departure, one sees an empty jar, an empty boat, a beardless man, or a crying crow on a dead branch. If one has to enumerate all these things it will be a long list, but a few more superstitions and taboos are noted below as they display a peculiar aspect of the village mind.

One should not eat neem or anything bitter on a Sunday. One should not give or purchase cow dung cakes on either a Saturday or a Tuesday. There is prohibition against cutting of bamboos on Saturdays, Sundays and Tuesdays. One would not sell anything hairy on a Monday, and paddy should not be sold on a Wednesday. Though there is no such restriction for their purchases on festivals and ceremonial days, one is not to boil paddy, husk it or fry it. On such days clothes are not be sent to the washerman, nor are they to be boiled for washing at home. One is also not to take any roasted food on these days. As it happened, on the day when puja offerings were being sent by the villagers to the place of Didi-Thakrun, our servant inadvertently purchased a few brinjals for our food. For this he was severely reprimanded by the daughters-in-law of our friend's family. All these are social injunctions that have to be strictly obeyed, and their sanction lies in the irrational fear of the unknown in the minds of our villagers. "This is an age-old custom which nobody has been seen to break. If it is broken some unusual event something disastrous may happen. Therefore it should not be broken." Such is the attitude of our villagers. Some even try to justify prohibitions and taboos with incomprehensible arguments based on planetary and stellar influences.

Before the topic is closed it is desirable to point out a few charms and amulets that are in fashion at Kanchanpur. To begin with, I quote a passage from "*Kanchanpur Revisited*".

> You come out early in the morning and at your door you see a naked boy of some ten years whistling to himself. He wears a string round his waist, and to the string is attached a punched pice. On his ankle there gleams an iron ring. If you ask him why he wears these things; he would wonder at your ignorance and would explain to you that since he had been born after his two elder brothers had died in their infancy, it is the custom to wear these protective charms.

The iron circlet round the ankle is known as (god) Dharma's shackles, and it is the general belief that Mama (god of death) can not take away such a child who wears god Dharma's chain. There are various other methods in which a village mother fights her battle against the god of death. A woman who brings forth children that do not usually live long, symbolically sells away her child as soon as it is born either to the midwife or any other woman of the village. By such sale, the goha of the child is changed. It no longer belongs to the mother and it is hoped that Death would not, therefore, be interested to take it Usually the sale price is one or more cowries and accordingly the child is named Ek-kadi (one cowrie), Do-kadi, Tri-kadi, Partch-kadi and so on. Sometimes the transfer is made on receipt of a khud (a broken bit of rice), in which case the child is named Khudiram. Sometimes a child may not be transferred, but he is given loathsome, repelling names such as Guey (faecal), Narule (hellish) or Pasha (putrid) in the belief that the god of death will certainly disdain to touch one so obnoxiously named. Also there is a custom of piercing the ear or nose of a new-born child in the hope that a defective infant is not fit to be taken away by any god.

Besides the above popular charms and practices, Kanchanpur has the good offices of a Grahacharya (astrologer) Pandit of the village of Bara Belun. He pays regular business visits to Kanchanpur. When I was first introduced to him, he greeted me with a Sanskrit couplet and gave me to understand that he was no less a person than the Darbar-Acharya (court astrologer) of the ex-Nawab of Murshidabad. He is famed for his accuracy of heavenly calculations and power of foretelling the future events of life from the horoscope of any person. He is believed to have powers to ward off the present and future evil influences working against his clients by various yajnas (ceremonial functions)—such as nabagraha jag santi-swastyayan or shyama-swastyayan and the like. Further, he prepares various charms and distributes effective kabachas (amulets) on payment of suitable fees. Thus he gives Lakshmi-kabach for prosperity, Nabagraha-kabach for success, Mafia-Bagala-habach for removing distress and difficulties, and several other kabachas for this or that purpose. It appears that our Grahacharya has a good clientele in the village, and the eager welcome what is accorded to him whenever he visits the place indicates Kanchanpur's profound faith in him.

CHAPTER 9

▼

CONCLUSIONS

Kanchanpur presents a drama of forces that play on New India's villages. Here is a type of rural culture that is rooted in traditions but has now to face the changes and developments due to independence and a changing civilization. Means of external contacts and relations with the outer social environment are ever increasing, and the old traditional structure of the village society is apparently quaking with the dynamism of the new age. Twenty-five years ago it appeared that Kanchanpur had not changed; now it is certainly changing. Since Independence came, Government itself has become an agent of change; but, after all, it has to be admitted that the rate of change is a great deal slower than is appreciated by our reformers and city-dwellers.

Viewed from the stand-point of space, the village has been brought nearer to the town of Vardhamana and through it to the bigger outside world. In the dry season, a bus runs twice or thrice a day on the Burdwan-Kusumgram road and Jeep trucks and motor lorries come to the heart of the village. The road is being metaled under the second five-year plan, and the villagers are looking ahead for the time when daily bus service will be a regular feature throughout the year.

The coming of the canal has been referred to. It has not only brought waters to the fields of Kanchanpur, but it has also caused the village itself to come closer to Vardhamana. The distance from Burdwan to Kanchanpur when the village is approached through the path on the embankment of the canal has been short-ened and one can ride on a bicycle even in the rainy season, if the weather has been dry for a couple of days.

In the economic sector, the noticeable change is that land has become an object of investment in the village world, and it is coveted by all the classes culti-vating or non-cultivating. As a result land has been concentrated in the upper caste, who are generally rich but do not hold the plow themselves. In Kanchan-pur at present 60% of the village lands are held by them, while only 10% of the lands are held by the agricultural castes. In consequence, there is a proportion-ately large growth in the number of agricultural labourers in the population, with a non-working landowning class on the top.

Changes from traditional caste occupations may be noted, and it seems that the caste system has been shaken mainly in its occupational aspect by the rude forces of the economic world. But the core of the caste system with its current esoteric background, its restrictions on intermarriage and commensality still remains entrenched in our village world.

The sails of the Zamindar and rent-receiving class have been deflated on the surface of village life. Machine-made goods have also displaced many of the old occupationists, such as the village weaver, the blacksmith, the oil-presser, the paddy husker and so on. Western medicine has come to be introduced in the vil-lages and the Kavirajs with their dasamula and rasasindur and other indigenous remedies have left the arena. Instead has come the allopathic physician with pen-icillin and streptomycin and similar such shafts in the quiver in his battle against the diseases of mankind. It may be noted that there is an unqualified homeopath in the village, but his practice thrives because he does not charge any fee, and at the same time distributes his doses of medicine very cheap. But in serious cases, the villager thinks it necessary to go to or call the allopath.

In cultivation, chemical fertilizers have come to be used. New varieties of paddy and sugarcane have been introduced, but for what particular reason and with what benefit are not exactly ascertained. Traditional agricultural processes are followed, and there is little technological improvement in the implements. The bullocks, the wooden plow, the hoe and the scythe still do their jobs. An improved pattern of sugarcane press, however, has come in use.

In the ways of living, tea has come to be used as a cheap general drink. Some families of the rich upper castes have introduced an element of wheat in their diet.

English pattern of costumes such as coats, shirts, chemise, saia, blouses, frocks and pinnies have been slowly introduced in our village, and have now become quite common. If we look at the inventory of semi-durable goods, especially of the rich upper castes, another list of English names is presented to our eyes—i.e., table, chair, shelf, dock, watch, bicycle, torch, petromax, hurricane lantern and so on. In the arena of marriage and home-making, what is first noticed is a rise in the age of marriage, especially amongst the upper castes. The present Indian legislators do not follow the shastric directive that girls are to be married before they attain the age of puberty. On the other hand child marriage has been prohibited in law. Still girls have to be given in marriage, as the customs of our village would still require it. Whether the parents or guardians have means or not, the girls must be married off. The difference from earlier ages only lies in the fact that the crisis is felt not at the eleventh year of the girl, but when she has passed her teens. Then it is time for the father, or any other guardian, to take recourse to any means—begging, borrowing or selling properties—but the girl has to be married, as the life of an unmarried girl is incompatible with the traditions of Kanchanpur.

The matchmaker has no longer his job; but all the marriages are arranged by the parents and relatives. Romantic love has not got any footing as yet in the village world, and no civil marriage has taken place in Kanchanpur. The marriage rites have not changed.

The feudal values of womanhood still prevail. The men do not share the household duties—they are not even expected to do so.

In the upper castes the joint family is even now the dominant type, though in the exterior castes the nuclear type is more familiar. In joint families, the mother-in-law is still the mistress of the house, and the "bou" has a subordinate place. The male dominance cannot be overlooked in the relation between husbands and wives in our rural families.

Primary education has been made free and compulsory, but the guardians do not think it convenient to send their girls to the school. The same is true for the labouring class boys as well.

The school has got its own site and building with some modern equipment such as tables, chairs and benches. This has contributed to the creating of a salubrious climate for growth of school life at Kanchanpur. The old disciplinary method of the village pathsala has vanished, and the child enjoys more liberty, if not more reverence. The children no longer play the truant and they have come to love the school as their own. Most of the students expressed that they love the school more than their home. The school subjects seem to cover in elementary lines all the studies which a student has to pursue in secondary or higher education. Formerly the mother tongue, and whatever they learnt became useful to them in future. But now-a-days the primary course attempts to be integrated to the secondary and higher subjects. But as most of the pupils drop away and do not go for the secondary course, their little knowledge in various subjects does not help them much in the future. The village guardians at least are apprehensive of the new education.

Kanchanpur, we have seen, is growing politically conscious. Here we can say that the village is moving out to embrace a new way of thought and form, that is, democratic faith and values.

A new type of leadership that acts as an intermediary between the official and the village world is also emerging. The new leaders come from the young educated group, and usually love to participate in social work and devote a substantial part of their life to such activities. They possess democratic leadership in them, and do not dictate through coercion and compulsion. At the same time they have to serve as a link between their village community and the outside official world—or various urban organizations and institutions. The new situation created by the elective Panchayat, development projects and urban connections etc. has brought them to the front. At Kanchanpur a young man of the Kayastha caste has emerged as an Adhyaksha at present. His relationships with the officials of the Headquarters and the Development Block, his links with the influential leaders of the District Congress, his devotion to social work in his community have placed him and his associates in the role of leadership. It is hoped that he will continue to head the community activities of Kanchanpur for the betterment of his village for the coming years.

Least change is noticed in the ritual structure of the village and the tenets and practices connected therewith. Slowness of ritual changes has been referred to in the evolution of the god Dharmaraj. There we have seen the indigenous form of worship of the original inhabitants firmly rooted within in spite of the layers spread over it by intrusive Buddhism and Hinduism. And Dharmaraj may be taken to be a symbol of the entire culture pattern of Kanchanpur. In spite of the already mentioned changes, in spite of the apparent ascendancy of the new age, Kanchanpur's culture is still ancient and medieval to the core. Its basic texture, depending on the age-old rice economy, on the position of the exterior castes as the backbone of agricultural labour, on its multiple society consisting of the hierarchical caste system with its esoteric background, on the feudal values of womanhood, on old fashioned ideals of marriage and home-making, and lastly on ancient beliefs and practices of religion, appears to be sufficiently tough to resist any abrupt change and keep its major content intact against the onslaught of the so-called modern forces.

Glossary of Terms

Abaran-devata—Encircling gods

Adi-deb—Original god—an epithet of Dharma or Buddha

Adhyaksha—President

Agrahayan—Bengali month corresponding to November-December.

Aguri—(or Ugra-Kshatriyas)—a caste engaged chiefly in husbandry.

Akanda—A kind of shrub (Calotropis gigantica)

Alna—A wooden frame for hanging clothes

Arran—The principal crop of rice; Winter rice.

Anchal—Region

Anna—The sixteenth part of a rupee

Annaprasana—The ceremony of giving rice for food to an infant for the first time

Annapurna—A Hindu goddess

Arat—Warehouse

Arundhati—Name of a star; also the name of the wife of the sage Vasishtha

Asan—Seat

Ashar-nabami—The ninth lunar day in the month of Ashar (June-July)

Asirbad—Benediction

Asura—Demon

Asvatha—Peepal tree; Ficus religiosa

Auksal—A temporary hut raised for extracting juice of the sugar cane and turning it into molasses.

Aus—Spring rice; literally ripening in a short time

Avatar—Incarnation

Ayurvedic—Relating to the Hindu system of medicine.

Baan—Flood
Babu—Hindu gentleman
Badal—Rains
Badhai—Name of a festival
Bael—Aegle Marmelos
Bagdi—A low-caste Hindu
Baidya—A high-caste Hindu
Baikuntha—Heavenly abode of the God Vishnu
Baisakh—First month of Bengali year corresponding to April-May.
Baishnab—A follower of Vishnu especially in the form of Chaitanya
Bakchur—A variety of rice
Bakula—Minusops Elengi
Bata-bhakta—Female votaries: or those Sannyasis who do not perform cremato-
rium rites
Bamun—A colloquial term for Brahmin
Bansnagra—A variety of rice
Baralat—The Viceroy of India in British days
Baraghar—Big hut
Baran—Ceremonial welcome
Barga—Class
Bargadar—Share-cropper
Banwari—A community organization
Bari—Little balls made of mashed pulse, dried in the sun, and used in curry or
fried separately
Basanta-Chandi—The name of the village goddess presiding over small-pox
Basanti Vernal—A Hindu goddess worshiped in the spring season—another
form of Durga
Bat—Ficus indica
Batasa—A light cake of sugar.
Bati Bowl Bayen—A low caste Hindu
Bene—Colloquial for Banik
Bhadra—A Bengali month (August-Septemher)
Bhadralok—Gentle folk
Bhakta-bhojan—A feast to the devotees
Bhag-chasi—Share-cropper
Bhandar—Store or treasury

Bharat—India
Bhat—Rice
Bhatar—A colloquial term for husband
Bhek—Assuming mendicants garb
Bhujna—Same as annaprasan
Bhut-yoru—Ghost-life
Bichuti—A stinging nettle (Tragic involucrata)
Bigha—About a third part of an acre
Bilat—England
Biri (Bidi)—A kind of cigarette
Bisarjan—Immersion ceremony
Bombai—A variety of sugarcane
Born—A variety of rice
Bostom—A colloquial word for Baishnab
Bou—Daughter-in-law
Brahma—A Hindu God
Brahmin—A Hindu caste, occupying the *Sanctum Sanctorum*
Brata—Vow
Byagra-Kshatriya—Same as Bagdi

Chaddar—A sheet worn as an upper garment
Chaitra—Last month of the Bengali year (March-April)
Chandal—A low-born caste
Charka—Spinning-wheel
Charaktala—The place where Charak (i.e. ceremony of swinging) is held
Charanamrita—Water in which the foot of a deity or Brahmin has been washed
Chasa—Plowman
Chatuinukhi—A variety of rice; bits as small as the nails of a sparrow
Chhabi—Picture
Chhal—Feigning
Chhai—Mat-roof
Chhatnatala—An awning under which the marriage ceremony is performed
Chhotolat—Literally the lesser lord; Governor of the province in British times
Chhotolok—Smaller men or debased men
Chun—Lime
Chunari—Manufacturer of lime

Dagra-salami—Fee to the village adolescents—paid for refraining from stoning any marriage party

Dai—Midwife

Dakhina—Fee to Priests; Southern

Dal—Pulse

Darbar-acharva—Court astrologer

Dasamula—A kind of indigenous medicine composed of the roots of vegetables

Devottar—Endowed for the support of an idol

Deulia—Carrier of the temple (i.e., palanquin) of an idol.

Dhali-Karma—A variety of rice

Dhane—Coriander seeds

Dharmaraj—A village god

Dhawa—Name of Kanchanpur's Muslims

Dhelabhangani—Same as Dagra-Salami

Dhruba—Polestar

Dhup-Sannyasi—Censer-carrying ascetic

Dhuti (Dhoti)—A piece of cloth usually five yards long

Didi-Thakrun—A village goddess

Dighi—An oblong tank

Digh-Pranam—Long prostration made to deity

Dingi—A small boat

Do-kadi—Two cowries

Dom—A low caste Hindu

Dud-kalma—A variety of rice

Dule—A low sub-caste among the Bagdis

Dull—A litter usually for carrying women

Duo—Goddess of Adversity in "Dingi" Festival

Durga—A Hindu Goddess

Durga-Mandap—An open shed where Goddess Durga is worshiped

Durva—A kind of grass

Ek-kadi—One cowrie

Fatua—A short-upper garment for males

Gandha-banik—Spice-dealer caste (jal-chal)

Gandheswari—A Hindu goddess, especially worshiped by the Gandhabanik caste

Gajan—A folk festival in honor of such village deities, as Siva, Dharma or Manasa

Gajaneswar—The presiding deity of gajan

Gamcha—Bathing towel

Genji—Guernsey

Ghat—Landing place in a tank or river

Ghatak—Professional match-maker

Ghatwal—A low caste Hindu; keeper of the passes

Ghee—Clarified butter

Ghorasal—A variety of rice

Goala—Milkmen (a caste)

Gobindahhogh—A variety of rice

Gop—Same as goalas

Gossain—A Baishnab Brahmin; a spiritual director

Goswami—Same as Gossain

Gokal—Period of cow-serving

Golancha—A kind of flower or shrub

Gonar—Bully

Gorai—A jal-achal caste

Goylachatar—Milkmen's court

Gotra—Lineage, race

Graha—Planets

Grahacharya—Astrologer

Gram-sabha—Village assembly

Grihini—House-mother

Gur—Molasses

Guru—Spiritual director

Gurumashai—A teacher in the village pathsala

Haimanti—Relating to Hemanta season (Oct-Dec.) for paddy, same as aman

Handi—Pot, usually made of earth and used for cooking

Hari—Another name for God Vishnu

Harijan—Beloved of God, a term used by Mahatma Gandhi for the low castes

Harircharan—Feet of (god)

Hari Haritaki—Myrobalan tree or fruit

Hat—Market

Hatisal—A variety of rice

Hattala—Market place Hooks

Hookah—Smoking apparatus
Hom—Sacrificial offerings to fire

Isaneswar—A name of Siva

jal-achal—Refers to castes from whom water is not accepted by the high castes
jal-chal—Castes from whose hands's water may be accepted
jat—Caste
Jatra—Village theater
jhingasal—A variety of rice
Jhoro—Falling paddy—a spurious variety
Jnati Agnates; kins
Jogadya—Another form of Goddess Sakti

Kabach—Amulet
Kabi—A debating entertainment by village poets
Kachheri—Cutcherry
Kalbarta—Fishermen caste
Kajule—A variety of sugarcane
Kak—Crow
Kal-Bhairab—A village god
Kati—Hindu Goddess
Kaliyuga—The fourth or present age according to the Hindus

Malakar—The gardener caste; florist
Manasa—The snake goddess
Mandap—An open shed
Mlechha—Unclean; non-Hindu; out-castes; savage tribes
Modak—Confectioner caste
Marai—Storehouse of paddy
Mashaipara—Ward of the schoolmasters
Mukta-dhowa—A ceremony in Dharmapuja, in which brushings and washings of the temple are thrown in tank
Mul-Sannyasi—Head ascetic in gajan festivals
Muri—Parched rice

Nabasakh—Nine branches, traditional nine castes from whose hands water is accepted

Natgar-Sankirian—Mass prayers and songs through city streets
Nagdi—Peon
Nagra—A variety of rice
Napit—A barber
Nama-Sudra—A low-caste Hindu
Narayan—A Hindu God; another name of Vishnu
Nataraj—Name of Siva, literally the king of dancers
Navanna—Literally new rice; the festival of first fruits
Neem—Margosa tree
Nilkantha—Another name of Mahadeb
Nil-Shasthi—The Shashti goddess who is worshiped on Nilpuja day
Niranjan—An epithet and name of Dharma and Buddha
Nirmalya—Cast-off flowers of god
Nishi—Night; Personification of night in the form of a female ghost
Nitya-seva—Daily worship

Ojha—Ghost doctor

Palash—Butea frondosa
Palki—Palanquin
Pallav-gop—Milkmen caste
Palui—A stack of straw
Pancha-devata—five deities of the Hindus, namely Vishnu, Siva, Sakti, Ganesh, and Surya
Panchanan—The five-faced god
Panchayat—A statutory village Council
Panchkari—Five cowries

Sadarjama—Revenue payable to Government
Saha—The wine-seller caste
Saiva—Votary of Siva
Sakta—Votary of Sakti
Sakti—The female energy of Divinity
Sala—Literally wife's brother; used as a term of abuse
Salgram—A black oval shaped plain stone representing god Narayan
Sambhunath—Name of Siva
Samkranti—Last day of the Bengali month
Sampradan—The ceremony of gift of a girl in marriage

Sandesh—A kind of sweetmeat
Sanjpuja—Evening worship
Sankalpa—Resolution before god
Sannyasi—An ascetic
Santal—A hill tribe
Santhal—Same as Santal
Sapta-padi—A marriage rite in which the bride and the groom walk seven steps together
Sara—A species of reed (Sakharum Sara)
Saraswati—Goddess of learning
Sardars—Chieftains, leaders
Sari—Women's wearing cloth
Shashthi—Goddess of fecundity and protectress of children
Satpak—A marriage rite, seven bindings
Satranj—A coarse Indian cotton carpet
Satyanarayan—Name of a god
Satyapir—A folk god or some saint of the Muslims
Sabha—Assembly
Sajjatolaru—Fee exacted for allowing the bridegroom to get up from vasarghar
Sevait—The manager or priest of an endowed temple
Shastric—Relating to Scriptures
Sida—A gift of rice, pulses, vegetables, oil etc.
Sil—Curry stone
Simul—Silk-cotton
Sindur—Vermilion
Sindur-dan—A marriage rite in which the bridegroom paints the bride's head with vermilion
Sindurtopor—Vermilion topped
Sinni—Offerings of sweets etc. to God (a word from Persian language)

Vaishnab—same as Baishnab

HINDU CUSTOMS IN BENGAL

Basanta Coomar Bose

Editor's Introduction

▼

Hindu Customs in Bengal was written by Basanta Coomar Bose who describes himself as Advocate, High Court, Calcutta. The book was dedicated "To My Wife, Part Authoress Of This Book" and was originally published by Girinda Nath Mitra (The Book Company Ltd.) in Calcutta. The date of publication is uncertain. The author states that the book was written in 1875. It contains references to personal experiences as early as 1858 and as late as 1926. It is not known how many editions were published.

Hindu Customs in Bengal describes intimate details of everyday life in Bengal, things which are utterly hidden from outsiders and probably not known even to the most dauntless of sociologists. Since the book is old, possibly some of the customs have changed, particularly after the onslaught of movies and television. However, in a social sense Bengal is a very conservative society and it is likely that the book still provides an accurate description of Bengali customs. Of course, only a Bengali would know and the book talks about things that Bengalis do not talk about.

Obvious spelling mistakes in English have been corrected. Otherwise the book is as the author wrote it. Apparent spelling mistakes of Bengali words have not been corrected since there is a natural variability in the spelling of Bengali nouns.

Richard Stevenson

AUTHOR'S INTRODUCTION

▼

I intend describing the customs that prevailed in Bengal half a century ago, many of which are either becoming obsolete or are not observed today. In process of time most of them will become obsolete, and I therefore think it necessary to record them for the benefit of posterity. There are customs in different parts of India, but as I happen to know very little about the customs prevailing outside Bengal, I shall confine myself principally to Bengal where I have spent the best part of my life. I shall make very few comments upon the customs as they may be unpalatable to orthodox Hindus, but they have no right to complain if mere facts are stated. I have no doubt that future generations will laugh at some of our customs but they will like to know what sort of people their ancestors were. If anybody asks what my justification is for writing such a book, my reply is that there is no book on the subject as far as I am aware. There are books on the several castes and sects among the Hindus, their feasts, festivals, and religious ceremonies. These books are concerned with the religious beliefs and ceremonies of the Hindus. I am not concerned with the religious beliefs of any person. In fact I shall try my best to avoid the religious aspect of Hindu customs and beliefs. I shall try my best to narrate facts as they are but shall have nothing to do with the Hindu religion, though it affects the daily life of every Hindu and influences almost all his daily acts.

The orthodox Hindus may feel insulted at my disclosure of certain facts but the world at large and our descendants have a right to know what sort of people the Bengalis of the nineteenth and the beginning of the twentieth century were. If they think concealment is the best policy, then I beg to differ from them. For long our customs were fashioned and beliefs imposed by the Brahmins often to serve their own purposes, but now education has made rapid progress among the upper classes and we have a right to judge which of these customs should be altogether abolished or modified. In fact my long experience tells me that English education has made deep inroads upon our beliefs and the following pages will show to what extent abolition or modification has taken place in our customs.

It might be objected that some of my statements are incorrect, but in my defense I must state that many of these customs obtained among my own kinsmen who are not inferior in social status to any Kayastha in Bengal and my knowledge of this subject is mostly derived from observing the practices of my kinsmen and neighbours. No doubt there are slight variations in different localities and in different families in the same locality, but in the main my narrative will be correct.

To avoid constant reference to the fact that many of our customs are becoming obsolete, the reader is to note that this book was written in the year 1875 when I was 55 years of age and had acquired mature understanding.

I shall divide the subject into separate heads: I shall begin with customs connected with pregnancy, next I shall take up the child's birth, his infancy, his adolescence, his marriage, and lastly his death.

Basant Coomar Bose

CHAPTER 1

▼

PREGNANCY AND
BIRTH

When signs of pregnancy first become manifest, the young wife is treated with the greatest consideration by the members of her family. The reason is very simple. Naturally everybody expects that first child will be a male one and is most glad when he gets his first son. This applies to all men, Hindus or non-Hindus. The word for a son is putra, derived form the root put and affix trai. Put is a hell and trai means delivery. So putra or son is one who delivers from that hell. So Hindus believe that the first son delivers his parents from hell. There is no knowing whether the child in the womb is a male or female. Everybody hopes for the best. This is the legacy left by Pandora for the human race. As everybody expects the mother to give birth to a male child, the pregnant mother is treated with the greatest consideration. If she gives birth to a male child, the mother's position is assured in the family. In ancient times all females were excluded from inheritance by the male agnates and today in all provinces outside Bengal the males living in joint family exclude all females. Though a Bengali mother would succeed to her deceased husbands estate if he dies without a son, still the ancient idea of helplessness of females is prevalent in Bengal. Further, the law of Bengal is a recent one, Jimutavahana, its author, being the fifth in descent from one of the five Brahmins who came to Bengal in 1075 A.D. at the invitation of king Adisura, and it must have taken some time to make the law of inheritance uniform throughout Bengal. Jimutavahana was a resident not of Bengal but of Assam, its king having made him his chief Pandit and so at first his influence was not great in Bengal.

No ceremony is observed till the fifth month, when the ceremony of panchamrita or the five nectars takes place. But during this period she cannot have the services of the barber or the washerman and her nails remain unpared and her clothes unwashed, but nothing prevents her from paring the nails herself or getting them pared by a maid servant or getting her clothes washed by a domestic.

On an auspicious day in the fifth month the barber pares her nails, the washerman takes her clothes to wash, the young wife anoints herself with mustard oil mixed with pounded turmeric and moong dal and then she bathes and wears a silk sari. She then takes panchamrita or the five nectars consisting of a mixture of (1) curd (2) milk (3) ghee (4) sugar and (5) honey. A priest is in attendance to recite some mantras to sanctity the holy ambrosia which she chaffs off. He must fast till she drinks the panchamrita. Afterwards she takes her rice and fish and vegetables in plenty. A boy and five married women, whose first-born children are still alive, eat with her out of the same dish. She cannot take rice again at night but if she feels inclined to take any nourishment she takes only milk and fruits. In some families the first ceremony takes place in the seventh month and is called saptamrita or the seven nectars when plantain and dab water (green coconut) are added to the above mentioned five nectars. Henceforth she can have the services of the barber and the washerman.

In the eighth month there is another ceremony called astambarikapuja when the goddess Astambarika is worshiped by a priest and the young wife wears a new sari and takes the blessing of peace from the priest.

In the ninth month the goddess Mahamaya is worshiped by the priest who cooks all the dishes for the young wife on that occasion. She must he joined in the ceremony by five other married women whose first-born children are alive, when they all sit together to breakfast and eat out of the same dish.

In the same month on an auspicious day she eats her first shad which means wish. The first shad must he given by the mother-in-law, and in well-to-do families all near relations and even the villagers are feasted. But often only females are invited on this occasion. The young wife bathes and then wears a new silk sari presented by the mother-in-law, and takes a sumptuous breakfast. After the first shad is over all the near female relations give her shad and she gets a new sari of cotton or silk and presents of sweetmeats and fruits or regular invitations to breakfast on each occasion.

The object of this round of invitations and presents is to keep the young wife in a contented and happy state of mind. Her slightest wish is attended to on these occasions. It is said that Seeta, when she was pregnant, wished to go out on a journey to see the ladies of the house of Valmiki Muni and her husband Rama took advantage of this shad to send her with his brother Lakshmana to the hermitage of the Muni, where Lakshmana left her behind in exile.

One thing is very strictly observed in all orthodox families. No female can undertake a journey in the eighth month of her pregnancy, nor ride a palanquin or carriage.

With the exception of shad, the above customs and rules are not generally observed in cases of subsequent pregnancies, and on these occasions she is not treated with the same consideration as on the first occasion and the round of feasts and presents rapidly diminishes.

When delivery is approaching a new hut is erected for the occasion and it must not touch any other hut or building, the reason being that no one can touch the hut or anything touching it after the delivery takes place without being compelled to bathe. This untouchability lasts 5 days. For this reason, in some families there is a permanent lying-in-hut or room detached from any other hut or building.

After the delivery takes place and the child cries, the ladies present join in making a noise with their tongues. This is called ulu. It is a sign of welcome to the newborn babe.

When the bridegroom enters the house of the bride on the occasion of his marriage this ceremony is invariably observed and even distinguished persons are received in this way. When the image of Durga is brought to the house for worship, it is also received with ulu. If the newborn babe be a son, the ulu is cried five times, but in the case of a girl, only, thrice. After this the midwife cuts the navel string, and after washing the child's body, asks the mother thrice if the child is hers or the midwife's. The mother says mine on each occasion, and the child is then placed on her lap. Five lamps are lighted after the child is born and they must burn continuously for five days and nights. They must be oil lamps and they all must burn mustard oil. There was no kerosene oil or tallow candles in India in the beginning of the nineteenth century. As the Hindus are opposed to any kind of innovation in social or religious matters, they will stick to the mustard oil and avoid kerosene lamps, tallow candles, gas or electric lamps on ceremonial occasions. Electric light was once introduced in the temple of Jagannath at Puri, but it had to be removed. During the Durga Puja a mustard oil lamp burns continuously for three days and nights in the house where the puja is performed. This burning of lamps is regarded as a necessary feature of all festive and religious occasions as fire is perhaps the only surviving Vedic god except Vishnu.

The mother has now to lie down for the rest of the day and night without taking any food. Her bedding consists of a mat and a pillow without a cover as every piece of cloth or linen or any other thing that enters a lying-in-hut during the first five days has to be thrown away after use and is never washed for future use. Even the mat and the mattress, if any, have to be thrown away. The mother is not generally provided with a mattress or a curtain for the first five days, though there may be plenty of mosquitoes in the hut. Sometimes but not always a pillow is not allowed and the mother rests her head on a wooden plank. On the first day she gets no nourishment. On the second and third days, she lives upon milk and sago, and it is only on the fourth day that she takes rice cooked in the hut itself. From the fifth day she takes a regular diet. A charcoal fire is kindled and placed in an earthen vessel, and this fire is kept up in the hut for a whole month and the young mother is practically roasted as every part of her body, particularly the abdomen, must be rubbed with a piece of cloth which is heated upon the fire. One result of this is that even very fair women, when they come out of the confinement room, have their skin tanned and their complexion very much darkened. This is intended to remove all humors from the body. Allopathic doctors have abolished this roasting of mothers and have introduced trained midwives and nurses into the lying-in room. One lamp must continue to burn during the whole month.

On the birth of a child it is necessary to inform all near relations of the event and there is music for two or three days after the birth. The servant who gives this information is rewarded with bakshish, and it is the rule that the father presents the cloth he is wearing when he gets the news. Of course the present is larger in the case of the birth of a boy. Near relations come to see the face of the child and present silver or gold coins to the child.

On the fifth day the mother comes out of the hut, anoints herself with mustard oil mixed with pounded fresh turmeric, moong dal, gila, methi, and her finger nails are pared by the barber and she afterwards bathes, wears a new cloth, and takes her child in her arms and pounds some paddy placed in the center and the four corners of a mat and puts some grains of rice out of the paddy into her mouth and eats them. From this day the mother and the hut become touchable.

On the sixth day a cow's head is placed in front of the door of the hut and a lighted lamp is placed upon it. This is a relic of the ancient custom which required the slaughter of a cow for feasting near relations on the birth of a child. Now-a-days a cow is regarded as sacred and an incarnation of Vishnu, and so cannot be sacrificed, and therefore a dead cow's head is substituted in its place and placed at the door. Orthodox Hindus will be astonished to hear that formerly Hindus ate beef. But this fact has been amply proved by Dr. Rajendra Lal Mitra in the Chapter on Beef in India in his work *The Indo Aryans*. The Vedas mention gomedba sacrifice. The Taittirya Brahmana of the Yajur Veda gives the following directions for the selection of the cow in a gomedha jajna; "*a thick legged cow to Indra, a barren cow to Vishnu and Varuna, a black cow to Pushan, a cow which has given birth only once to Vayu, a cow having two colors to Mitra and Varnua, a red cow to Rudra, a white barren cow to Surya, etc.*"

The Grijya Sutra speaks of Sulagava or spitted cow i.e. roast beef. The Asvalyana sutra gives directions to eat the remains of the offering. The Taittiriya Brahmana gives the following directions to cut up the carcass: "*Separate its hide so that it may remain entire. Cut open its breast so as to make it appear like an eagle with spread wings. Separate the four arms, divide the arms into spokes, separate successively in other the 26 ribs, dig a trench for burying the excrements, throw away the blood to the Rakshasas etc. O slayer of cattle, O Adbrigu, accomplish your task, accomplish it according to rules.*"

The Gopatha Brahmana of the Atharva Veda gives in detail the names of the different individuals who are to receive shares of the meat for the parts they take in the ceremony. The following are a few of them: "*The Prastota is to receive the two jaws along with the tongue, the Pratibarta the neck and the bump, the Udgta the eagle-like wings, the Neslita the right arm, Sadashya the left arm, the householder who ordains the sacrifice the two right feet, his wife the two left feet, etc."*

In the Rig Veda also mention is made of eating of beef and in Mandal 10, Sukta 89, verse 14, we find mention of slaughter houses for cows. Even such a late writer as Manu in Chapter 5 of his Laws which relates to diet, verse 18, declares as lawful food, *"all quadrupeds, the camel excepted, which have one row of teeth."* All ruminating animals have but one row of teeth, therefore the goat and the cow are both included in this category, and both are therefore lawful food. Medhatithi, the commentator of Manu, is of the same opinion. As regards the horse sacrificed in the Ashamedha it was comforted with the idea that it was going to the gods, Rig Veda 1.162, Verse 21. *"Here thou diest not, thou art not injured, by easy paths unto the gods thou goest"* but there is no such solace given to the cow sacrificed in the gomedha. Modern pundits say that the cow sacrificed in the gomedha jajna was revived afterwards, in other words there was a resurrection of the cow, but how could that be after its parts had been eaten and digested by participants, its hide removed and its entrails buried? The parallel of Jesus Christ cannot apply. His body was entire; only there were four holes in his arms and legs, the hole in his side being an addition by St. John. So there is great difference between the resurrection of Jesus with his entire body and the resurrection of the cow with its dismembered and digested body. In fact the Vedas do not give any support to this modern explanation of the Pundits, who are generally speaking, not versed in Vedic literature. In fact I doubt if 1% our so-called tithed Pundits in Bengal has ever read the Vedas. They recite the Gayatri everyday, and because the Gayatri is a part of the Rig Veda (iii 62. V. 10), they satisfy their conscience by thinking that they read the Vedas every day, which is the duty of every Brahmin to do.

In the Vedas we find mention of all sorts of sacrifices. Even the sacrifice of human beings (Purushameda jajna) is mentioned, but as this matter is foreign to my subject, I shall confine myself by simply stating that human sacrifice was enjoined by the Vedas for the attainment of supremacy over all created beings and that the Taittiriya Brahmana of the Black Yajur Veda gives directions as to the kind of human being to be sacrificed before a particular god. It says, to a divinity of the Brahmana caste a Brahmin should be sacrificed and so on till it comes to the one hundred and seventy-ninth god and ends by saying, to the goddess of hope for attainable objects a virgin is to be sacrificed. So one hundred and seventy-nine different kinds of human beings were sacrificed to as many deities.

Now-a-days in all these jajnas, no one will sacrifice a cow, a horse or a man. This is owing to the rise of Buddhism which prohibited slaughter of animals as there is no knowing whether any ancestor or any other near relation of the performer of the jajna or has not transmigrated into the body of the animal which was going to be sacrificed. This injunction of Buddha was embodied in the edicts of Asoka which forbade the slaughter of animals, and Asoka having been the emperor of the whole of Northern India, his edict, which had the force of law, stopped the killing of all animals. Even now no orthodox Brahmin will eat the flesh of any goat which has not been sacrificed before a deity, though formerly even cows were sacrificed for the entertainment of guests who were called gognas or cow killers as a cow was killed for their entertainment. Thus the conclusion is clear that the cow's head represents symbolically the cow slaughtered on the sixth day of the child's birth on the occasion of a feast to celebrate the happy event.

On that day an important ceremony takes place. Six kinds of very small unburnt earthen vessels or rather toys are brought from the potter's shop, sixty of each kind. These consist of sixty pots with covers, sixty lamps with stands, sixty kartals and sixty mridangas (both musical instruments), besides sixty larus (sweetmeats), sixty plantains and khai (fried rice). The sixty pots are filled with rice, dal, dried chilies, etc., and other things. There are also sixty leaves of the bakula tree. The Brahmin priest performs a jajna, and the leaves after being chopped in cow's ghee are burnt and some jajna faggots are burnt upon a layer of sand. After the ceremony is over, young boys and girls who are invited on this occasion scramble for the earthen vessels, and I remember having taken part in some scrambles. The clay is not burnt lest it should injure the youngsters, and the result is that most of the earthen vessels are broken into pieces. However, the youngsters enjoy the fun very much and the khai, larus and plantains are distributed amongst them. Brahmins tread upon a gamcha (towel) and leave the dust of their feet upon it. The priest takes some curd and the gamcha into the hut and leaves them there. The child's forehead is made to touch the gamcha containing the dust.

Some ladies take their evening meal before nightfall and enter the hut and shut the door which is not generally opened during the night for a whole month. They keep vigil alternately during the whole night and the child is not allowed to be on its bed. It must spend the whole night on somebody's lap. On that night the god Brahma comes and writes on the child's forehead its whole future life. Nothing can alter his decrees. I do not know what characters Brahma writes and do not know if any characters are visible on the forehead of any Hindu. Of course

Brahma never comes to the house of any non-Hindu to write his destiny on his forehead as he is untouchable by the gods. Perhaps the characters are written with invisible ink as no one can find any trace of writing upon any Hindu skull. However, I leave this matter to the learned Brahmins and my orthodox readers to decide as I understand very little of the mysteries of the gods. This Brahma is called Bidhata or Fate. Hindus and many non-Hindus believe in kapal (forehead) or kismet which is the same as fate, the idea being that each man's fortune is written on his forehead and nothing can alter the decrees of fate. The Mohammedans also believe that every man's fate was written from eternity in the Book of Fate, a book of vast extent in which the future of everyman is written, (Koran Ch. VI). Even Jesus speaks of the elect who will be saved. (Mat. XXIV. 31. Mk. XIII. 20. 27). If the child is not on the lap of someone then some evil spirits will enter the room and affect the child's destiny before the entry of Brahma.

On the evening of the eighth day another ceremony takes place. It is called atkalui or eight kaluis. On this occasion all the boys and girls of kinsmen and neighbours are invited and sing a few songs addressed to the child. On the sixth day the kinsmen and near relations are invited to witness the ceremony and there is music and great rejoicing but on the eighth day only children are invited and they get parched kalais and rice and sometimes sweetmeats but no other food is given to them, and they gladly return home wishing well of the newborn babe.

On the twenty first day the mother comes out of the hut, anoints herself with mustard oil, turmeric and methi, bathes, wears a new cloth and the floor of the hut is smeared with cow dung mixed with water, and she finally leaves the hut on the 30th day, when she bathes, wears a new cloth and enters her own apartment with the child in her arms amidst cries of ulu and the beating of musical instruments. All the linen, mats, mattresses and other things except bell metal plates used by the mother are thrown away. Thus ends the first month of the infant's life.

There is music in the house for two or three days after the birth of the child and also on the sixth, eighth, twenty-first, and thirtieth days.

CHAPTER 2

▼

RICE TAKING

When the boy is six months old or the girl seven months old the rice taking ceremony takes place. If for some reason the child cannot take rice at that age, then it takes rice two or four months after, that is, the boy must be six, eight or ten months old and the girl seven, nine or eleven months old.

The ceremony is very elaborate. At nightfall of the day previous to the day fixed for the rice taking ceremony, all the married ladies and their unmarried girls go out in a procession with a small kalsi (pitcher) accompanied by music and they visit all the houses in the neighbourhood and every housewife pours a little water into the pitcher. The houses of the untouchables are avoided, as their water is polluted and can be of no use in an orthodox household. The ladies then return to the house and afterwards a puja is performed with the water brought by them. Rich people sometimes offer the sacrifice of a goat to the goddess Kali, the greatest destroyer of evil in the whole Hindu pantheon. Next day very early in the morning a little curd is given to the boy and the married ladies and their young daughters again go out in a procession accompanied by music to fetch water, this time from a tank in the village. A married female relation carries this water home. In some families the parents carry this water to their home. This kalsi is placed in one of the principal rooms in the inner apartment, and upon it is placed a twig of a mango tree, a dab (green coconut), a bunch of kathali plantains, called kabari in East Bengal, and the whole is tied together with a newgamcba (towel). An idol is painted on the kalsi with vermilion. This ceremony is called adbibasb. In some families the ladies do not go out on the previous evening to fetch water but all ceremonies and processions take place on the day the rice taking ceremony takes place.

In the morning the ceremony begins. A shraddha is performed and the ancestors are offered pindas and a Brahmin priest officiates. The boy's nails and toes are pared and the washerman bathes him. The boy wears a red silk dhoti and a chaddar and sometimes a silk shirt. He wears on his head a coronet made of pith, mica, and tinsel, beautifully colored. The rich man's son is decked with gold and silver ornaments and other kinds of jewelry. For the first time in his life he wears gold bangles, gold necklace, gold waist chain, and silver anklet with jingling bells, besides other ornaments, but no Hindu can wear any gold ornament below his or her waist, the only exception being the rulers of states and their queens.

The infant is now made to sit on apiri (wooden seat) painted in various colors. A winnow is placed before him and the following twenty one articles are placed upon it:

(1) a lighted lamp burning mustard oil
(2) paddy
(3) grass
(4) sesamum
(5) wheat
(6) rye
(7) jute leaves
(8) moong
(9) maskalie
(10) myrabollam
(11) mustard oil
(12) vermilion
(13) turmeric
(14) gila
(15) methi
(16) boar's tusk
(17) conch shell
(18) pestle
(19) dhuna (incense)

(20) white sandal paste

(21) red sandal paste.

Then five names are written on a black stone plate by the priest which must agree with the zodiacal sign of the boy's nativity. Then five wicks are soaked in mustard oil and placed in front of each name. That name before which the flame rises highest is adopted for the boy's name, so that when the boy attains manhood his name may spread throughout the country. The priest mentions that name into the father's ear who mentions it into the mother's ear and the boy gets that name. Most boys also get a false or nickname. This is to deceive the spirit, which, when he comes to attack the boy, is misled by the false name and is unable to identify or injure the boy.

After the boy has got his name he is placed on a palanquin and, accompanied by music and near female relations and children, is carried to the several temples in the village and the boy's head is lowered in the presence of the presiding deity of each temple. After his return home he is seated on his mother's lap and the boy is made to play with cowries and rice or some near female relation does it for him. Then all the ladies present perform a ceremony called baran which is performed by the trembling of the fingers and alternately showing the front and back of the palms. Then the boy's forehead is made to touch the winnow which is raised for the purpose. Then all the relations give him presents beginning with the mother. Then he is taken to the outer apartments and all the male relations and invited guests take him into their lap and give him presents. In rich families land is given to the boy so that he may live in ease and plenty upon its produce.

The boy is then taken inside the house and is seated on the piri and if there be any prasad of a god, that is, anything which had been offered to him, then a drop or particle of this prasad has to be put into the child's mouth otherwise a particle of rice boiled in milk and sugar has to be given. Then balls of rice are taken near his mouth and thrown into the sacrificial fire. This is done by a very near relation, but the maternal uncle, if present, is preferred to all others. Two stone plates are used, in one of which prasad and portions of the dishes are placed and on the other the five names are written.

On this occasion all near relations and a large number of guests are invited. Rich people invite all the people of the village on such auspicious occasions such as rice taking, haircutting and marriage, etc. No meat is offered to the guests as no animal sacrifice can take place on that day. If thought necessary the sacrifice takes place the previous day. The guests are given luchi, rice, fish, vegetables, dahi, khir, sandesh, and sweetmeats. Rich people sometimes add polao to the dishes. The abolition of sacrifice on such occasions is evidently due to the influence of Buddhism which at one time was the prevalent religion in Bengal. It has been mixed up with the Hindu religion and the two together have given birth to the Tantric religion, which is the prevalent religion in Bengal.

CHAPTER 3

▼

HAIR CUTTING

When the boy is two years old, his hair is cut after some religious ceremony is performed. This hair cutting ceremony may be performed at home or if the parents had made a vow to cut the hair before a particular goddess then the parents take the child to the shrine and the boy's hair is cut there, after performing a puja of the goddess. In East Bengal the most celebrated shrine where the Hindus flocked to have their children's hair cut for the first time was that of the goddess Kali in village Chachurtala in the Dacca District, now in the bed of the Padma since July 1926, where I was taken to have my hair cut, seventy years ago. This ceremony is not of much importance, but a puja is performed and the Brahmins get something.

CHAPTER 4

▼

CHURAKARAN

The ceremony of Churakaran or ear piercing also takes place after the child is two years old. The ceremonies of this occasion are very elaborate and almost the same as those which are performed on the occasion of a marriage. In fact it is commonly said that there is no difference between the two ceremonies except that a bride is wanting. Water has to be fetched from the neighbours' houses and from a tank by the ladies on two successive days accompanied by music as on the occasion of the rice taking ceremony. The sradh of the ancestors must be performed. The boy must wear a red colored silken dhoti and a silk chaddar and a coronet of pith and the winnow with its twenty-one articles must be placed before him. A jajna must be performed and the services of the barber and the washerman are necessary. The child is placed on a slightly raised platform of earth upon the four corners of which four plantain trees are planted, and a string, which passes through perforated moochhies, that is, small earthen plates, is hung round the trees. The child sits on a piri and it is the duty of the washerman to bathe him, his perquisite among other things being the cloth which the boy was wearing when he bathed. The lower lobes of the ear are pierced with a thorn and then two gold or silver pins are placed in the hole and they must remain there until the wound heals but if they are removed too early the holes will close up. The holes are very necessary as a man or woman without any hole in his or her ear is unable to touch any water which is to be offered to the gods, and this rule is strictly observed in orthodox families. The boy is also to be carried in a palanquin to the idols and in fact all ceremonies in connection with marriage have to be performed on this occasion and as I shall fully describe the ceremonies in connection with marriage, it is unnecessary to anticipate them here.

CHAPTER 5

▼

HATEKHARY

When the boy is five years old, the ceremony of hatekharia takes place and a jajna is performed by the family priest, but no pindas are necessarily offered to the ancestors. Hatekhari literally means chalk in hand. The young boy wears a red silk dhoti and chaddar and is seated on a painted wooden plank (piri) and a piece of chalk (khah) is placed in his right hand and by the priest and he is asked to scrawl with the chalk over some characters written by the family priest on a black stone dish. Such people invite their kinsmen and relatives on these occasions but it is not compulsory to do so.

Both the above ceremonies, that is hair cutting and writing, are prescribed for male children only. Daughters have not to have their hair cut or be initiated into the mysteries of writing. It appears that in ancient times Hindu women were not prohibited from acquiring learning. Instances of highly educated ladies writing books or engaging in disputations on philosophical subjects with the most learned sages are to be found in Sanskrit literature. Ghosha, the daughter of Kakshivan, composed Rig Veda X.39. The names of Gargi and Maitrayee are well known to all Sanskrit scholars and their disputations are recorded in books, and Lilabati has left a treatise on Mathematics. But whatever might have been the rule in ancient times, in the first half of the nineteenth century, Indian women were prevented by social rules from acquiring learning. Education even of males was at very low ebb. Almost all learning was confined to Brahmins and to Sanskrit literature. The village guru who taught all the young boys knew the three R's only, Reading, Writing, and Arithmetic, and the reading of the adult was confined to half a dozen translations into Bengali, including metrical translations, of the Ramayana and the Mahabharata. Printing had not made much progress and books were very scarce and very dear. The Brahmins could only teach Sanskrit which their women did not like to learn and there was no school for the education of girls. The first girls' school was established by Mr. J. E. D. Bethune in Calcutta in the middle of the last century and the first girls' school in East Bengal was started in my village Malkhanagar by my father at the suggestion of some young kinsmen in the year 1865. This caused daladali (factions) in my village which spread throughout the whole of Vikrampur, the most celebrated and advanced Paragana in East Bengal and this daladali lasted three or four years. It was like a battle between the ancients and the moderns. All sorts of social weapons were used and the whole of the Brahmin and the Kayastha communities, the two principal ones, were divided into two hostile camps. There were five unmarried girls not exceeding 10 or 11 years of age with whom the school was started. Nevertheless, as I have already stated, there was bitter party feeling and the school came to untimely end, but today there is a school in my village which nearly 50 unmarried girls attend, and the parents of every unmarried girl think it necessary and wise to send their girls to the school, as today no uneducated child will be selected as a bride by any Brahmin or Kayastha. Such are the changes which time has made in our society. My grandmother could never write, my mother learnt Bengali after her marriage, my wife knew it before her marriage, and my daughter-in-law knows English. Such is the progress of education and enlightened ideas in our society caused by the progress of time and English education.

CHAPTER 6

▼

HOLY THREAD

The ceremony of taking the holy thread or upanayana, which the three superior castes must perform, takes place when the child is five to nine years old but the utmost limit of performing this ceremony is fifteen years three months. Here again the ceremonies are almost the same as in Churakaran. There is a peculiar custom in connection with this ceremony. For twelve days the boy is confined to his room and cannot see the face of any low class man and in the case of Brahmins they cannot see the face of any non-Brahmin and if they do they will lose brahamtez or the vigor or light of the god Brahma. Sradh and adhibash have to be performed, the boy has to fast till the ceremony is over, which is the invariable custom in all ceremonies including even the rice taking ceremony, although the child is six to ten months old. In churakaran and upanayan ceremonies there must be, as already stated, adhibash, sradh, visit to the idols, giving of a feast to friends and relations, presents to the boy from the mother's relations, then from paternal relations and afterwards friends.

Formerly only the Brahmins had the sacred thread in Bengal. As the five Kayastha immigrants from Kanouj intermarried with the aboriginal Kayasthas of Bengal who were mostly Buddhists, the Brahmins thought that they were degraded as the aboriginal Buddhist Kayasthas had no sacred thread. The descendants of the five newcomers also gave up their sacred thread and therefore no Kayasthas wore the sacred thread in Bengal. In the year 1901 or soon after an agitation began among the Kayasthas of Bengal and they claimed to be Kshatryas whom they divided into two classes, the sword bearers and the pen bearers, the duty of the former being to fight and of the latter to write, and they asserted that the real administration of the country in Hindu times was entirely in the hands of the pen bearers. It appears that the Kayasthas of Northern India called Lalas wear the sacred thread and in imitation of them the Kayasthas of Bengal began to wear the sacred thread and this movement is still going on.

Among the Vaidyas of West Bengal some of them formerly wore the sacred thread but Vaidyas of East Bengal wore no sacred thread. But now almost all the Vaidyas of West Bengal wear it and many of the Vaidyas of East Bengal have commenced to wear it. Now the Vaidyas claim to be pure Brahmins. The origin of Vaidyas in Bengal is very obscure. Formerly they said that they were the descendants of a Brahmin by a Vaisya woman. Whether they were married or not was left uncertain. Now, as I have already stated, they claim to be pure lineal descendants of Brahmins and have begun to call themselves Vaidya Brahmins which means physician Brahmins, the word Vaidya meaning a physician. Speaking for myself I do not know anything about the real origin of the Vaidyas and I doubt very much whether anybody really knows anything about this matter. A very high authority informed me that Vaidyas were originally Kayasthas who took to the profession of medicine and thus formed themselves into a separate community This is not at all strange. In Vedic times there was no division of castes. The Purusha Sukta (Rig Veda X.90.) contains the only passage in the Rig Veda (V.12) about the origin of caste, an account of the separate creations of the four castes. It is a palpable forgery, as in verse 12 it is stated that the Brahmin was the mouth of the Purusha and the Sudra his feet, and again in the next two verses it is stated Indra and Agni were produced from his mouth (V.13) and the earth was produced from his feet (V.14). Therefore verse 12 is an interpolation and European Sanskritists are of the opinion that the language of verse 12 is written in modern and not Vedic Sanskrit. Every householder in Vedic times could perform a jajna but owing to the principle of the division of labour some people became versed in the Vedas and got the mantras by heart and their services were required to perform jajna and they gradually became a separate caste. Similarly these Vaidyas have become a separate caste. Their pretensions are very high. They claim Raja Ballal Sen of Bengal to be a Vaidya, but they forget that Raja Adisur, the grandfather and immediate predecessor of Banal Sen, invited only Brahmins and Kayasthas from Kanouj and no Vaidya was invited and there is no tradition as to how they came to be settled in Bengal which in Vedic times was beyond the pale of civilization. They rely upon the fact that Ballal was a Sen and among Vaidyas there are Sens, but there are Sens also among inferior classes of Kayasthas, gold merchants (an untouchable class) and betel leaf growers and others. So this identity of patronymic does not assist us much in solving this question. Banal Sen introduced Kulinism only among the five Brahmins and five Kayasthas who came from Kanouj but not among the Vaidyas. This shows that he had no regard for the Vaidyas who claim him as one of them. Further Adisur had the patronymic of Sur and Surs are Kayasthas and no Vaidya bears such a patronymic.

Some ancient copper plates have been discovered and manuscripts found which show that Ballal belonged to the Kshatriya caste and the Kayas thus claim to be Kshatriyas but no Vaidya will ever claim to be a Kshatriya. This is a matter which is involved in very great obscurity and I leave it to the decision of my learned readers.

This holy thread movement has taken hold of the country and even Namasudras, the lowest of the untouchable castes, have in many places in Bengal adopted the sacred thread. This movement has been so rapid that the time is not far distant when they will all adopt it and they will be followed by all other castes in Bengal, so that all Bengalis will in time wear the sacred thread. The Namasudras have gone so far as to change their patronymics. They were formerly called Mandals, but after the adoption of the sacred thread they assumed the patronymics of the Brahmins and now call themselves Banerjees, Chatterjees, etc. This upwards movement is advancing in such rapid strides that the Rishis or tanners of skins and hides call themselves the descendants of the Vedic Rishis and they will adopt the sacred thread without any loss of time.

CHAPTER 7

▼

MARRIAGE

I shall have to deal with this subject a little elaborately. All other ceremonies are one sided, but here there are two parties and various considerations arise before a marriage takes place. In Bengal, as is well known, the two principal upper castes are the Brahmins and Kayasthas. The Brahmins again are subdivided into three main subdivisions, the Rarhis, the Vaidics, and the Varendas. The Vaidics again are divided into two branches, the Western and the Southern. There can be no intermarriage between any two of these subdivisions. No doubt lately there have been such intermarriages but the parties thereto belong mostly to the reformed Hindu religion and are not followers of the orthodox Hindu religion. The origin of the Varendra is somewhat obscure and there are different stories regarding their advent to Bengal. They are called Varendra because they were originally settled in Varendra in Northern Bengal, that is north of the Ganges or Padma and west of Brahmaputra. The Varendras allege that they belong to the original stock of the Rarhis but the latter do not acknowledge this kinship. The Southern Vaidics came from Southern India, the Western Vaidics came from Western India and are numerically superior to the Southern Vaidics. As regards the Rarhis, tradition says that king Adisur, the first orthodox Hindu ruler of Bengal, wished to perform a jajna but found no Brahmin priest fit to officiate in it as Bengal had previously been a Buddhist country under the Pal dynasty. So he wrote to the king of Kanouj to send some learned Brahmin priests to perform the ceremony. Five Brahmins were sent and they were accompanied by five Kayasthas. Dr. Vincent Smith in his *History of India During the Hindu Period* does not admit Adisur to be a king of Bengal. But Bengali social rules are based upon his invitation to the Brahmins and Kayasthas.

After the jajna was over the king requested them to settle in this country and gave them grants of villages. They were originally settled in Rarh, the county west of the Ganges and therefore they are called Rarhi Brahmins and Dakshin Rarhi Kayasthas but some of the Kayasthas settled in Bengal which originally meant the whole country lying to the east of the old Ganges now called Bhagirathi and Hoogly, west of the old Brahmaputra, south of the Varendra country and to the north of the Bay of Bengal. These Kayasthas are called Bangaja Kayasthas. The Dakshin Rarhi Kayas thus intermarry among themselves but no intermarriage can take place between the Dakshin Rarhi Kayasthas and Bangaja Kayasthas. I am not aware of any marriage, except one, between Dakshin Rarhi and Bangaja Kayasthas having taken place in the nineteenth century, but Kayasthas are becoming more and more liberal and several such marriages have recently taken place.

After Adisura's death his successor King Ballaj Sen, the most famous among the modern kings of Bengal, and the father of Lakshana Sen, the last king of Bengal, divided the Rarhi Brahmins into two classes, Kulins and non-Kulins. The non-Kulins were again divided into several classes, such as Suritri and Bangshaja. The Kulins represent the highest class among Rarhi Brahmins and they cannot marry any Bangshaja girl. If they do so, they become Bangshaja.

Their first wife must be a Suritri and their second and subsequent wives are Kulins, and when I was young I knew the son of a Kulin Brahmin who had more than hundred wives, as marriage was a profession with them. During the last fifty years such plural marriages have not taken place, but most Kulin Brahmins are practically obliged to marry a Suritri and afterwards a Kulin girl. A Suritri girl can be given in marriage to a Kulin or a Suritri but a Kulin girl can be given only to a Kulin. The Bangshaja subdivision is swelled every day by Kulins who have intermarried with them, as intermarriage with them degrades a Kulin into a Bangshaja. The Kulins regard the Bangshajas as very inferior in rank, and on ceremonial occasions, particularly in marriages, the Kulins will not interdine with them, and are therefore rarely invited on occasions of marriage of Bangshajas who are practically social outcastes of Kulin Brahmins. The rich and ambitious Bangshajas are very desirous of giving their daughters in marriage to Kulin Brahmins and I know instances in which very heavy ponas (dowries) were given to the bridegroom's parents for inducing them to give their sons in marriage with the daughters of Bangshajas. In one instance in this century the pona of Rs. 35,000 was given to the bridegroom's father by the richest Bangshaja zaminder in the district of Barisal. The Bangshajas usually marry amongst themselves unless, as just stated, a Bangshaja thinks of paying a heavy bonus for a Kulin bridegroom, The Kulins again are divided into several melas. Some melas are so low in the estimation of Brahmins, such as Kishorekuni, that if a man of a superior mela marries a Kishorekuni girl he at once becomes a Kishorekuni which is the lowest of melas. Ballal Sen alone is responsible for the division of Rarhi Brahmins into the above mentioned three classes. Subsequently one Debibar Ghatak framed very strict rules regarding the marriage of Brahmins which are still followed. He was a great Ghatak or family genealogist. On the occasion of the marriage of Kulin Brahmins a ghatak or family genealogist, on each side, must be present and if any dispute arises about the social position of the parties to the marriage, the two family ghataks present must settle it.

The Bangshajas find it very difficult to get brides and they have to pay a heavy pona or bonus to the father of the bride which usually is Rs. 100 per year of the bride's age, so that if the girl be twelve years old her price is Rs. 1200. Cheap brides also can be had. People take a boatload of Bangshaja girls. They may not be Brahmin girls at all but they are passed off as such and Bangshaja bridegrooms buy these girls from out of the boatload. These girls can be had at cheaper prices and therefore poor people buy these girls. Instances have been known when Mahomedan girls sold out of the boatload have been passed off as Bangshaja girls. One such girl after her marriage ordered the servant to bring a cherag, which is a Persian word for lamp, a word always used by the Mahomedans but never by the Hindus. On cross examination she was discovered to be a Mahomedan, but she was not driven away by her husband and she remained in the family, as such a procedure would have entailed loss of caste, and the matter was hushed up.

The Kulin Brahmins, who lose their social status by marrying Bangshaja girls are called Bhangas or broken. After four or five generations they lose their patronymic in East Bengal where there are more Kulin Brahmins than in West Bengal. The Banerjees, Mukherjees, and Chatterjees are then called Barorys, Mukhutys and Chathatys.

Ballal Sen had nothing to do with the Vaidics and they had no Debibar Ghatal among them, so their rules of marriage are not complicated. They only follow the ordinary rules of Hindu law regarding consanguinity and affinity like all other Hindus but they have a peculiar custom amongst them. Their children marry at a very early age and it often happens that two pregnant Vaidic women settle the marriage of the babes in their wombs provided they be of different sexes and so it sometimes happens that the wife is a few months older than the husband, a thing unheard of among any other class of Brahmins or non-Brahmins in Bengal. In upper India no such rule regarding seniority is observed amongst the superior or inferior class of Brahmins or non-Brahmins, and I know instances amongst Brahmins and Kshatriyas in Bihar where the wife was senior in age to the husband.

Ballal Sen divided the Kayasthas into Kulins and non-Kulins and the latter are called Moulicks in West Bengal and Bangals in East Bengal, the word Bangal literally meaning a native of Bengal. The five Kayasthas who accompanied the five Brahmin priests to Bengal were made Kulins, but one of them, Purushottam Dutt, was degraded from his kulinism for some reason or other. In West Bengal he is ranked among the Mouliks but in East Bengal he has a much higher position, though he is not a Kulin and as he belonged to the Madogollya gotra, he is called Madgollya in East Bengal and is socially higher than a Bangal but lower than Kulins in East Bengal. Similarly the Mitras are Kulins in West Bengal but Mouliks in East Bengal, and Guhas are Mouliks in West Bengal but Kulins in East Bengal. Boses and Ghoses are all Kulins in West Bengal, but some of them have become degraded into Mouliks in East Bengal and the rest are Kulins.

Besides the descendants of the five emigrants, there are eight superior Kayasthas in West Bengal and seventy-two other subdivisions of inferior Kayasthas. In East Bengal besides three Kulin and semi-Kulin families of Ghose, Bose and Guha and the Magollyas, the rest are treated as of almost equal rank, but the descendants of Kulins, degraded from Kulinism, are ranked higher.

Besides the Dakhin Rarhis and Bangajas, there are also two other classes of Kayasthas, the Uttar Rarhi and the Varendra. Uttarrar is the country to the north of the Hoogly and Burdwan districts and Varendra, as already stated, is to the north of the Padma, and west of the Brahmaputra river. The origin of these Kayasthas is obscure. The Varendra Kayasthas were probably the original inhabitants of Bengal. Uttar Rarhis say that they are new settlers.

These Kayastha, have no Ballaly system among them but they recognize superiority and inferiority amongst themselves. There is nothing extraordinary in this. Even among Chandals, one of the lowest castes in Bengal, there are higher and lower subdivisions. In fact, this rule obtains among Christians and Mahomedans also and perhaps throughout the world. Every English peer tries his best to marry into the family of another peer; every Mahomedan of low rank tries to give his daughter in marriage to a Sayed and thus ennobles himself. So it might be said that in imitation of the Kayasthas of Eastern and Western Bengal, the other Kayasthas have introduced amongst themselves a modified system of Kulinism, but Ballal never introduced this system among them and it is difficult to ascertain how this modified system of Kulinism originated.

Now it is necessary to state the rules and customs regarding marriage amongst these four subdivisions of Kayasthas. Let me premise by saying that intermarriage between these four subdivisions never took place before 1897, but the institution of a society called the Kayastha Sabha in the year 1901 has much advanced the views of the Kayasthas and they have come to regard themselves as children of a common ancestor called Chitragupta who is regarded by the Hindus as a god presiding over the deaths of all mankind. In fact Brahma, the Creator, may be called the Registrar General of births, and Chitragupta may be called the Registrar General of deaths. There is a movement throughout India to assimilate all Kayasthas into one common fold and as Kayasthas are the most liberal among all Hindus, just the reverse of Brahmins, it is hoped that all the Kayasthas of India will soon intermarry amongst themselves. Almost every year Kayasthas from all parts of India assemble in a general meeting in some big city in India and discuss this and other social customs and pass resolutions for amalgamation. The last meeting was held in Jaunpur in the year 1925, in which a resolution was unanimously passed to the effect that it is desirable that the Kayasthas of Bengal, who are descendants of Chitragupta, and the Sribastabya, Ambastha, Shaksen, Mathur, and other classes of Kayasthas do intermarry and dine together. Even today Kayasthas belonging to the several subdivisions of Bengal and the Kayasthas of other provinces do often interdine and in all annual sessions of the All-India Kayastha Association or of the Provincial Associations Kayasthas interdine but I have rarely heard of Brahmins of different subdivisions interdining. In fact the orthodox Brahmins do not interdine with persons belonging to other subdivisions. I may be permitted to foretell that the Kayasthas of India, who are as much advanced in intelligence and education as the Brahmins themselves, but less illiberal than they, will at one time be the social leaders of India. They will be the first to introduce intermarriage amongst themselves and by degrees abolish all distinctions of caste which have barred the social progress of India, and the Brahmins will come last, their education and self interest standing in the way of their making much progress in the leveling of the Indian races. Many intermarriages have taken place since the commencement of this century between the Dakhin Rarhis and the Bangaja Kayasthas as there is no doubt that both these people belong to the same stock, having descended from common ancestors. Of the Kulins amongst them, all trace their descent from the five Kayasthas who accompanied the five Brahmins who came from Kanouj to officiate at Adisur's janja in the year 994 Shak, corresponding to 1072 A.D., according to Golap Chandra Sircar Shastri.

Regarding marriage customs, I shall begin with the Dakhin Rarhis. The Boses, Ghoses, and Mitras are the only Kulins among them. The Guhas and Duttas, though descended from two of the five companions of the Brahmins brought down to Adisur's court, are not recognized as Kulins. The eldest son of the Kulin must marry for the first time a Kulin girl. There is a peculiar custom among Kulin Kayasthas, both of East and West Bengal. They count their pedigree from the common ancestor which is called parjya and the boys and the girls must belong to the same parjya. The younger sons of West Bengal Kulins are at liberty to marry either a Kulin of the same pedigree or a Moulik girl. In rich Moulik families and in all Moulik families near Calcutta there is no such thing as intermarriage between two Mouliks. Formerly Kulin boys only used to get large dowries or pona but now the tables have been turned upon the Kulins who have now to pay large dowries to Moulik boys. I have known instances where a Moulik boy got Rs. 10,000 in cash from a Kulin father-in-law as dowry, besides other gifts on the occasion of his marriage. Formerly Kulinism was a very valuable asset but now, owing to the progress of the democratic spirit, Kulinism has become an empty name and now everything depends upon the boy's education and his worldly prospects and blueness of blood does not now count much.

Among East Bengal Kulins there is no fixed rule that the eldest son must marry a Kulin girl but among them the principal rule regarding marriage is that there must be giving of a Kulin girl to a Kulin boy and taking of a Kulin girl into a Kulin family within three generations, otherwise the Kulin is socially degraded and ceases to be a Kulin. In East Bengal there are many people who are descended from the original stock of Kulins but have become Mouliks, but in West Bengal such a thing rarely happens as the only condition imposed upon them is that the eldest son must marry a Kulin. Another rule prevails among Kulins of East Bengal though not in West Bengal. In East Bengal certain tracts of territory are excluded from the residence of Kulins and if any Kulin settles in such a tract he ceases to be a Kulin, but there is no such rule among Kulins of West Bengal; they can settle anywhere they like in Bengal. The promulgation of this rule in East Bengal is generally attributed to Raja Paramananda Bose of Bakla in the district of Barisal. He was the head of the Kulins in East Bengal. It is said that on the death of his maternal grandfather he became the Raja of Bakla and put to the sword all his maternal relations and banished his younger brother who settled in the western portion of the Dacca District outside Vikrampur, and he passed an edict that if any Kulin resides in any portion of Dacca District outside Vikrampur he ceases to be a Kulin.

In East Bengal there is no rule prohibiting intermarriage between two Mouliks who often intermarry amongst themselves and do not follow the rule prevailing in West Bengal prohibiting intermarriage between Mouliks. As a Kulin boy demands heavy dowry on account of his being both a boy and a Kulin, the poor Mouliks of West Bengal who are forced to give their daughters in marriage to Kulins have to incur large debts on the occasion of the marriage of their girls, though if they have boys they have a chance of recouping themselves by exacting heavy dowries from Kulins, when their son will marry. But if he has no son but many daughters and is poor, he is a ruined man. It is not so in East Bengal where Mouliks rarely demand dowry and in the last century such a demand by Mouliks, particularly from Kulins, was unheard of. Formerly it was the invariable custom for a Moulik to pay dowry, big or small, if he married into a Kulin family. Kulin boys and girls had to be paid for by Mouliks and even now the fathers of Kulin girls sometimes get large dowries. In West Bengal Kulin girls get no dowry but in East Bengal the father of Kulin boys and girls get dowries but the rate of dowry of a Kulin girl in East Bengal has become much lower than it was a hundred years ago.

I shall give an example of such a dowry. My grandfather's brother's daughter was given in marriage about the beginning of the last century to a Moulik and my paternal grand uncle got a very large dowry which was not counted but measured in a bouta. A bouta is a cane basket which can hold sixteen seers of paddy and a heapful of rupees that must have amounted to between 15 and 20 thousand. The bridegroom was very rich and it was the first marriage of his family into our family, regarded as one of the highest Kulin families in East Bengal. This was an extreme case. The usual dowry for a Kulin girl is between two and three thousand rupees or even less in East Bengal.

There are certain differences in the customs of East and West Bengal. In West Bengal the bridegroom's party goes to the bride's house and some of them spend the night of the marriage there and are feasted and return home the next day with the bride, but it is not so in East Bengal. There the bridegroom's party remains in the bride's house for three days and nights and then returns home with or without the married pair. In West Bengal the marriage feast takes place the night of the marriage, but it is not so in East Bengal. There no marriage feast takes place at night, the bridegroom's party receiving shidha or raw articles of food which their Brahmins cook for them. On the next day a regular feast takes place with meat, fish, and other eatables. In West Bengal, particularly in the towns, all classes dine together but in villages such promiscuity is not permitted. In East Bengal Kulins do not allow any Moulik to partake of the marriage feast sitting in the same room with them. The Mouliks must sit in a separate room. This rule is strictly observed. In the marriage feast the bridegroom's party and the bride's party sit to breakfast in the same room if they are Kulins. There is a peculiar custom in East Bengal which is still in vogue. A Moulik bridegroom is not permitted to go to the house of a Kulin bride to marry her. The Kulin bride goes to the Moulik bridegroom's village with her near relations and a residence is assigned to the bride's party. Just before the marriage the bridegroom gets on a palanquin and accompanied by near relations and musicians goes to the bride's residences and the bride gets upon another palanquin and follows the bridegroom to the latter's house where the marriage is performed. However, this custom is gradually being abolished and the marriage of Moulik bridegrooms now often takes place in the Kulin bride's house but as the kinsmen of the Kulin bride will not join in the marriage feast with the Moulik bridegroom and his kinsmen, such marriages take place in towns where a house is hired for the purpose. In West Bengal it is considered derogatory for the bride to come and get married in the bridegroom's village or house. But in East Bengal it is not at all considered derogatory, not even among Brahmins. The custom of the bride going to the bridegroom's village to get married is laughed at by the people of West Bengal. But this is not a rare thing in the civilized world. Where did George IV and Edward VII of England marry? Did they travel to the Continent to marry? Rather the brides came over to England for the marriage.

There is a modified Kulinism among Uttar Rarhi and Varendra Kayasthas though its origin, as already stated, is obscure. Most probably they have introduced it among themselves in imitation of the Dakhim Rarhi and the Bangaja Kayasthas. They also observe the rules and customs prevalent in East and West Bengal.

Kulinism which was introduced by Raja Ballal Sen among the five Brahmins and the five Kayasthas brought down by Adisur from Kanouj has permeated all ranks of society in Bengal. I have known some sweepers claiming superiority in social position over other sweepers. This is natural and I believe that Kulinism in some form or other prevails in every ranks of society throughout the world, with this difference that Brahmins permanently lose their kul by marrying a girl of an inferior rank and I believe that this custom of Brahmins is peculiar only to them. In other castes a man may be temporarily socially degraded by marrying a girl of a very low caste but within the subdivision of his own caste, but if he afterwards marries into a high family he recovers his position. But it is not so among Kulin Brahmins. Once they lose their kul they can never recover it.

As regards the ceremony of marriage it is almost the same as that of Churakaran. A priest performs some ceremonies in the bridegroom's house on the previous day and white sandal paste is rubbed over the bridegroom's forehead. The remnant of the sandal paste is sent to the bride's house with a silken or cotton sari and some sweetmeats. The bride's priest performs a similar ceremony with that sandal paste over the bride's forehead. In the evening the ladies of the house fetch water from neighbouring houses and the goddess Kali, the protectress from evil, is worshiped with that water. Next, day, at early dawn, the bride and the bridegroom take some curd and some ceremonies are performed by the ladies of both the houses accompanied by the sound of conch shell and music. Afterwards sradh is performed by some kinsman. In the evening one or more relations of the bride go to the bridegroom's house or lodging as the case may be and bring down the bridegroom and his party to the bride's house. The procession must be accompanied by music and lights. In towns rich people spend lots of money on this procession and display fancy choukies, some of which are made of tinsel. When the procession approaches the bride's house, all these choukies are looted by the spectators. In East Bengal all expenses in connection with the journey, food and conveyance of the bridegroom have to be paid by the bride's father if the parties are both Kulins or Mouliks but it is otherwise in West Bengal where each party pays its own expenses. When the bridegroom's party arrives at the bride's house the first carriage must contain the bridegroom, and all the other guests must follow him in their carriage or on foot. The barber takes the bridegroom in his arms and takes him inside the house where he is seated on a velvet sheet with velvet bolsters on his three sides. The bridegroom must be very well dressed and is generally accompanied by a small near relation but in Calcutta two Jewish girls accompany him and fan him. The bridegroom is heavily garlanded and everyone of his party must be garlanded. The bridegroom's party sits round him. But there is a peculiar custom among Kulins in East Bengal. My kinsmen claim precedence and insist on sitting on a velvet sheet (masland) near the bridegroom and will not allow anybody else to sit there. Rival Kulins object to this, and once there was a regular fight on the occasion of the marriage of the sister of the late Mr. Mon Mohon Ghose, the well-known Barrister of the Calcutta High Court. Since then, where my kinsmen go, no seat is provided for anybody and they and all other Kulins remain standing when the marriage ceremony takes place. This is really a barbarous custom but no one will yield and therefore this custom will remain in force for many years. If anybody is inclined to sit, he must go to some other room and take a seat, as, for the above reason, no one gets a seat near the place where the marriage is performed. But in places where my kinsmen are not invited, seats are offered to Kulins who occupy the place of honor and the Mouliks sit behind them.

Before the commencement of the marriage the bridegroom is taken into the inner apartment and is there made to sit on a mat or carpet with the bride in front, with the ladies round them who perform the baran ceremony and the bridegroom goes back to the place of marriage.

When the marriage ceremony begins, all the relations of both the parties are asked to come to the place where the marriage takes place. In some families the marriage must take place under the sky and in some families in a covered place or a room. The priests recite the necessary formula which the father of the bride or his representative has to repeat, then the bridegroom is asked to stand and the bride goes round him seven times keeping him to the right. In some families a male relation takes her in his arms and goes round the bridegroom. In some families in East Bengal the bridegroom and the bride are both raised on two piris (wooden seats) which are held aloft by people called nafars or hereditary slaves who live on rent free land and have rent free land to maintain them. This was our family custom also, but now my kinsmen hold the piri and have dispensed with the services of the nafars. These nafars are a privileged class. If they have no food at home they begin service in their master's house and take their food there. They always accompany the marriage party of their master, and get as their perquisite all that is left after eating of the sidha given to the bridegroom's party. When the bridegroom gets his breakfast on the day after the marriage the nafar gets all the plates and cups in which rice and the dishes are served. The bride and the bridegroom are now confronted. The bride's veil is removed and the pair is asked to look at each other. The bride is brought to the place of marriage just before she moves round the bridegroom. After they have looked at each other a yellow thread is tied round the right wrist of each of them and the bride's father is made to repeat the formula of giving away the bride and the, bridegroom repeats the formula of acceptance, coupled with a promise to guard her honor, and to maintain her. Then there is a ceremony called saptapady, the wife taking seven steps, her feet being urged by the bridegroom's gentle kick from behind. After this the bridegroom receives a dakshina of gold. Instances have been known where a Kulin bridegroom has insisted on receiving a large amount of dakshina as no marriage is complete without it. Fortunately such instances are rare. After the receipt of dakshina the marriage is over and the parties are considered lawfully wedded. After this the bridegroom is taken to the female apartment and there he is received by the ladies of the bride's party. The pair sit on a mat or a carpet placed upon the floor and they play with the ladies with rice and cowries as emblematic of wealth.

The poor bride and bridegroom have to fast almost the whole day. Before marriage they can take only milk and dahi and no solid food. After the marriage they get some sweetmeats to eat but no regular food, but everybody in the house and all guests are sumptuously fed. The mother of the bride fasts the whole day, but the mother of the bridegroom, if not a widow, takes seven regular meals in the course of the day. This custom arose out of a curious legend. It is said that Kartic, the god of war, was on his journey to marry when he suddenly remembered to have left something behind, and he returned home and found that his mother, the goddess Durga, was taking a sumptuous feast and he asked the reason. She replied that she was taking this sumptuous breakfast because after his marriage it might be that his wife would not give her proper nourishment and it was therefore that she was eating to her heart's content. This reply struck Kartic as extraordinary and he resolved not to marry lest his wife should starve his mother. The result is that Kartic is still a bachelor and all mothers of bridegrooms, if not widows, enjoy seven meals on the day of the marriage whereas the mother of the bride has to fast the whole day until the marriage is over.

Hindu religion or shastras do not insist that the marriage should take place at night but such has been the custom all along. Moreover the marriage cannot take place at any hour of the night but must be performed in an auspicious moment. The almanacs fix the time when the marriage is to begin and when it is to end, and after the marriage is over a Brahmin priest performs a yajna which is not always compulsory in the case of some Dakhin Rarhi Kayastha families but is always compulsory in the case of all superior castes, Brahmins or other Kayasthas.

After the happy pair has played with rice and cowries they get their supper and are led to the nuptial bed. In East Bengal they are allowed to spend the night alone without any disturbance, but in West Bengal the room in which the nuptial couch is laid is filled with ladies who chaff away the whole night with the bride-groom, who is not permitted to sleep but who is rather exposed to all sorts of tricks by the ladies present at the marriage, a most barbarous custom.

On the day after the marriage there is another ceremony which is called bash-ibibaha and the Brahmins perform the worship of the sun and the happy pair, after bathing, go round the four plantain trees, at the four corners of a square, which had been planted on the previous day and there is a small hole inside the square called a miniature tank, in which some water is poured and the happy pair throw their wedding rings into the water which they pretend to try to find out of the muddy water. After this ceremony is over there is no other ceremony to be performed, except on the tenth day on which occasion the pair is taken inside the above square, and the water which had been brought from the tank on the first day and preserved in a jar with a figure of an idol in vermilion is poured upon their bodies. Five myrabolams, grass and paddy which had been presented to the bridegroom at the time of the marriage with a golden ring and which had been tied in a corner of his dhoti are thrown away.

After the bashibibaha is over the married couple get some refreshment, as until this marriage is over they are not permitted to take any food, though the bride and the bridegroom had practically fasted on the day of the marriage. On the tenth day also until the ceremony is over they cannot take any food. In fact on every ceremonial occasion the parties concerned have to fast until the ceremony is over. Even the priest who officiates at any ceremony has to fast. During the three days of Durga puja, the priests cannot take any cooked food at all and take slight nourishment after the day's work is over, and it is only on the night of the third day when all the rites in connection with the puja are over that they can cook and eat their rice. Christians have much faith in the rite of baptism, but Hindus must baptize every day before performing any religious ceremony and must also fast until the religious ceremony is over. Roman Catholic priests perhaps also observe this custom. I was once traveling with a Roman Catholic priest who told me that he had taken no dinner. I offered him some biscuits which I had with me; he looked at his watch and he said that it was past midnight, therefore he could not take any food until he had said his prayers in the morning. I believe this baptism and this fasting have been introduced into Christianity in imitation of the Hindus, with this difference that Christians think that one baptism in one's lifetime is enough, whereas Hindus are of opinion that they must baptize every time they perform any religious ceremony. That baptism and fasting are very important ceremonies is proved by the fact that Jesus fasted forty days and nights after his baptism, (IV Mat. 2.)

The Mohammedan religion also enjoins fasting for purification. In fact all Mahomedans are directed by the Koran to fast every day during the month of Ramadan, (Ch. II. V.181.) At night they can take refreshment, but when one can clearly distinguish a white thread from a black thread by the daybreak they begin the fast until night and their fast is so strict that they cannot even swallow their spittle or even bathe, and Algazali reckoned fasting one-fourth part of the faith. So the institution of fasting is not peculiar among Hindus though it seems somewhat strange that on the day of marriage, the happiest event in one's life, one should have to live upon curd and milk only.

On the day of marriage a big feast with lucbis, fish and all sorts of eatables is given to the bridegroom's party, and to all kinsmen and relations, male and female. This is the rule in Calcutta and in some towns, but in villages the marriage feast is given at noon of the day after the marriage, as no social feast can take place at night. On this day meat and pilau are also served, as goats may be slaughtered on this day but not on the previous day.

On this occasion frequent disputes arise regarding payment of caste money. If a Kulin gives his son or daughter in marriage with a Moulik, his kinsmen are entitled to have bedai and in all cases each house gets some cash payment which varies from rupees two to five, in our family, besides mustard oil, betel leaves, dabi and fish. Sometimes kinsmen do not give these things or pay any cash money but promise to pay them after they have got money from the Moulik.

They sometimes fail to keep their promise and the kinsmen insist on realizing all previous dues before joining in the feast. I have known an instance in our family when the quarrel lasted from noon to midnight. As the parties could come to no agreement there was no feast and most of the eatables had to be thrown away. This rule is still in force at least among my kinsmen, who are regarded as the highest Kulins in East Bengal.

On this occasion, in my younger days, I used to see every invited kinsman send his servants with the necessary piris, thalis, cups, and glasses to the host's house and they arranged the seats for their masters, the host supplying only salt, lemon and water and no plates of any kind. The first thing to be served was pilau accompanied with meat curry. After everybody had filled himself with these two dishes a little rice was served, then moong dal, fried fish and an acid. After these were consumed, dahi, hkir, and paramanya or rice cooked in milk and sugar were served. There were no sweetmeats such as shandesh, rashgolla, pantooa, amriti in those days. The females were served with other dishes in addition, such as fish curries, etc. The villagers also got fish and vegetable curries and dal but very little pilau or meat. Such was the custom in our family when I was young. But now the host provides everything and plantain leaves have been substituted for thalis (bell metal plates). The pilau which is served is prepared with fresh pure cow's ghee, but sometimes turmeric is mixed with boiled rice and a little ghee is added and this pilau is for the guests, the bridegroom's pilau being prepared in the usual way with good ghee.

On the occasions of these feasts Kulins and Mouliks do not eat together, the Mouliks being accommodated in a separate room. In fact there can be no inter-dining between Kulins and Mouliks during the ten days that the marriage festival lasts and I know of Kulins who strictly observe this rule even today. Some of my kinsmen ate rice in the house of a Moulik on the occasion of the marriage of a Moulik, who married a girl of our family, and each of my kinsmen who ate got Rs.500-0-0 for simply eating rice in his house. My brother and first cousin married the daughters of the richest Kayastha in East Bengal who did not dare ask us to eat rice in his house. Let it be understood once for all that everything turns upon the eating of rice; luchies or any other preparation of wheat can be eaten almost everywhere, even though cooked by a modak (sweetmeat seller). But no rice can be taken if cooked by a man of an inferior caste or by a servant. This is a universal rule in Bengal among the orthodox people.

On the second day, after the bashibibaha is over, all the ladies of the house and the invited female guests give presents of cloth, cash or jewelry to the bride and bridegroom.

On the third day of the marriage there is no ceremony. The bridegroom's party and kinsmen are treated with luchies and sweetmeats but not rice at night. This is called dry food and the nuptial bed is bedecked with flowers and the married pair get new dhoti, chaddar and sari which they wear before going to bed.

It is the invariable custom among all Brahmins, Kayasthas, Vaidyas, and all rich people, that the bridegroom and the bride must wear a red silken cloth at the time of the marriage. This is a very ancient custom, for we find that the poet Kalidas says that when Shiva went to marry Parvati he was dressed in China silk, the words being Chinansuka pattabastra. Formerly silk could come only from China, as we find from Gibbon's History, Chapter 40, Vol. VII, page 92 that, "*till the reign of Justinian the silkworms, who feed an the leaves of the white mulberry tree, were confined to China.*" The price of silk was so high that, "*Aurelian complained that a pound of silk was sold at Rome for twelve ounces of gold*", page 94. Gibbon also says that two Persian monks who had long resided in China, soon discovered that it was impractical to transport the short-lived insect but that in the egg numerous progeny might be preserved and multiplied in a distant climate, and they, after a long journey arrived at Constantinople, imparted their project to the emperor and were liberally encouraged by the gifts and promises of Justinian. They returned to China, concealed the eggs of the silkworms in a hollow cane, and returned to Constantinople and hatched the eggs. This led to the introduction of silkworm throughout Europe and Asia and silk became gradually less costly.

There are other customs in connection with marriage which are prevalent in all castes. For instance, during the ten days that the marriage festival lasts, the husband and the wife must spend the night together except on the second day when after nightfall the husband is not permitted even to see the face of his wife and must sleep in a separate room, the reason being that there is a legend to the effect that Lakshindhar was bitten by a deadly serpent because he, notwithstanding the injunction of the goddess Manasha, the presiding deity of serpent, slept with his wife on that night.

It is said that Lakshindhar disobeyed the injunction of the goddess and slept with his wife in a hermetically sealed room, but, as the fates would have it, there was a very small hole in the wall and the goddess sent the thinnest venomous snake called Kalinda to bite him, and Lakshindhar was bitten and died of the bite, though revived by the goddess at the intercession of his wife. Therefore no Hindu is permitted to sleep with his wife on the second night.

There is another custom. During the ten days of the marriage the married pair are not obliged to observe any auspicious day for undertaking a journey; in fact all these ten days are auspicious for them for any undertaking. There is another custom. Immediately after the father or his representative has repeated the formula of the gift of the bride, the ends of their cloths are tied together and they should remain tied together for the rest of the night, and also on the occasions of the performance of the rites previously mentioned, which are performed on the second and the tenth days, the ends of their cloths are tied together.

There is a peculiar custom among the Vaidays. When the bridegroom enters the house of the bride a winnow containing kasla (a water fruit) is brought by the bride's party to be touched by the bridegroom's forehead. The object of this is to make the bridegroom henpecked and it is supposed that in future the husband will do every thing at the bidding of his wife. This is opposed by the bridegroom's party and sometimes lathis decide the battle, ending in some broken heads and bloodshed. It was my misfortune to attend one of these marriages where some heads were broken and blood spilled.

When the married pair go to the bridegroom's house, they must wait till nightfall before entering it. This is the custom in East Bengal. The bride's palkee precedes that of the bridegroom's and she alights first and then her husband. A cloth is spread upon the ground and she walks upon it, followed by her husband, the ends of their cloths being tied in a knot. When they have proceeded a little, another piece of cloth is laid upon the ground, or the first one is turned over and they proceed thus till they enter the room of their house. They sit on a mat with pith crown and tiara on their heads and they play with rice and cowries and the next day the ladies of the bridegroom's house and kinswomen came to see the bride's face and give her presents of cloth, jewelry, or gold or silver coins, the bride in turn giving saris to the ladies present. On the first night the bride must not eat any food prepared in her husband's house but she brings her food with her from her father's house and eats it. In some families the bride is made to hold a live kai fish in her hand and stand on a stone plate with milk in it.

On the day after her arrival the mother-in-law gives a sumptuous breakfast to the bride which is served on bellmetal plates and cups which become her property and she gets a new silk sari. This food is given by the bridegroom with his own hands and he must ask her to eat.

The married pair go back to the bride's father's house and after spending a night or two there return home. This is called dirgaman or second coming. It must take place within ten days of the marriage, otherwise the bride will have to wait for in auspicious day when her husband goes and brings her home.

When a newly married woman and her husband came to the latter's house far the first time they are received by all near relations. They are received with ulu and the blowing of conch shells, besides music. This blowing of conch shells is necessary in all ceremonial occasions and is intended to scare away the evil spirits. If there be earthquake or an eclipse there must be blowing of conch shells as both these events are attributed to the action of evil spirits who must be scared away. On ceremonial occasions there is blowing of conch shells in the house where the ceremony takes place but in the case of eclipses and earthquakes there is blowing of conch shells in every house. The reason is curious. If a man blows the conch shell on these occasions the evil spirits will leave his house and go to his neighbour's house and it is therefore that the latter thinks it his duty to drive the spirits away and the spirits go to the house of a third man whose duty again is to drive them away and so on, so that the whole country resounds with the blowing of conch shells, with the result that the evil spirits do not find any resting place anywhere and are obliged to leave the country. An eclipse is caused according to our Hindu astronomers by the demon Rahu which literally means shadow but in Vedic times he was known by the name of Svarbhamu,(Rig Veda V.40). It is quite natural that the evil spirits should be driven away, otherwise they would devour the sun or the moon, but the earthquake is believed to he caused by the shaking of the tortoise or of the hood of the endless serpent upon which the earth rests and these are not evil spirits, and I can find no reason why they should be scared away by the blowing of conch shells.

After the arrival of the newly married wife in her husband's house, all near relations male and female go to see her face and the next day there is a regular levee, when the pair sit on a mat and everybody comes to see her face and gives them presents, when the bride's veil is removed from her forehead. She must then shut her eyes in East Bengal but in West Bengal this rule is not observed and she sees her visitors. She touches the feet of everyone who is superior in pedigree and age to her husband and everyone puts some grass and paddy upon her head as tokens of blessing. The mother-in-law must commence this ceremony. As to the custom of touching one's feet, the invariable rule is that a wife will touch the feet of every one who is senior in age and relationship to her husband. Those who are his juniors will touch his feet and his wife's feet too. In fact her position in this respect and in most other respects is that of her husband whose ardhanga or half body she is.

As to the putting of grass and paddy upon the head, it is the invariable custom in Bengal for females to put them on the head of everybody who appears before them on the Dasami day after the Durga puja is over. They will either touch the feet of the visitor or the latter touch the feet of the ladies, but the grass and paddy must be put on the visitor's head by the females. On ceremonial occasions and return from a long journey this ceremony is also observed.

If the newly married wife be the daughter of a Moulik and her husband be a Kulin, the husband's kinsmen and kinswomen are invited to a breakfast at her husband's house and each family receives half the bedai paid to each of the guests who were invited to attend the marriage and a few extra rupees for some petty items before any Kulin accepts the invitation. Each of the married kinswoman receives a sari for eating with her and those whose feet she can touch get another cloth each. But this does not permit the newly married wife to touch the foot of her Kulin kinsmen. If she wishes to do so then she must again pay another half bedai to the head of every family among her kinsmen and give the kinsmen a feast or she can amalgamate the two feasts together. This last ceremony is called pakashparsha or touching cooked food. On this occasion, when all the guests are seated for breakfast she enters the room and puts a handful of rice or pilau upon each plate beginning with her husband's and retires. Then the servers come and serve other dishes as usual and the breakfast commences. Every family which partakes of this breakfast is bound to take food cooked or touched by her, but if she does not perform this paksbaparsha ceremony then no kinsman is bound to take any cooked food touched by her. But female kinswomen will simply eat with her in the same room, if she performs the first ceremony called boubbat or a wife's rice taking. This only raises her to a level with her other kinswomen, Kulin or

Moulik, but if she performs the ceremony of pakashaparsha then she raises herself to an equality with kinswomen who are daughters of Kulins. Nevertheless no outsider Kulin is bound to eat any food cooked or touched by her unless some money is paid to him. This practice is rigidly observed in East Bengal, but there is very great laxity in this respect in West Bengal where for all practical purposes Kulinism has been abolished, in so much that every educated Moulik bridegroom receives a pona or dowry from his Kulin father-in-law sometimes to the extent of Rs. 10,000 in hard cash, besides presents. In East Bengal also Kulinism is on the decline and some Moulik bridegrooms accept pana, though the amount may be very small and hardly exceeds Rs. 1,000. Formerly all Moulik brides and bridegrooms had to pay dowry to marry or be married into a Kulin family but now this rule is not always observed. If the Moulik bridegroom be highly educated or belongs to a highly respectable or a rich family then no papa is demanded from him; rather in some cases he expects pana.

But in the case of a Moulik bride her father must pay some pana to a Kulin bridegroom. It is the prevalence of the democratic ideas brought in by English education that is levelling up the people of this country and removing all barriers among sub-castes. Now-a-days such marriages take place between people as could not possibly have taken place fifty years ago. Even the Brahmins have begun to intermarry into different sub-castes, and if Brahmins, the most conservative people in India, can do so, the more liberal sections of the community will naturally do something more and I believe the time is not far distant when there will be intermarriages between all castes, the Legislatures having paved the way by passing a recent Act called "Gour's Act," No. 30 of 1923, which enables Hindus to marry one another, irrespective of caste.

In the marriage procession of rich people there are plenty of musicians and lights and in cities there is a long train of carriages, but the poor people cannot afford to bear the expense. In towns motor cars and motor buses have replaced the horse drawn carriages, the result being that there can be no musicians or light bearers walking on foot.

Formerly among the upper classes marriages took place between infants, and fifty years ago it was very difficult to find a bride who was more than twelve years of age but now-a-days, except among the poor, marriages rarely take place before the girl is at least fourteen years old and the bridegroom has just finished his college career and entered service or is going to finish his studies soon. These grown up boys object to be led in procession and therefore there is very little hubbub in the marriage procession now-a-days.

In towns also there is one peculiar custom. When the bridegroom's party enters the bride's house all sorts of well dressed uninvited strangers enter the house with them and partake of the marriage feast. Therefore the bride's father has to make arrangements for a much larger number of guests than that estimated by the bridegroom's party. As the marriage takes place soon after the bridegroom's party arrives it is very difficult to find out who these uninvited strangers are. In villages there is no such difficulty. No outsider is permitted to sit in the marriage feast and as the feast must take place in the daytime it is very easy to detect all interlopers and to eject them. In towns, particularly in Calcutta and its neighbourhood, the marriage feast takes place at night. It is not so in villages where people observe the strict rule of Hindu society that no ceremonial feast can take place at night. The rule is so strict that the feeding of Brahmins at night does not count as a virtuous act, but feeding Brahmins at daytime is always reckoned as a meritorious act. If Brahmins are fed by a non-Brahmin the Brahmins must get some dakshina but no dakshina is given if the feeding takes place at night. The reason is that this feeding does not add to the virtue of the host and will not count in the next world. In fact the word bhojan or feast is restricted to feeding people in the daytime.

As mentioned, fifty years ago marriages took place between infants. The girls rarely exceeded the age of twelve and it was a meritorious act on the part of their fathers to give them in marriage preferably in the eighth year when the gift of the bride was considered as the gift of the goddess Durga. So great was the merit of such a gift. The merit decreased every year and if the girl was twelve years old the father incurred sin in giving such a grown-up girl in marriage, because Raghunandan says that if a girl attains puberty before marriage her father goes to hell. It was for this reason that when a bill was introduced in the legislative Council nearly forty years ago to raise the age of consent to twelve years, there was agitation in Hindu society, the Hindus thinking that if the marriage is deferred till the girl attains puberty the soul of the bride's father will be condemned to hell. But now Hindu society, at least of the upper classes, has much advanced in liberal ideas and even orthodox Hindus have to wait till their daughters exceed the age of puberty for the simple reason that no well educated boy can be had at a very tender age and if the bridegroom is a grown-up one, as he must be if he has finished his education, he will disdain the idea of marrying a little girl. Now-a-days, there is a great demand for grown-up girls because the bridegrooms are grown-up boys who never think of marrying before they have graduated or finished their academic career. In my time when I was young I never heard of the marriage of a graduate if he was in affluent circumstances and I believe that among my contemporaries I was the first man to marry after I had joined the bar. Now-a-days the rule is just the reverse. Two years ago, when the age of consent was raised to thirteen there was no commotion in Hindu society. So great is the advance of liberal ideas in our society.

Marriages are proposed by common friends and relations or by professional marriage brokers and the bridegroom's party sees the girl but the bride and the bridegroom, half a century ago, never saw one another before marriage. Fifty years ago I know only of three cases, including mine, in which the bride was seen by the bridegroom before the marriage was settled. But now-a-days after the parents have approved of the bride, the bridegroom goes and sees her and the final choice rests with the bridegroom and sometimes with the bride also, particularly when the bride is a grown-up girl aged about eighteen to twenty-five, as marriages of such girls are not very rare.

After the marriage is settled there is something like a formal agreement between the parties, not necessarily a written one but a ceremonial one. On an auspicious day some very near relations of the bride are invited to the bridegroom's house to a feast. A Brahmin accompanies them, recites some mantras, puts grass and paddy—the necessary emblems of blessing—upon the bridegroom's head and rubs some sandal paste upon his forehead. The bride's father gives to the bridegroom a sovereign. The Kulins among the guests get some money, and the party is feasted, but in East Bengal they will not take any rice in a Moulik's house and they will only take some dry food, but in West Bengal everybody partakes of rice with many fish and vegetable dishes and sweetmeats. A piece of paper is daubed with a vermilion mark on the top and several items which the bride's father agrees to pay are written down, consisting of the amount of the dowry, and the several items of jewelry with their weights and fineness entered therein. In East Bengal only the amount of the dowry is written, no mention is made of the jewelry, but it is not so in West Bengal which is much richer than East Bengal. Another reason is that East Bengal people rely upon the word of the bride's father that he would give proper jewelry, but in West Bengal every item of jewelry must be noted down with its weight and fineness. This ceremony is called patra in West Bengal and patipatra in East Bengal. On another auspicious day the bridegroom's father and his near relations go to see the bride and there a similar ceremony is repeated but nothing is written on paper; only the bride gets a present of jewelry and a Brahmin officiates. On both these occasions the father of the bride and the father of the bridegroom invite their own relations to their house and they are present at the ceremony and join in the feast. After this ceremony the marriage is, according to Hindu custom, irrevocable and if by some mishap the bridegroom dies before marriage, it is very difficult to get a bridegroom because the bride is recognized as the widow of the deceased and widow marriage does not prevail in this country, though legalized in 1856.

There are some peculiar customs relating to marriage among certain sects of the Vaishnavas, or the followers of Chaityana. They are divided into two classes, the householder and the mendicant, as among the Buddhist, from whom Chaitanya has copied many customs. The customs relating to the householder Vaishnavas are the same as those among the general Hindu population. The mendicants are those who have renounced the world and live, generally speaking, by begging and on charity. They live together as a separate community under the leadership of a local guru or spiritual guide. The householders do not take meat but take fish and vegetables like the general body of Hindus. The mendicants do not take meat or fish. The marriage customs of some mendicants are very peculiar. If anyone of their community wishes to marry, then he has to pay a fee of Rs. 1-4-0 to the guru. Then unmarried Vaishnavis or widows are made to lie down in a room and their bodies and faces are covered up and he is asked to remove the covering over some one's face from among these females. He removes the covering, sees the face, and if he likes the particular woman and she agrees, there is an end of the thing and no further marriage ceremony is necessary. But if he does not like to marry her, he pays a further fee of Rs. 1-4-0 to the guru and removes another covering and goes on paying this fee till he makes his selection and the woman agrees, when he has to pay no more fee. So there is no formal marriage between a Vaishnava and a Vaishnavi. It is rather a concubinage. At any time, a Vaishnava can divorce a Vaishnavi whereas there is no divorce according to Hindu law, and both parties may marry again.

On the first night of this marriage the guru sleeps with the bride and must cohabit with her. From next day the so-called husband may approach her. This is called guruprasady, prasad means what is left after eating or enjoying. The enjoyment of this guruprasad is considered a devotional act and enhances the religious merit of the partaker. Be it understood that the guru in ninety-nine cases out of hundred is a Brahmin and therefore this custom was probably introduced by them for their own benefit. The householder Vaishnavas do not generally follow this guruprasady system but I have known such cases among them also. This is not a matter of astonishment. In the Malabar country in Southern India, the Nambudri Brahmins have abolished marriage among non-Brahmins and this for their own benefit. There are more degrading customs among certain castes of Hindus than among any other civilized people. Hindus boast of their civilization which the orthodox Hindus ascribe to the Brahmins, but what have the Brahmins done to elevate the lower castes or some hill tribes in India? The reader will be astonished to learn that in certain parts of India on the death of a wife the husband marries his eldest daughter, and on the death of the husband the wife marries her eldest son. Similar custom, I understand, prevails in some parts of Mid Africa but I do not know if such custom prevails in any other part of the world. There were marriages between brothers and sisters in Egypt. Cleopatra, though of Greek descent, married her brother. He was the last king of Egypt, and on his death she succeeded to the throne. Similarly Darius the last king of Persia married his sister. In Burma we find that its last king Thebaw married his step-sister Supya Lat. The story of Oedipus' marriage with his mother may no doubt be cited against the Greeks but the parties knew not each other. The Greek ambassadors to the Court of Atilla speak of his marriage with his daughter. This shows such marriages were not rare among the Mongolians but those ambassadors refer to similar incestuous marriages in Egypt, Persia and India. I have already cited the cases of the Persian, Egyptian and Mongolian and Burmese kings but I am not aware if any such custom prevailed in India except as stated above and I am of opinion that the charge laid against civilized Indians in that respect is not true. The inquisitive reader is referred to the Report on the *Census of India* in 1911, Vol. I, page 230 et seq. (Re: Marriage) and Guizot's *History of Civilisation,* Vol. II page 422.

The third wife of a Hindu cannot be a human being, as she is certain to be, carried away by death. Therefore when a man is going to marry for the third time, he has first to marry a pigeon, on whom death will soon come down, and then he marries a human wife, who is thus the fourth wife, to whom death may be propitious, having devoured the previous bird wife.

Kulins extort money from Bangals in East Bengal in various ways. When they go to the houses of the latter on the occasion of a marriage, they will demand and get some money for gramdarshany or seeing the village, then for chulakhudany or digging the ground for making a hearth to cook their food. Before marriage they had extorted some money for attending the patipatra ceremony when the marriage is finally settled. After the marriage when they leave the place, the Kulins get bidai, or leave money, which varies from ten to twenty-five or more for each Kulin. The Brahmins, gomastas, servants, the barber, the washerman who usually accompany them all get some money, and the Bangal has to pay the cost of the food and the hire of the boat or railway fare both ways. Kulins, who usually travel third class, travel second class or even first class when attending a marriage at a Bangal's house.

If a Kulin son-in-law is invited to a marriage in his Bangal father-in-law's house he gets his sidha, bidai, and everything the other Kulins get but no money for seeing the village as he had seen it before. He will lodge with his kinsmen but his wife lives in her father's house with her children as no Hindu can demand any money from his maternal grandfather on any ground and will eat in his house though his father will not do so within ten days of the marriage.

There are various customs which it is unnecessary to relate but there is a peculiar custom prevalent in West Bengal which requires notice. The bride's father must send presents to the bridegroom's house every month of the year, thus :

(1) In the month of Baisak the presents consist of mangoes, sandesh, towels, baris made of dal, and prepared betel. The bridegroom sends to his father-in-law's house mangoes, sandesh and betel.

(2) In Jaisth, the bride's father sends mangoes, jack and other fruits, bari, piri (wooden seat), sandesh, betel and towel, and on the occasion of Jumai Sasty, which takes place in that month, the jamia or bridegroom gets all sorts of sumptuous presents such as dahi, bhir, sandesh, rasagolla and other sweetmeats, betel nuts and spices, a pair of dhoti and chaddar, banians, shirts, handkerchiefs, socks, shoes, scents, soap, towel, looking glass, brush, comb and prepared betel.

(3) In Ashar on the occasion of the Rath, dhoti, chaddar and some cash are sent. If the bride is in the father-in-law's house she gets from her father, bodice, dhoti, alta, vermilion, pineapple, mangoes, jack and other fruits, dahi, khir and sandesh and prepared betel.

(4) Nothing particular in Sraban.

(5) In Bhadra hilsa fish, sandesh, all kinds of preserves, dahi, vegetables, sak (creeper), prepared betel are sent.

(6) In Aswin on the occasion of the Durga Puja some presents have to be sent to the bridegroom as in Jaisth on the occasion of Jamai Sashthi. Besides this all the members of the family of the bridegroom get dhoti, chaddar and sari and the bridegroom also sends dhoti, chaddar and sari to the members of the father-in-law's house. In East Bengal this custom of sending presents during Durga Puja is observed in the first year after the marriage but in subsequent years only the bridegroom and the bride get wearing apparel from the bride's father and nobody gets any present.

(7) On the occasion of Bhaifota, or mark on the brother's forehead in Kartic, all married sisters give presents to their brothers of dhoti and chaddar, betel and its spices, and sweetmeats, and the day after the Bahifota the brothers are feasted by their married sisters.

(8) In the month of Agrahayan, winter clothing, such as shawl, banian, hose, handkerchief, mirror, comb, scents, shoes, cauliflowers, peas, oranges, bari, yeti fish, lobster, dahi, sandesh and betel are sent to the bridegroom's house.

(9) In Pous, cakes have to be prepared and sent to the bridegroom's house and with them the following articles are sent: grapes, pomegranates, and other Cabuli fruits, hard khir, chhana, sugar, sujee, ghee, flour, khaja, moong, maskkalai, til, mustard oil, molasses, coconuts, new rice, pair of sari for the bridegroom's mother, towel, piri, basket, cooking vessels and prepared betel. Similar articles have to be sent from the bridegroom's house for the bride's mother.

(10) In Magh, on the occasion of the Saraswati puja, the following articles are sent to the bride if she is in her father-in-law's house, otherwise not: yellow colored cloth which must be red bordered, alta, vermilion, tip, sweetmeats and betel nut.

(11) In Falgoon, on the occasion of the Dol puja the bride's father sends the following presents: red abir, sugar, futkalai, murki, and other sweetmeats, dhoti, chaddar, coat, shoes, handkerchief, hose, banian, scents, mirror and brush, and some cash. This is for the bridegroom. The bride will get some cash, rose-coloured cloth, chemise, bodice, golden embroidery, ribbon, hair pin, alta, vermilion and tip.

(12) In Chait, on the occasion of Charak festival, the bridegroom will get dhoti, chaddar, scents and some cash. Vide Kayastha Patrika for Sraban, 1330.

The giving of these presents is compulsory in the first year of marriage in West Bengal. In East Bengal, as I have already stated, the married pair get dhoti, chaddar and sari on the occasion of the Durga puja but in West Bengal these presents must be continued by rich families, though on a lower scale. In East Bengal there is no cash payment except on the occasion of the Durga puja when amounts varying from rupees twenty-five to three or four hundred are sent by rich people to their sons-in-law's house. After the married pair get children, their children also expect clothing from their mother's father and the maternal grandfather has to present his grandchild with a cup and spoon for feeding him and toys when he is a year old. The cup and spoon may be of bell metal but rich people prefer to present silver articles.

It was the custom, particularly in West Bengal, to send presents of cloth and sandesh, to the bride or bridegroom on receipt of all invitations to marriage. This present must be sent before the marriage takes place. But now this custom is dying out for various reasons. In the first place, the price of a piece of cloth and of a seer of sandesh has doubled within recent years, and secondly, a movement was set on foot by the late Mohini Mohan Roy of the High Court Bar to abolish this custom and the custom is dying out.

Rich people used to send a brass jar with some other articles with every letter of invitation to a marriage but this custom is also dying out.

The Kayastha Shabha, founded about a quarter of a century ago, started a movement for the abolition of dowry, and, it has made some progress. This system of dowry is a most pernicious system and it is one of the causes of the delay in getting one's daughter married. Because a father could not afford the dowry demanded from him, his daughter, Smehalata, burnt herself to death by pouring kerosene oil on her cloth and putting fire to it. All grown-up daughters, particularly of Mouliks of West Bengal, should worship the memory of this Senhalata, who sacrificed her life to save her family from ruin.

As regards the lower castes, it is unnecessary to say much. They try to imitate the customs of the upper castes as far as their means permit. Among them the bridegroom almost invariably pays some dowry, and the bride is often of tender age. Among the Chandals the bridegrooms are generally grown-up people and the brides very young, and among the Patials (mat makers) the price of the bride is one hundred rupees per year of her age.

CHAPTER 8

▼

PUBERTY

Formerly girls were married when they were very young. Manu says that a father who gives his daughter in marriage in her eighth year has the merit of bestowing Gouri or Durga in marriage, and the merit decreases every subsequent year and if the girl is married in her eleventh or any succeeding year when she is expected to attain the age of puberty, the father who bestows such a girl in marriage goes to hell. Therefore orthodox Hindus must give their daughters in marriage before the completion of the tenth year. When the Government introduced the Age of Consent Bill in 1890, there was heated controversy throughout India among Hindus and numerous meetings were held in Calcutta and other places to protest against the Bill, and Manu was quoted everywhere, though even then many girls were married after the maximum age prescribed by Manu. But when the age was increased two years ago from twelve to thirteen, there was no noise anywhere. Such is the progress of civilizing influences in operation in this country. This is due to the spread of other than Sanskrit education, an education which did not allow people to think out of the groove of our ancestors. But now-a-days girls are much older when they are given in marriage, in most cases after they attain puberty. Formerly girls never exceeded the age of twelve or thirteen when they were married but now-a-days very few girls of these ages are married. This is the rule among the upper classes. Among the lower classes the old rules still prevail to some extent but among them also grown-up girls are given in marriage. Among the upper classes formerly boys married when they were in school, now very few school boys are married. The bridegrooms are usually students of the college classes and in many instances they marry after they have commenced to earn money. Half a century ago it was very difficult to find a bridegroom who had finished his education and commenced to earn money but now-a-days such bridegrooms are to be found in plenty. As formerly the bride was young when married she usually attained puberty after marriage. But in this century boys and girls are not usually, at least among the upper classes, married at such early ages. Now it is not unusual to see graduates and people earning money marrying for the first time. Among girls also, fourteen is about the minimum age of marriage and now-a-days many graduate girls are married for the first time. In fact girls above twenty years of age are not very rare, though a generation ago it was a rare thing to find a spinster above that age. The result is that among the upper classes girls usually attain puberty before marriage.

When the girl attains puberty after marriage, ulu is uttered by the females and the young wife is confined in a room for four days and is not permitted to see the sun or the face of any male person. She lives on a vegetable diet and milk during these five days. The members of the family and kinsmen who are invited on this occasion make themselves merry in the house of the young wife. A small trench is dug and water is poured into it and people are brought to the trench and made to sit in it. Sometimes somebody is brought in by force. A regiment of boys and grown-up people go to a house, seize somebody living in that house, bring him by force and compel him to sit in the muddy water of the trench. Sometimes this water is thrown upon people standing near by. In the afternoon these kinsmen get a light repast of parched rice, dahi, and khir, sugar and molasses. On the fifth day the girl comes out of the room, bathes and wears a new cloth. Garbhadan is prepared consisting of cow's dung, urine, milk curd and honey and she is made to drink it. The image of a boy is made with pounded rice and water and thrown from her navel on the ground through the inside of her cloth. The object of this is that she is expected to give birth to a male child. In the evening the husband and wife sit on two seats side by side and then a priest worships the setting sun and the husband repeats some mantras at the dictation of the priest. On that day kinsmen are invited to dinner which usually consists of luchi, vegetables and sweets. If for any reason this so-called second marriage cannot take place within sixteen days, then it can only take place on a Thursday or Sunday, after she gets her menses again.

If the girl be at her father's house, he is bound to send this happy news with a few rupees to his son-in-law's house and vice versa, so that the merry-making can take place in both the houses.

During the period of menstruation, the woman is untouchable in East Bengal. She sleeps on a separate bed which no one can touch, unless he bathes afterwards. Her bedding, mat, bed covers and blankets after the expiration of three nights, are washed and she bathes and becomes touchable. Before her first pregnancy, she must bathe before the cock crows, which is very painful in the cold season. But this rule is not observed if she does not become a mother within three or four years after her puberty.

In West Bengal, she is not untouchable, but she cannot cook anything during two days. Madras follows the custom of East Bengal but there the rule is very strict, as the woman cannot enter any room and lives in a separate hut.

CHAPTER 9

▼

WIDOWHOOD

A married woman becomes a widow not at the moment of her husband's death but when his body is reduced to ashes. She then lays aside all the ornaments on her person, bathes, wears a new washed borderless white dhoti, as there is sizing in all new unwashed dhoties. For the first four days she and her sons live only upon milk and fruits. On the fifth day she and her sons can eat atap rice cooled by her eldest son in an earthen pot. She can also take ghee, milk and plantains but no salt or sugar. She continues this during the whole period of mourning. On the eleventh day of the moon she observes fasting. There is a difference between the customs of East and West Bengal. In East Bengal she can take milk and fruits on the eleventh day but in West Bengal she is absolutely prohibited from taking any nourishment. Non-Hindus will be astonished to hear how rigid is the fast of a widow in West Bengal. If she is ill, she cannot take any medicine, if she is thirsty she cannot drink any water, if she is hungry she cannot take any food.

In fact nothing can go down her throat. It is usual to put some Ganges water into the mouth when a man or woman is dying. But on the eleventh day of the moon no Ganges water can be put into the mouth of a dying widow in West Bengal, but Ganges water is poured into her ear instead. This is a most cruel system practiced in West Bengal. There is fasting among Mahomedans and Catholics. The Mahomedans are directed to observe fast during the whole month of the Ramadan (Koran Chapter II) and Mahomed used to say that fasting was the

"Gate of religion" and that the odor of the mouth of him who fasteth is more grateful to God than that of musk. Algazaly reckons fasting one fourth part of the faith. When the Mahomedans fast, they cannot bathe or swallow their spittle. But this injunction is for the day time, for the Koran permits Mahomedans to eat after sunset and to continue eating until one can distinguish a black thread from a white thread. The fast of the Catholics is the mildest of all. Their priests do not eat anything after midnight until they read their morning prayer. It is difficult to say whether the Bengali widow's fast or the Mahomedan's fast is the more severe and exhausting. The widow's fast lasts during twenty-four hours in a fortnight but the Mahomedans' fast is for twelve hours only but it lasts for a month. Mahomedans also are not permitted to drink in the day time or take a clyster or injection. The Jews also observe the fast in the same way as the Mahomedans. In fact the fasting enjoined in the Koran is taken from the Jews. In East Bengal the rule is not so strict. Widows can take anything but rice and cooked vegetables. They can take unleavened bread, fruits and milk, but on four days in the year they observe strict fast. Those days are when the god Narayana goes to bed, when he turns on the left in his sleep, when he turns on his right side in his sleep, and on the day of Bhim ekadashi and if, she likes, on Sivaratri. Widows of West Bengal taunt those of East Bengal with eating on ekradashi days but they forget that in this respect the widows of East Bengal are more civilized than their sisters in West Bengal. This observance of ekadashi lasts during the lifetime of the widow. The sons also observe ekadashi for one year after their parent's death but they can take fruits and milk.

Two days after the performance of the sradh by the eldest son, the widow takes rice with vegetables, ghee, milk, and everything which a widow is permitted to eat. She can take only one meal a day and that during the daytime. No widow can take any rice after nightfall, nor are widows permitted to take meat, fish, eggs, maskkalai, and moosor dal and pui and some other vegetables. The only animal food a widow can take is milk and its preparations. A widow cannot cook her food in a vessel which has not been scoured and washed and if it be an earthen vessel it cannot be used for a second time. A widow must eat her food in the kitchen or in an adjoining room, as her cooked food cannot be removed from one house to another under the open sky and she cannot eat the leavings of food or eat from any plate which a person has used for eating. If any person while eating has touched any cooked food then no widow will take it, the only exception being in the case of the spiritual guide who takes a large quantity of food on his plate, eats a portion and leaves the remainder for his disciples to eat, which they do with the greatest devotion.

A widow must eat out of a stone dish, a brass plate or a plantain or other leaf. Every male Hindu or a married woman can eat out of bell metal plates but the use of a bell metal plate is prohibited to a widow; she can use bell metal cups for putting her cooked food in them but she cannot eat out of a bell metal plate. Of course no orthodox Hindu can use a China plate as it is made of clay and if any one eats rice out of it then it is spoiled and cannot be used for the second time and must be thrown away. In fact no earthen dish which is once used for the purpose of eating can be used again by a Hindu and it must be thrown away. Even an earthen glass cannot be used twice for drinking water out of.

No widow can remarry, though the law was passed in 1856 for the remarriage of widows. Nearly a hundred widow marriages take place during the year but lately societies have been formed in East and West Bengal for the advancement of widow remarriage. Formerly widow marriages took place among the lower classes but as they try to imitate the upper classes, among whom there is no remarriage, the lower castes are giving up the custom. Widows cannot take ordinary salt; the only salt they can take is rock salt. Widows cannot wear any dhoti which has a colored border or colored body but in some cases I have seen black or green bordered dhotis to be used by widows. These were exceptional cases. The use of a red-bordered dhoti is absolutely prohibited. Widows also cannot eat any food cooked on the previous day; even unleavened bread baked on the previous day cannot be taken on the next day, the only exception being khai or parched rice. They can never take any chira unless it is prepared from atap paddy at home by her own caste people. Even khai bought from the bazaar cannot be eaten and must be prepared at home. In the evening the widows take a slight repast. Rich people take milk and fruits but young widows take luchi or unleavened bread with vegetables in addition. Old widows generally crop their hair. It seems that red color is absolutely prohibited to widows. They cannot use any cloth or chemise upon which there is a single red thread and they cannot use any vermilion. Generally speaking, widows are very strict and orthodox. They do not allow any one to touch them after their bath and before breakfast and if any one touches them they immediately bathe again. My grandmother never allowed me to touch her before her supper. If I accidentally touched her she would forego her night repast. But in some cases a few drops of Ganges water are sprinkled upon the widow's person which serves the purpose of a bath. It is unnecessary to say that a widow's food can be cooked only by one of her sub caste or by a person of a superior caste. No person of a lower caste can cook her food. She will not drink any water fetched by a servant of inferior caste or allow any one of an inferior caste to touch her food or drink. Formerly widows did not drink any pipe water but now many of them do so. No widow can wear shoes or slippers or any bodice. Her dress consists of a white dhoti and now-a-days a chemise and in winter a thick cotton or woolen chaddar.

Widows of gentle families eat rice once from sunrise to sunrise and when it is daylight but I have ascertained that in Bihar even Brahmin widows can take rice in the day and again in the night, just as a married woman does. As already stated, a widow in West Bengal must totally fast on the eleventh day of the moon, and she cannot take any food, drink, or even medicine on that day but this rule does not obtain in East Bengal except in portions thereof. They can eat every cooked food but rice, dal and cooked vegetables. They usually take unleavened bread or khai and milk. Widows take slight supper at night. In East Bengal respectable widows never take parboiled rice and their rice must be cooked in a separate room and the smell of cooked flesh or fish should not enter their cook room. In West Bengal respectable widows sometimes take parboiled rice cooked in a hearth where fish and flesh had been just cooked, only the hearth must be wiped with water and a rag. Sometimes cow dung is mixed with the water. If a widow who has given birth to only one son hears the sound of a flute while eating, she must stop eating.

CHAPTER 10

▼

DEATH

Before death it is usual to take the dying man to the Ganges and just before loss of consciousness the body is immersed up to the navel in the sacred water and the dying man is made to repeat some mantras, the idea being that if a man dies in such a state he gets the same benefit as dying within the sacred limits of the town of Benares. It is the Hindu belief that if a man dies there he goes direct to Shivalok or the abode of Shiva. Some even go as far as to say that such a man becomes a part of Shiva, which is the same thing as Nirvana, the *summum bonum* of human existence. The above rule cannot apply to people living at a distance from the Ganges. In their case the dying man is removed to the place where a tulsi plant has been planted. In all cases the body of the dying man must be removed from his room and placed under the sky. The Hindus justify this upon the grounds that if a man is gasping for breath, he should be taken to the open courtyard where he gets plenty of air and feels greater ease, but they forget that the gasping is caused by the loss of vital power and not by any insufficiency of air contained in the room. The real explanation is that if a man dies in a room the whole floor must be removed to the depth of some inches and a puja must be performed, otherwise his spirit will hover round the room. So this rite is derived not from hygienic laws but from the dread of evil spirits, an ingrained belief of all orthodox Hindus. After death some kinsman or other person of the same caste must remain near the dead man, touching his body or the bier or bed on which he is laid, as the moment he removes his hands from the body or the bier or bed, evil spirits will enter the dead body. Near relations and other people collect and remove the body to the place of cremation. One rule is strictly observed; no one of an inferior caste can touch the dead body or bier or bed so that castehood sticks to a man until he is burnt to ashes. The sons of the deceased put their shoulders to the foot of the bier which is always towards the house and the head is always towards the burning ghat. In the case of old and well-known people there is a sankirtan party which precedes the bier. Those who carry the bier repeat the name of Hari. When the body is taken to the cremation ground, it is bathed by pouring water upon it and it is made to wear a new cloth; a Brahmin reads some mantras and the body is afterwards placed upon the funeral pyre with its head towards the north. If the deceased be a male, he lies upon his breast with his face downwards, but if a female, she lies upon her back. Then the sons and other descendants of the deceased turn round him seven times, keeping the dead body to the right and each holding a lighted faggot in his hand. Then the eldest son puts a lighted faggot into the mouth of the deceased and the others follow him. Wood is gradually piled upon him and some sandal wood and ghee are thrown into the fire. Rich people use no other wood but sandal wood in cremating the dead. In East Bengal the usual custom is to cut down a mangoe tree and burn the deceased with its wood, the reason being that raw mangoe wood burns freely. Friends also throw some ghee and sandal wool upon the fire at their own expense, thinking it to be a meritorious act and there is a well-known saying in Sanskrit literature that he who stays in the cremation ground is a friend. Therefore the usual rule is that all friends and near relations are informed and they go to the cremation ground but no one whose wife is in the family way can go to the cremation ground. When the cremation is nearly over, each of the sons and kinsmen present throws seven small pieces of wood into the fire. This ceremony is called saptakastha or seven pieces of wood. After the body is completely cremated the place is washed by the eldest son and the Bhuimali gets the kalsi or water jar.

Afterwards all the people who took part in the cremation take a dip in the river or tank. It is necessary that the head must go under the water, pouring water upon it is not enough and does not purify the whole body. Then the sons wear new borderless white dhoti and chaddar and white collars with a piece of iron attached which they must continue to wear during the whole period of mourning which is ten days among Brahmins and Chandals, twelve days among threaded Kayasthas, fifteen days among threaded Vaidays, thirty days among non-threaded Kayasthas and Vaidays, and all other castes. The widow changes her sari and wears a white piece of cloth without any border and removes the ornaments from her person. This she does after the return of her sons from the cremation ground, as theoretically she is not a widow until her husband's body is completely reduced to ashes. Henceforth she wears a borderless white dhoti for the remainder of her life. The sons wear white dhoti and chaddar. Four small earthen pots are hung in the four corners of the house or the room in which the deceased lived and water is poured every day into these by the sons to quench the thirst of the spirit just emerged from the fire, and a mantra addressed to the soul of the departed is recited at the dictation of the priest, asking him to quench his thirst by this water.

This continues during the whole period of mourning. The sons and their mother cannot sleep on comfortable beds nor sit upon any comfortable seat. Their bedding consists of a blanket spread upon straw; pillows are also made of straw, and their seats consist of woven kusa grass about a cubit square, and whenever the sons go they must carry the seats with them. This kusa grass seat is the orthodox seat of Hindus. In big feasts they sit upon this seat while eating and—in all religious ceremonies—the participants must sit upon this seat. This is a relic of the Vedic times. In all religious ceremonies this kusa grass is used and a ring made of the kusu grass is placed upon the water contained in a copper vessel which is used in all religious ceremonies. During the first four days the widow and the sons cannot take any rice. They subsist upon fruits, milk, coconut, and moong dal soaked in water. Excepting the milk no other food can touch the fire. On the fifth day a new earthen vessel is washed, put upon the fire and water and atap rice are poured into it. The mother and the eldest son only can cook this rice. No additional water can be poured into it nor the gravy thrown away. Then the eldest son must take down the pot from the fire. Only ghee without salt and milk without sugar but with plantain can be taken with the rice and nothing else. No other dish or any other eatable is allowed. At night only fruits and milk are taken. This food must be taken during the whole period of mourning and the only seat upon which the widow and the sons sit is the kusa grass seat, and the only covering for their body in summer is the chaddar but if they feel uncomfortable they can use a shawl or any woolen chaddar over the cotton chaddar which thy must always wear round their bodies. No sewn garment can be used and shoes and slippers cannot be worn. This state of things lasts during the whole period of mourning.

The widow and her sons must bathe every day and recite mantras, but sometimes the eldest son only recites the mantras. In fact, in the cases of the younger sons the rules are somewhat relaxed and it is considered enough if the eldest son observes the rules strictly. Now-a-days sugar and rock salt have been introduced in the food. On the eleventh day of the moon, the sons cannot take any rice; they must live upon milk and fruits only. As regards daughters there is a distinction. Married daughters observe these rules for three days only but the unmarried daughters are ranked in this respect in the same category as sons. There is a peculiar custom. If for any reason the earthen pot cracks while rice is being boiled and the rice falls into the fire and is spoiled, another pot cannot be used. The sons must pass the day without taking any rice. A new pot must be used daily and the old one thrown away. After the bath the sons wear their chaddar, and the white dhoti is dried in the sun but the mother wears a new dhoti as she has no chaddar to use after the bath. The sons and their mother cannot have the use of the barber or the washerman.

On the fourth day a small ceremony is performed called Chaturtha and some Brahmins and near relations are fed. On the tenth day those who assisted in the cremation are invited to a feast.

On the last day of the mourning the family barber comes, shaves the head and beard and pares the nails but a tuft of hair must be left on the top. The parties then bathe and wear new dhoties and chaddars which had been previously washed, as no Hindu will use any unwashed cloth on any ceremonial occasion. The washerman gets as his perquisite all the dhoties and chaddars cast off by them.

The next day the sradh is performed. A raised vedi has to be erected a cubit and quarter high and either 4 or 8 or eight cubits square and a covering placed upon it. All sorts of silver or brass ware and new cloths are placed upon it or in an adjoining place. No gold will be accepted by a Brahmin except of the lowest class. Therefore no gold can be used. The eldest son recites mantras at the dictation of the priests. A bull calf is brought to the place and branded with a hot piece of iron and set at liberty. The goalas or any other Hindus take it. Formerly it was sacrificed and eaten. I refer the reader to my observations upon cow killing in connection with the placing of a cow's head at the door of the confinement room. Some female calves also are similarly distributed. Large numbers of people are fed, all the kinsmen and near relations being invited to the feast as well as the villagers.

They are sumptuously fed. No animal food can be offered on this occasion. Beggars also come; they are either fed or paid in cash. Brahmin Pandits are also invited; they are paid in pieces of silver and cash, the silver utensils used at the sradh being cut into pieces and given to the Pandits according to their merits. It is very easy to decide on the merit of each Pandit. They are divided into five classes, the lowest ones get eight annas in the rupee, next in order ten annas, the next twelve annas, then fourteen annas, then a full rupee. If the performer of the sradh intends to pay, for example, sixteen rupees to the first class pundits then he pays eight rupees in cash and eight tolas of silver; the rest get their bidai in similar proportion.

The other Brahmins are also paid and each pandit gets a sidha consisting of all necessary articles of food. A sidha for one man is usually a sidha for half a dozen people. Hindus are very extravagant on occasions of marriage and sradh, specially the latter. They think that the more they spend the greater will be their religious merit and the efficacy of the sradh and therefore their ancestors will ascend higher in heaven. I was invited to the sradh of the Maharaja of Burdwan, Mahatap Chand Bahadur, which took place in 1879, and I saw there heaps of silver and brass vessels, besides cots, elephants, horses, etc. The silver vessels were not generally finished articles as they have to be cut into pieces. Heaps of rupees there were, all distributed among Brahmins and the poor. It must be understood that none but Brahmins can get any share in this distribution; the beggars only got eight annas each, their number exceeding a lac. The Kayasthas and other castes who were invited got only board and lodging. The principal part in the religious ceremony consists in the offering of pindas which consist of cooked atap rice and plantain in the case of Brahmins and the threaded Kayasthas and Vaidyas and of raw atap rice and plantains, in the case of other castes. It is a strange thing that the plantains used in most religious ceremonies, such as sradh and Durga puja, must be of the worst variety; the best ones are never used. At the time of actually offering these pindas the officiating priests must be of the Agrandani class, they being the lowest in the scale of Brahmins.

A very large number of people are fed on the occasion of a sradh. People from distant villages come to the feast and the beggars get food and copper as well. All kinsmen and relatives are given luchis, vegetable curries, dahi, khir, sandesh, but no kind of animal food is given.

On the occasion of a sradh there are music and religious songs. In West Bengal the singers are generally women and the songs relate to the Was or doings of Krishna and Radhiki. In East Bengal there are music and religious songs by amateurs in the case of the sradh of old people and female singers are not hired for the occasion. It is strange that Shiva the God of death is not addressed in these songs. Guests have to pay some money as presents to the singers.

After the sradh is over and the sun sets, the eldest son cooks atap rice, fish, and vegetables and carries them to the ghat and leaves them there with a light burning. This food is intended for the departed soul. If the deceased be a widow then no fish is given to her.

This finishes the sradh ceremony. The widow and the sons had been fasting the whole day, which is absolutely necessary on all ceremonial occasions as already stated. They now take some refreshments which consist only of milk, moong dal soaked in water, plantains and other fruits. They must sleep on the same bed as before and also on the next day when they are required to observe all the above rules, as, correctly speaking, the period of mourning includes the day of the sradh and also the next day. On the second day after the srahd, kinsmen and sometimes friends and near relations are invited to a midday feast, as a feast at noon is the only feast recognized among Hindus on ceremonial occasions. Then the sons and the guests sit together for breakfast. Fish is first served, then the nearest kinsman takes in his hand some fish which had been served to him, and gets up and he then gives the fish to each of the sons and grandsons of the deceased and asks them to eat the fish. Then he goes back to his seat and everybody eats a little fish. Then other dishes are served and eaten by the sons and the guests. Meat is also served to all. After the feast the sons wear their shoes and their ordinary dress and at night they sleep upon their ordinary beds. In fact after the feast, the period of mourning is actually over and the sons have not to observe any rule in connection with the mourning, but on every eleventh day of the moon they abstain from taking rice but live upon milk and fruits. This rule must be observed during a whole year and during this period the children of the deceased cannot eat rice at any house excepting a kinsman's, nor contract any marriage, unless in the case of grown-up daughters, when an urgent sradh is performed for purification.

After the monthly sradh the sons perform sradh every month on the same lunar days as the day of the death; and on the twelfth lunar day a yearly sradh is performed in which the deceased parent and ancestors up to third degree and their wives are offered pindas. Some people perform this annual sradh as long as they live. In East Bengal all friends and relations come to see the sons of the deceased to condole with them, but in West Bengal the sons have to go out to see their friends and relations and announce the death of their parent; only very near relations and friends coming to condole with them. In East Bengal people do not follow this custom. They generally do not leave the house during the mourning period.

When a married woman dies, her forehead is painted with vermilion and she is dressed in a sari with red border or a red silk sari and is cremated in this dress. But in the case of all males and widows, the dhoti which the deceased wears just before cremation is white. If a young man's wife dies, then some friends must propose another marriage at the cremation ground, before the body is burnt to ashes. This ensures an early marriage. The most eligible bride for a widower is his late wife's sister, just as the most eligible boy to adopt is the brother's son.

CHAPTER 11

▼

FOOD

Orthodox Hindus take sacrificial meat of goats and sheep and venison and no other meat. They eat almost all kinds of fish except gajar and shout. In East Bengal they eat the flesh of the tortoise, but not in West Bengal where it cannot be had. Turtles are eaten in the Barisal District by all people. In the Burdwan and Hoogly districts shell fish is eaten and if fried in ghee is regarded as a delicacy.

Ordinary Hindus eat the flesh of goats and sheep even if they are not sacrificed before any idol. Hindus never take beef or ham or pork or fowl, though in ancient times beef was not a prohibited article of food and Yajnavalka is reported to have said that he ate beef provided that it was tender, (Sacred Books Of the East, Vol. 36. p.ll) and Manu makes it an allowable food, (V.18). As to pulses, widows cannot take moosori and maskalai and orthodox people will not eat moosori on Sundays. When I was young the Chandals used to eat wild boars. I saw that a wild boar, which was killed, was taken away by them for eating, and that was about sixty years ago. But now the Chandals, the lowest classes of Hindus in Bengal, are beginning to imitate the manners and customs of the superior castes and have ceased to eat the flesh of the wild boar. Formerly widow marriage was prevalent among them but now in imitation of the superior castes they have abolished that custom. The Chandals have gone so far in imitating the superior castes that many of them have taken the sacred thread and call themselves Banerjees, Chatterjees, and Mukherjees, etc. As to vegetables, Hindus eat almost all kinds of herbs but widows make some exceptions.

Grown-up Hindus generally take two meals, one at noon, the other after nightfall. They cannot take two regular meals in the daytime as it is prohibited by the Shastras. They rarely take any lunch and never any chotahazri. But now-a-days tea drinking in the morning and in the evening has been introduced in many families and they take some slight nourishment with the tea. Fifty years ago 1% of Hindus took tea but now more than 10% have adopted the habit of tea drinking. In towns nearly 25% take tea every day. In Calcutta the lowest classes almost invariably take their morning tea. On ceremonial occasions the Hindus generally fast and in many parts of Bengal the widows have to fast on the eleventh day of the moon, and in the case of males and married women it is considered a merit to fast on special occasions.

No Hindu will cook or eat any food during the progress of an eclipse, as it is the general belief of all Hindus that eating food at such a time will bring on chronic diarrhea. The origin of this idea is very curious and illustrates how superstitious beliefs arise. The eclipse is called grahana in the vernacular and chronic diarrhea is called grahani. These two words are not at all connected nor is the pronunciation alike. But some fanciful etymologists have derived the word grahani from grahana. In fact resemblance in pronunciation is the cause of many superstitions. A harmless vegetable is called gosingha which means the horn of a cow which it resembles. Therefore no widow will take that vegetable, but in the district of Barisal it is not called gosingha but it is called rekha and therefore widows eat this vegetable. Similarly the word tula has two meanings; it means a scale (Libra of the Zodiac) and it means cotton, the result being that when the sun is in Libra in the month of Kartic no orthodox Hindu will use a cotton quilt at night. Such is the origin of some superstitious beliefs. There are some customs in connection with eating. In Northern India any man who does not belong to the untouchable class can touch almost any cooked food and people of superior castes take it, the only exceptions being cooked rice, dal and unleavened bread. But in Bengal no inferior caste man can touch any cooked food intended for any superior caste but, strange enough, anyone who is not untouchable may bake the unleavened bread of superior caste, though orthodox Brahmins and Kayasthas refuse to take such bread. As to loaves, it was not regarded as allowable food by Hindus. More than half a century ago loaves and the meat of fowls were placed in the same category but now-a-days, excepting orthodox Hindus, everybody eats loaves although baked by Mahomedans, and in many houses the flesh of the domestic fowl has been introduced.

There is a peculiar custom among Hindus. Almost all cooked dishes are regarded as untouchable. If anybody touches a vessel containing rice or any cooked food he has to wash his hands and, as already stated, no inferior caste man can touch any such vessel and if he does no superior caste man will eat out of that dish. This is called sakari which is untranslatable into any other language.

There is a sect of Hindus who will wash their hands if they put betel leaf into their mouths, as the betel being an article of food connects the mouth and the hand, but these are extreme cases. There are exceptions also on the other side. Ordinary Hindus will buy sweetmeats from a sweetmeat shop and eat them but orthodox Hindus will not take any sweetmeats so bought from a shop excepting sandesh and resagolla which are prepared only with sugar and chhana. When Hindus sit together to eat, their seats are generally wooden planks or kusa grass seats placed on the floor.

These seats must not touch one another and no Hindu will touch another person who is also eating by his side. Among Brahmins this rule is very strictly observed. No one except the mother and the wife can touch a Brahmin while he is eating; if he does, he will stop eating and get up and wash his hands and mouth. This is a most barbarous custom. Some Brahmins do not allow their wives to touch them while they are eating. As the mother is regarded as a goddess by all Hindus they make an exception always in her case. The position of the mother is so great among Hindus that there is a well known saying that the mother and the home are superior even to heaven. The reason why nobody is allowed to touch a Brahmin while eating is a very curious one. Eating is regarded as a yajna and nobody should touch a man while he is performing a yajna. In Europe, when people sit together to eat the man who is first served begins to eat, but it is not so among Hindus. They must in begin at the same time and with the permission of all. The man who is highest in rank among them says, "Let us begin", and then they begin to eat. Before commencing to eat the orthodox Hindus must recite some mantras, put a few grains of rice upon the floor and take a few drops of water into the palm of the hand and drink it and then commence eating. In regular feasts the Brahmins must be served first and then the other castes. Formerly in West Bengal Brahmins would leave some remnant of food upon the plantain leaf from out of which they were eating, and the other castes would sit on their seats and begin taking those remnants. But this custom is grad-ually dying out and everybody now insists on getting a fresh plantain leaf for his plate. All the diners must rise together. If anybody rises the rest will stop eating and get up. Therefore the usual custom is to enquire whether everybody has fin-ished his meal. After they get up they wash their hands and mouth and are offered betel leaf and tobacco. If Brahmins are feasted they get dakshina which varies from one anna to one rupee per head. But if a Brahmin invites non-Brah-mins then every non-Brahmin will give some dakskina to the Brahmin host, the result being that the Brahmin diner or the Brahmin host must get some money from the non-Brahmin in all cases. This is regarded as a meritorious act.

English dinner consists of a few courses, but a vegetable dinner in Bengal, when many people are invited, consists of many dishes, though the number has been very much reduced of late. In one case many years ago, I remember there were more than sixty dishes. When many people are invited and there is not enough space in the house, guests are fed in batches and are sometimes obliged to sit in places which were never intended to be used as dining rooms. The place is swept and besmeared with cow dung mixed with water and the food is placed upon a plantain leaf, and sometimes it is torn and the food is mixed with the cow dung, but if two plantain leaves are placed one upon another this does not hap-pen. In Europe the host or hostess sits at the head of the table and the principal guest sits on his right and so on. But in Bengal the host does not generally sit to take his dinner before others have eaten and the womenfolk take their dinner after all the males have been served. If the number of guests be few then the host sits with them but he gives the place of honor to the guests who are held in high-est esteem. It is not usual for girls to sit with the males unless they are very young. The usual order of serving the dishes is as follows: first rice is served to all, then ghee and salt, and then fried fish or vegetables are served. In East Bengal this dish is usually bitter khesari dal. In West Bengal khesari dal is rarely used and there-fore some bitter vegetable dish is served instead, then some pungent dishes are served, then fish curry, then pilau and meat curry then some chatni, then dahi and sandesh and in East Bengal khir with sugar and plantain, rice boiled in milk and sugar.

These are the usual courses served in a breakfast or dinner. In West Bengal they begin with two luchies and some vegetable dishes, then they are served with rice or pilau as the case may be. In East Bengal luchies are never eaten with rice or pilau. The usual rule is that gentlemen are first served, then the ladies, lastly the lower classes. There is a strange custom in Bengal and perhaps throughout India. On big occasions poor people and strangers who had not been invited sit down to eat and are fed. In parts of the district of Barisal genuine pilau, made of rice, meat broth and ghee, is a rare thing. Only the bridegroom is served with it. His brothers and other relations do not generally get it. Then pilau is prepared by coloring the rice with turmeric and putting a little ghee over it and mixing them together. In other parts of Bengal real pilau is served to the principal guests.

Hindus have a very unsocial custom about eating. No two castes can dine in the same room according to strict Hindu custom. The orthodox Brahmin even today will not dine in the same room with a non-Brahmin and no one while eating can touch another diner. A dish containing food cannot be touched by anyone while eating, even by any part of his body or even by his washed left hand or his dress. If he does, the food will be thrown away or given to lower class people. A husband cannot see his wife eat; if he does, then the wife will cease eating and get up, otherwise Alakshmi or the goddess of poverty will overtake them.

After a Hindu has eaten his food the dishes and cups are removed and the place washed with diluted cow dung; otherwise no one will pass over the place and no one will sit there to take his food. Diluted cow dung is the greatest purifier amongst Hindus. An unused place can be made fit for use even as a dining room, if wiped with a rag with some diluted cow dung. In places where Ganges water is easily available, no cow dung is necessary; this water is considered enough to purify a place. This diluted water and the rag are rubbed every day over the floor of rooms and the floor and plinth of huts and even the courtyard gets a sprinkling of this sacred water every day to purify it. The cow dung is very sacred, and it is ordained that if anybody has to expiate a religious or social offense, then he must eat cow dung.

Orthodox Hindus never take the milk of a cow before three weeks have passed after calving, when they give some milk to a deity and then begin taking it. Similarly they never eat any mango or other well-known fruit before it has been offered to a deity. No one can mix salt with milk unless curdled. If he does so, it becomes beef. Nor can anybody mention the word beef while eating. If any one does so, the rest will stop eating and get up.

After Dussera and before Sharaswati puja no orthodox Hindu will eat the hilsa fish. On the occasion of Sharaswati puja a pair of hilsa fish is bought, a vermilion mark is placed on each and grass, paddy and jute leaves and a lighted lamp are placed on a window and then presented to a goddess with the sound of ulu.

CHAPTER 12

▼

MISCELLANEOUS

When a Hindu wakes up from his sleep, before he rises he must say "Durga, Durga", then he gets up, salutes the sun and after his ablutions must brush his teeth, cleanse his mouth, then leave the dhoti he had been wearing at night, recite his morning prayers and then commence his business whatever it may be. Then he changes his cloth, performs his puja and sits to eat. He takes a siesta if he has no business to look after, then he gets up, washes his face and mouth, does some business if any, or plays with dice or cards and in the evening recites his evening prayers, spends the evening as he likes and then takes his dinner and goes to bed. In England I understand people go to places of entertainment or otherwise enjoy themselves after dinner and usually go to bed after midnight but it is not so in Bengal or in India where people go to bed soon after their dinner is over. Hindus are very fond of betel; they begin to chew it after breakfast and go on chewing it until they go to bed at night.

Young people and infants do not observe the above rule. They eat four times a day and do not usually sleep in the daytime nor do they perform any puja, only Brahmin boys have to recite the Gayatri on three occasions, morning, noon and evening. This is the usual routine of the life of a Hindu. An orthodox Hindu will never start a journey on a day which is not auspicious. He consults the almanac, finds when it is auspicious to start on a journey, and then starts. If it be a long journey, two earthen kulshis full of water with two small twigs of a mango tree are placed on the two sides of the door and a deity is painted upon each kalshi with vermilion and when he starts he has to salute them. No Hindu will start when the two constellations of Aslesha and Magha are in the ascendant, nor on a full moon or a new moon night or on the first or last day of the month, nor during an eclipse or a week after. Before he starts he must salute his parents and other elderly people who are present to see him off. If he once starts on an auspicious day he can break his journey as often as he likes, provided he nowhere stays three nights, but if he does so, he must again consult the almanac and find out an auspicious day.

When a Hindu leaves his house if anybody sneezes or calls him by name or a house lizard (tikitiki) makes a noise then he must reenter his house and make a fresh start, and when a Hindu goes on a journey he considers it lucky if a jackal passes by his right side or a dead body is carried by his left side.

No Hindu will sleep with his head towards the north nor will he sit to eat with his face towards the north. They justify their diction in avoiding the north, when they sleep on the ground that it is prohibited by the Shastras. Now they base it on a scientific ground, something connected with electricity as the magnetic pole is towards the north. How far they are right I am not in a position to say.

No Hindu woman will take the name of her husband under any circumstances and it is not generally proper for a woman to take the name of any ancestor or ancestress of her husband or his elder brother or cousin. It therefore frequently happens that the name of a relation or a servant is changed if it happens to be the same as that of a person whose name it is not proper for her to take.

A married woman must wear a bordered sari and at least some ornaments in her arms. Poor people in Eastern Bengal wear bangles of conch shell, and glass churies in Western Bengal. The use of these bangles is conclusive of the fact that her husband is alive. In East Bengal rich women also use these bangles but in West Bengal they must wear an iron bangle; otherwise people will take them to be widows. Old widows, particularly of the lower castes, sometimes wear bordered dhoties but the color of the border can never be red. Married women put vermilion upon the forehead and the head and when so doing if any other married woman be present she must put similar marks of vermilion upon her forehead and head. Married women are permitted to take betel but no respectable widow will take it. If a married pair go to a place of pilgrimage or perform any religious act then the virtue is equally divided between them. If a wife goes alone the whole virtue will be hers but if the husband goes alone then his virtue will be equally divided between him and his wife, although she takes no part in the acquisition of this virtue. A married woman will never sit or stand on the right side of her husband, she must always be to the left. A newly married wife is not expected to speak to her husband in the presence of anybody nor is she expected to speak to any elderly relations, male or female, on her husband's side and during her lifetime she cannot speak or appear before her husband's elder brother or cousin or maternal uncle. These two persons can see her face only once. I understand that in Bihar the father-in-law is also included in this category. She can speak only with young females and in a very low voice. If she has to convey any idea to her mother-in-law or to other old female relations, she smacks her lips and thus draws their attention to her and she speaks by signs.

This state of things does not last long. Her state is really pitiable as she goes into a strange family and has great difficulty in communicating her wishes. Young women generally do not speak with elderly strangers or even servants; if necessary they use the third person singular and not the second person singular. A newly married wife addresses her mother-in-law as mother and she addresses other relations by the relationship her husband bears to them but will never call any elderly person by name. Similarly her new relations address her by the relationship she bears to them and nobody will call her by name. No newly married wife will eat with any male in the same room. She will eat with females and infants only. It is the invariable custom among Hindus that men and women eat separately, just as the ancient Greeks did, but this rule is not observed if she is an elderly woman when she is supposed to be above many restrictions. For instance young women never go to the outer apartment or courtyard. But elderly women do not always observe this rule. In a place of pilgrimage or on a journey they appear in public and many restrictions disappear. When a wife goes to her father's house, her father bears all expenses of the journey but when she comes to her own house her husband bears the expenses and furnishes the escort, but if the wife be the daughter of a Moulik and her husband be a Kulin, her father bears the expenses of the journey both ways in East Bengal. The newly married wife must rise very early from her husband's bed otherwise people will laugh at her.

Hindus must meet one another on the Dashahara day, or the day after, and touch the feet of Brahmins and of elderly relations. Male or female and the males embrace one another, and even untouchables are permitted to embrace the superior castes. The women, young or old, put some paddy and grass on the head of each male and touch the feet of their elderly male relations. The Romans had a similar custom which took place on the twenty-first of February every year, when even bitter enemies had to meet and embrace one another. This is a very good social custom. Even if after the lapse of some time after the Dashahara two Hindus meet, they must perform the same ceremony. Strictly speaking this ceremony continues till Kali puja, three weeks after, but generally speaking it lasts for nearly two months.

No orthodox Hindu will take any ghee with his rice if somebody else had eaten out of the plate which he is using. The result of this is that formerly no non-Brahmin could take ghee with his rice as he usually sat to breakfast out of a plate which a Brahmin had eaten out of.

Orthodox Hindus drink charanamitra or the nectar of the foot. This foot is the right of an idol or of a Brahmin who is a god incarnate, as Manu, who extols the Brahmins to the skies, says (1.98-101)

98. *The very birth of Brahmins is a constant incarnation of Dharma, God of Justice; for the Brahmin is born to promote justice, and to procure ultimate happiness.*
99. *When a Brahmin springs to light, he is born above the world, the chief of all creatures, assigned to guard the treasury of duties, religious and civil.*
100. *Whatever exists in the universe is, all in effect, though not in form, the wealth of the Brahmin; since the Brahmin is entitled to it all by his primogeniture and eminence of birth.*
101. *The Brahmin eats but his own food and wears but his own apparel; and bestows but his own in alms: through the benevolence of the Brahmin indeed, other mortals enjoy life.*

Some water is poured upon the big toe of the idol and given to Hindus who drink it with great devotional feelings. In the case of a Brahmin, who is generally unshod, he first washes the big toe of his right foot, then dips it into a vessel containing water and people drink it. I have seen my grandmother fetch water and get the charanamrita of our family priest, drink a few drops, sprinkle a few drops on her head, and keep the rest for future use.

If a Hindu digs a pond, its length must be north to south and the breadth from east to west. It must be sanctified by a ceremony performed by Brahmins before its water can be used. Mahomedans dig their ponds in the opposite direction. Their length is from east to west and breadth from north to south, with the result that no Hindu will drink its water or use it for any purpose.

This difference in customs between Mahomedans and Hindus is shown in other ways. Hindus use the front side of the plantain leaf when they use it for a plate, but Mahomedans will use the back side of the leaf. Hindus have been digging their tanks and using plantain leaves for plates before Mahomed was born. So this opposition to Hindu customs was started by the Mahomedans, who follow the converse rule. Hindus must have the kachha, as without it they cannot eat their food or perform any religious ceremony. The only exception to this rule is the Vaishnava who is a Bhikary, or beggar, who has renounced the world and who, like the Mahomedans, bury their dead. No orthodox Mahomedan will wear a kachha.

If any one praises the beauty or plumpness of an infant, then the mother or near female relation of the infant, if present, will throw a little spittle on it, to avoid the evil influence of the speaker, and if a woman after combing her hair has to throw away some hair which comes out of her head, she has to mix the rejected hair with a little spittle and throw it away.

If a creeper thrives well, and the passersby are likely to envy it or to speak well of its growth, then a black pot with a white cross mark is suspended near it. All this is to avoid the influence of evil spirits.

If a house lizard (tiktiki) makes a noise, then all present must say true, true, true (satya, satya, satya). The reason of this is unknown. No one should offer anything to another, specially if of superior rank, with his left hand. If the right hand is engaged, then he should touch the elbow of the left hand with his right fist. It is very unmannerly to offer anything with the left hand and people take offense if that is done.

No son or a much younger man or an inferior man will smoke or drink wine in the presence of his father or any elderly relation. It is highly improper to do so. So father and son can never drink wine or smoke together.

Hindus sit on piris or other seats when eating, and they cannot touch one another when eating rice. If they do so, the Brahmin or other superior caste man will stop eating, so they can never sit at table for eating. Although the ancient Greeks and Romans used tables for dining, it is strange that Hindus never copied their custom. The Greeks sat or rather reclined on sofas placed on three sides of the table, the other side being left open for the service of the dinner. The Romans also sat at table and Plutarch says that Julius Caesar, when he came to Rome after his Proconsulship, entertained his countrymen on twenty-two thousand tables, each accommodating nine people. Hindus cannot use any knife, fork, or spoon as they cannot use their left hand when eating, as the hand which touches any cooked food becomes polluted. The Greeks and the Romans had knives and spoons, but Hindus have only lately introduced them in their households. They had ladles only. As to forks, it was unknown even in Europe till the end of the sixteenth century and they are mentioned for the first time in England in a letter dated 1611, when the writer says that forks were introduced into England from Italy.

No one should enter a room containing an idol with his shoes on. All religious ceremonies must be performed with bare feet and preferably with a silk dhoti and chaddar on. All cotton cloths worn while in bed or used the previous day when eating must be washed, but no silk cloth need be washed though worn for days together.

Orthodox Brahmins will never touch a Chandal or a Mahomedan or a Christian. If they do so, they must purify themselves by bathing.

No Brahmin should be asked to give fire or burning faggots. The origin of this superstition is unknown. But if one asks the Brahmin to give him some wood he will give him the burning faggot.

If one is called by another, some superstitious Hindus will not answer the first call but will answer the second call, as the first call may be by some evil spirit.

It is not permissible to tread on the shadow of a Brahmin, the lord of creation according to Manu, and if by accident a non-Brahmin's foot touches the body or foot of a Brahmin, the former must touch the feet of the Brahmin, but if the two persons are of equal rank and of the same caste, the offender merely salutes the offended person; but if the offender be a man of inferior status or caste or a junior relation, then he must touch the feet of the offended person.

If a man has to pass by a very high personage, he must not show his back to him, but walk sidewise so long as he is within sight of him.

To address a man three forms of speech are used, as "you sir", "you", and "thou". An elderly man, an ancestor or ancestress, uncle or aunt is addressed as *apany* or "you sir" or "madam", as *Sie* in German; an equal as *toomy*, "you"; a younger man, a son or nephew or a servant or a low person as *tui*, "thou".

In villages, where there are very few or no chairs the women sit on the bare floor, so that the back of their dhoti becomes dirty in no time, but in towns and in the houses of rich people in the mofussil, chairs and benches are always used, and even in the mofussil women are offered piris (low wooden seats) to sit on.

A newly married wife wears many ornaments including nose-ring and ear-rings. In East Bengal she must wear two conch shell bangles on her wrists, and in West Bengal an iron bangle, sometimes covered with a thin gold sheet. Usually a married woman wears a bangle or churries on each arm and dispenses with the silver anklets which she wore at the time of her marriage. A woman must change her cloth every morning and wash her cloth in the evening after washing her body. In fact every woman bathes twice, except that in the evening bath she does not pour any water on her head as in that case her hair would remain wet the whole night which would bring on an attack of cold and it would dishevel her dressed hair.

Every one must salute the light when the lamp is lighted in the evening, just as everybody must salute the sun when he comes out of his room after rising from his bed. The Hindus regard light or fire as the principal form of energy. They have abolished every other principal god of the Vedas, and Fire, who is invoked in the very first sukta of the Rig Veda, the oldest book of the Hindus, is still worshiped by every Hindu. The Vedas often speak of yajnas, and yajnas were performed almost every day and Fire must be worshiped in every yajna. I believe that Fire was the most worshiped god of the Hindus. With their limited knowledge of chemistry and physics, they believed that the Sun was the preserver of life, and in this they were perfectly right.

In West Bengal if a Kulin is asked his name he will say that he is so and so, Ghose Das or Basu Das, etc., as the case may be, but in East Bengal no Kulin will add Das after his patronymic, except at the time of marriage or other ceremony. This addition of Das is owing to the evil influence of Brahmins who have tried their best to lower the Kayasthas to the level of all other castes. Raghunandan, the founder of the Bengal school of Dharmashastra who flourished in the beginning of the sixteenth century and was a contemporary of Chaitanya, has gone so far as to say that excepting Brahmins, all other people in Bengal are Shudras. Now-a-days all threaded Kayasthas call themselves Barmanas, and have omitted the word Das after their names. My kinsmen whether threaded or not, call themselves Barmans, and use that word in all ceremonial occasions.

Inferior classes of people have a hankering for big patronymics. The oilmen have the patronymics of Kundu and Pal, the wine sellers that of Shaha, and the moment they become rich, they becomes Roys, and sometimes Roy Choudrys, and other people have assumed other patronymics, but at the time of marriage or other ceremony they must revert to the original patronymic and in invitation letters to such ceremonies they must write their original patronymic after their names.

Kulins have also changed their patronymics. This is owing either to their eminence or to government service in Mahomedan times. My kinsmen of Malkhanagore are called Basu Thakurs, the Ghoses of Gabha are called Dastidars, the Guhas of Banaripara are called Thakurtas, the Boses of the Chandsy are called Muzumdars, the Boses of Radhanagar are called Sarbadhicarys, the Mitras of Ula are called Mustafis and there are other similar patronymics by which these highest class of Kulins are known throughout East and West Bengal.

Bengal Hindus have the very bad custom of chaffing with their granddaughters and grandnieces and sisters-in-law. Sometimes they propose marriage with them and sometimes use obscene language. They chaff with the children's mothers-in-law and aunts-in-law, and the rule is that a man may chaff with the alternate generation so that no man will chaff with his daughter or niece but with her daughters. Similarly one will chaff with his children's mothers-in-law or aunts-in-law, but not with their daughters, but again with the daughters of these daughters.

After the Kali puja, there is a ceremony called Bhratridwitya. The sisters put the mark of white sandal paste on their brothers' foreheads, and give a dhoti to each of them. The next day the brothers are invited to a sumptuous feast. The first ceremony takes place in some families the day after the Kali puja and the second the next day. In some families both ceremonies take place on the second day after the Kali puja. There is an invocation to Death to prolong the lives of the brothers.

In Jeyt, there is a ceremony called Jamai Sasty when the son-in-law gets dhoti and chaddar and other presents, and a sumptuous breakfast. The children of the mistress of the family who perform this ceremony also get cloths and it is believed that the lives of her progeny will be as long as the combined length of the thread in the cloths each of them gets. The Bhratridvitya is compulsory everywhere but this Jamai Sasty is an optional ceremony, but compulsory in certain parts of West Bengal.

If an infant is born after the death of his immediately preceding brother then the newborn babe is formally sold to some female for a few cowries, not exceeding nine, or for some broken rice and the purchaser resells the child to its mother in consideration of a shidha (present of articles of food such as rice, ghee, dal and other articles) and the child is called by the number of cowries for which it was sold, such as Acowrie, Docowri, etc., but there is no sale for one or two gandas of cowries, therefore there is no such name as Charcowri or Atcowri. If the sale is for some broken rice then the child is called Khudi from khud (broken rice). This is to deceive the evil spirit which is supposed to be deceived by the maternity of the child and so cannot wreak its vengeance on the devoted head of its natural mother's children.

On hearing the news of the death of a very near relation, paternal or maternal, it is usual to bathe. A man must bathe after the period of mourning is over, during which time he cannot have the use of the barber and therefore on the last day of the period of mourning every Hindu gets his nails pared and his beard shaved and afterwards he bathes. It is unnecessary to say that no man can be clean in person unless he bathes and I believe this custom of bathing was introduced among the Jews in imitation of the Indian custom. Jesus had to bathe before the Holy Ghost descended upon him and all people of Christian faith have to bathe before they can enter into the fold of Christianity.

If a woman has her monthly curse she is considered as unclean. In West Bengal she is not permitted to cook for others but her touch is not pollution and she sleeps in the same bed with her husband. In East Bengal such a woman is considered as unclean. Nobody can touch her and if he touches her he must bathe. She must sleep on a separate bed and cannot use any mattress, and the mat and the improvised pillow must be washed on the fourth day. During the period of three days she cannot perform any religious ceremony or say her prayers. In Madras I understand they go to an extreme. There is a hut separate from the main building for the use of such a female as she is not permitted to enter a building and pollute it. In East Bengal the cloths she wears during this period cannot be used by her before they are washed by the washerman. If my opinion were asked I would decidedly prefer the East Bengal custom. It is more sanitary and healthy to the husband and the wife.

During the period of mourning on the death of a kinsman no Hindu can take any animal food and in the case of the death of a father or mother no Hindu can accept any invitation to dinner or breakfast at the house of anybody except that of a kinsman. On the death of an ancestor or ancestress other than parents; the people of West Bengal must remain unshod during the whole period of mourning, but it is otherwise in East Bengal where the strict rules of mourning are observed only in the case of the death of one of the parents.

In the last century there was a fine custom of hospitality to wayfarers. It was called atithisheba or feeding the wayfarers. There were no inns in those days and articles of food could not be bought everywhere. So rich people gave food or sbidba to every wayfarer who arrived in their houses and demanded hospitality. In some families the days were distributed among the kinsmen. We had to receive all such wayfarers after the twenty-seventh of the month till the end of it. But now there are inns everywhere and good roads and shops where one can buy articles of food and cook them. Therefore this custom now prevails in rich families only. According to Hindu custom no atitbi can be asked whence he came before he is fed.

Englishmen are very fond of kissing one another. Indians never kiss any one but infants and a husband will never kiss his wife in the presence of anybody. Indians kiss cheeks, not the mouths but the mother kisses the mouth of her young baby. The kissing of the mouth was not prevalent in Europe in ancient times and it is said that the daughter of Hengist introduced it into England. The Indian practice is more cleanly and sanitary.

As regards the female dress, no one can show her person as Europeans do. The breast must be entirely covered. Mahomed had to enjoin this in the Koran (Ch. X)CM and the back cannot be shown at all. Only the right arm is visible sometimes. When a woman appears only before her relatives, she is somewhat negligent in her dress, but when a gentlewoman leaves her house, only her feet and half of her face and portion of her right arm are visible. In cold Europe there is a display of the person, particularly in nights, but in hot India, the rule is just the reverse, and Indians wonder how Europeans bear the intense cold of their country with such scanty covering of the body.

Formerly the dress of a female consisted only of a sari in which she covered her whole body and her head, as every married woman must be veiled when appearing before anyone. In East Bengal there are two turns of the sari below the waist but in West Bengal there is only one turn which somewhat exposes the person. But nowadays ladies wear chemises at home under the sari so their persons are always well covered. Now one can see Hindu ladies wear a bodice or other kind of European dress but they never wear a gown like a European lady, though some advanced ladies wear their sari in a gown like fashion in imitation of the women of Northern India which looks much nicer than the usual mode of using a sari.

Bengali ladies formerly never wore shoes and very few used slippers after evening when the day's work was over. Now shoes have been introduced in many Hindu families but no one can wear shoes or slippers when at her prayer or devotion or when entering a temple.

As regards the male dress, formerly it consisted of a dhoti but when a man left his house or village and went elsewhere he put a chaddar on his bare body; afterwards they wore a short coat up to the waist tied by two strings on the two sides of the chest, then pirans or shirts were then gradually introduced and now shirts with stiff linen cuffs have been introduced over which the chaddar is placed. This chaddar was used for various purposes such as a handkerchief, an umbrella or a sheet to cover the person, but now umbrellas have come into general use and a handkerchief is carried in the pocket; therefore chaddars have become useless and there are many people who never use a chaddar when going out in the street.

Hindus formerly did not wear shoes as they are made of the hide of a cow, a sacred animal. They used wooden sandals with a knob in them between the big toe and the next toe. They were very cheap and lasted long, but now everybody wears shoes which are very dear, though they were very cheap formerly. I remember to have bought a pair of shoes for me in 1858 for five and half annas but its leather was not well tanned. Now such a pair of shoes would cost three or four rupees.

Every respectable Hindu keeps a horoscope for his son. In West, Bengal a horoscope is kept for the daughter also, but in East Bengal no such horoscope is kept. The reason is very simple. Each horoscope gives the gan of the infant and there are three gans, Deva, Nara and Rakshasha, that is, God, Man and Rakshasha. The bride and the bridegroom may both be of first two gaps or either of them, but if one of them be of Rakshasha gan, the other must be of Deva gan. Otherwise the Rakshasha will eat or kill the other, but no Rakshasha can kill any person of the Deva gan. If the bride be a Rakshasha then she will soon be a widow if her husband be not a Deva and in the reverse case the bridegroom will soon he a widower. Hence whenever there is a proposal of marriage, the two horoscopes are consulted to see if the gans are in proper order. The Eastern Bengal Hindus do not keep any horoscope for their daughters to avoid this hindrance to the marriage of their girls thinking, that where ignorance is bliss it is folly to be wise.

No boy can marry on the day of the week when he was born, nor in the month when he was born. The eldest son cannot marry in Jeyt, which also means senior, or in Agrahayana which means foremost. But some people do not exclude the whole month but exclude the first thirteen days. Similarly there can be no marriage in Bhadra to Cartic, Pous, and Cheyt, but in East Bengal only Pous and Cheyt are considered as unholy for marriage but Aswin is generally avoided. The reason of the exclusion of these three months is given in all almanacs. If the marriage be in Bhadra, then the wife becomes a woman of the town, if in Aswin, then the wife will die, if in Cartic the wife will be a sickly woman Thousands of such marriages take place every year in East Bengal, with no such untoward result; still the people of West Bengal will persist in avoiding these months. Sundays are always excluded as it is a neutral day and the marriage will be fruitless, that is, there will be no issue of the marriage, which is the sole object of all Hindu marriages, according to the Shastras. There are other restrictions to marriage but they are not generally observed. The bride should be an even number of years old, counting from the conception. The curious reader will find all these prohibitions and restrictions in the Almanac.

One of the ten commandments of God to Moses was not to take his name in vain. But the Hindus follow the contrary rule. Half the names of Hindus are the names of deities, the idea being that the more one takes the name of a deity the better for his salvation.

A younger brother cannot marry unless the elder brother is married, or he promises not to marry.

Formerly women used to tattoo their foreheads, and the lower classes their arms also, but now no gentlewoman will tattoo herself. Married women and grown-up girls paint the edges of their feet and the tips of the fingers with alta (lac dye) in West Bengal and this custom is being gradually introduced in East Bengal. It is a very old custom and is mentioned by Kalidas in describing the personal appearance of Parvaty in his Kumara-Samvhaba. It need not be said that all grown-up girls and women must veil their faces. This is also enjoined in the Koran.

No Hindu will pass under the outstretched arm of any person as the Hindu belief is that the owner of the arm will have boils in the armpit.

If any one sneezes then the people near him will utter jiba (live) thrice, else death will overtake him. If anybody yawns then he will put his right hand near the gaping mouth and strike his middle finger with his thumb and make a noise to drive away flies which might enter his mouth.

No Hindu will kill a cat in any circumstances. If he does he will give salt and dakshina to a Brahmin and perform a penance.

If a dog enters a cook-room or a dining room then all the cooked food must be thrown away, the vessels and utensils scrubbed and washed, as dogs are considered very unclean and if anybody touches a dog he must bathe.

If a cow dies an accidental death, the owner must place a rope round his neck and remain speechless for one year and subsist by begging. Such is the veneration for the cow, regarded as an incarnation of Vishnu, although the Vedas and Manu allow its flesh as lawful food and the former enjoined cow sacrifice (yajna).

There are a thousand and one customs, but they are not of much importance and I pass them over lest I should tire the reader's patience.

Now let me conclude, but before concluding, let me pay my tribute to the late mother of my father, to my late mother, to the mother of my children who is part authoress of this book, and to the mothers of my grandchildren and to all Hindu mothers for their intense love for their children, their astonishing self-sacrifice and their devotion for the welfare of their children. It is for this reason that the Hindu mother is regarded as a goddess, as she truly is. I do not wish to disparage other mothers, but a Hindu mother is truly divine. May all mothers follow their example and attain godhead like them. I close with a salutation to all Hindu mothers and implore their blessing.

To order additional copies of this book contact:

Lionheart L.L.C.

1-480-396-0899

www.lionheartllc.com

lionheartllc@cox.net

978-0-595-36233-2
0-595-36233-8